COVENANT
and
CONSENSUS

By

CORA E. CYPSER

Published by

KIM PATHWAYS

*Dedicated to
all those who feel responsible
for the future
of earth*

Page Maker sketches by Cora E. Cypser
Cover design by Myra

Printed in U.S.
by BookMasters
Ashland, Ohio

Special thanks to Pat, Ken, Valery, Myra, and Rudy for constructive help.

Inquiries regarding requests to print all or part of *Covenant and Consensus* should
be addressed to KIM PATHWAYS.

To order directly from the publisher add $1.50 to the price for the first copy and
$.50 for each additional copy. Send check or money order to KIM PATHWAYS.

Opinions expressed in this book are not necessarily the views of the publisher.

For more information:

KIM PATHWAYS
101 Young Road
Katonah, NY 10536

CONTENTS

Contents

Contents

Contents

PREFACE

Does anyone ever read introductions? I never used to read them, but recently I discovered that to read introductory material makes it easy to decide whether or not to read the book. In college courses with a certain page reading assigned, one read only the paged assignment, skipping all the beginning pages and going for the meat of the book. Now that the freedom to choose what I read belongs to me, I have turned into an introductions *monger*. Often after reading the introduction, I can freely decide to skip the whole book.

If you are an introductions monger like myself, at this point you have probably made up your mind about this book. You may have decided that my style is too informal, and that no knowledge at all could possibly be gleaned from such a chatty individual. You may be right. However, in defense of my book, I should like to say that Socrates, too, was chatty, and that he bequeathed to us an excellent teaching tool. There are at least two methods of learning. The first method is when one is dealing with precise subject matter, such as chemistry; one has to put down carefully and correctly what others have found to be true statements. In the second case where much of the material rests on suppositions and hypotheses, the writer has to be questioning and must diplomatically prod the readers to think creatively. An authoritative tone does not usually inspire creativity. To write a book and set down facts precisely and clearly is a difficult and time consuming job. To write a book that inspires experiential learning is an even greater challenge.

In this book my desire is to get the reader to think about the whole purpose of history. Yes, we are having an interesting time here on this cute little world as it flies through space, but where are we going? Where do *you* think humanity is heading? Just what is history, anyway? Could we define history as an expression of God? Or would it be better to define it as an expression of humanity? Cats don't seem to have much of a history, as seen by them. I'm not sure if cockroaches have history, engraved somewhere in their inner consciousness, but humans seem to uniquely have recorded history, and also have an unrecorded form of history that they carry around with them in their genes, or in something called culture, or in deep recesses in their minds. But doesn't God have something to do with human history? How about God having a history, for certainly God was here before we were here? We sometimes talk about "God breaking into history," as at the moment of the Exodus, or with the Virgin Mary at Fatima. Or is God in *ALL* history? Or is history somehow an aspect of God? Are God and history some sort of phenomenal process? Can we do anything individually or collectively to aid in the process? These are really tough questions.

If you are the kind of person who reads introductions, you have probably decided by now whether or not you will read this book, but before you shove the book aside entirely, I would like to tell you about some other topics I am curious about. I have questions about our human structures, such as law, government, and community, and I would like you to think about what all these structures have to do with our relationships to God and to each other. I also wonder how these relationships (both to God and others) could be improved. My overriding question about all these structures is, "How do they look when we hold them up to the bright light of the great commandment of love?" In this book we can attempt to sort out some of our reactions to these questions.

PART I

The Way
It Is

Chapters 1 through 6

PART I

To discuss covenant and consensus, it is necessary to speak about the _who_ that is in covenant, and the _who_s that have possibilities of being in consensus. For that reason in chapter one we turn our thoughts to the peculiar ways of collective humanity, in chapter two we progress to the unknowable ways of God, and in chapter three we speak of the responsible individual. We investigate ways that humanity has worked together in groups (chapter four) and the collective dream that humanity has for its future (chapter five). Chapter six speaks of ways of liberating humanity from itself.

Looking out at our particular forest from the viewpoint of just one of the trees, I find the forest to be a remarkable place. It takes many trees to make a forest. I realize that every tree is entitled to its own point of view, and that one tree cannot know the design of the whole forest.

This is the way it is with the human being. It takes many of us to make a community. But aren't our ways wonderful! What a marvellous God must have created us! There are such possibilities of life and love in us. There is a seed of God in us that we are capable of recognizing, and, wonder of wonders, we may be enabled to bring this seed to fruition!

What do we do with our potential godliness? These first six chapters examine human and godly interactions in the environment of earth. God has given us many pathways to choose among, many marvellous thoughts to think, many astounding abilities to exercise. Let's meditate on these gifts and try to know God's will for us in our stupendously crafted world.

1

THE WAY

OF

OUR WRITHING WORLD

1.1 THE SEARCH FOR ORDER

Covenant and *consensus* may sound like pretty dry topics to discuss when confronted with a world in agony. *Covenant* may bring to mind old and decaying forms, with the backwardness of elitism. *Consensus* may make us think of Robert's Rules, and long meetings that we have suffered through. Let us try to get a new perspective on these old words; let's think of them as having to do with our relationships with God and with our fellow humans. If we look at them from this improved perspective, *covenant* and *consensus* may be for us the words that designate the most important actions that can occur in the human race. They have possibilities of being able to influence the whole world into attitudes that encourage the Queendom/Kingdom of God in our midst.

Individually we can never have things just the way we want them to be, and, likewise, collectively, we will never achieve the perfect government. Perhaps the best we can do is to keep tracking after the elusive goal of peace among nations. One definition for peace might be continued non-violent actions in a positive direction. As the centuries flow by, many human beings have given of their energies to assist in this search for a peaceful world order.

The human race has been around a long time, yet it continues to behave in approximately the same manner. It strives to have orderly government, yet graft and corruption stalk on every side. It makes statements about ethical behavior, yet yields to its less worthy impulses. It dreams of a Utopia, yet connives with weapons and entanglements, and creates an environment with the density and

3

intensity of the jungle.

There have been breakthroughs of wisdom shining forth making this continual return to decadence and violence more noticeable. Socrates advised us in our personal desires, to question and to realize what we were doing. Plato described a positive democracy, and some of his directions were implemented. Buddha gave the world an eight-fold path towards perfection. Alexander created a world empire that temporarily acquiesced to his easy governance. Jesus told us what God was like, and how to achieve the beloved community. Mohammed proposed a life of submission to God's will. None of this wisdom was ever fully implemented. We have many good tools to use, but we lack the will power to pick them up.

There should be great incentive to try these tools, for, collectively, we appear to be a pretty miserable lot. However, it seems as though the majority of humanity is too busy fighting everyday decay to worry about the larger problems of the world, past, present, or future. Socrates would advise, "Know thyself!" Do we know who we are, where we are going, the purpose of our life, how to treat other people, how to worship God? Individually, on the surface, most of us don't really seem to care about these things. It is much easier to discuss who will win the next ball game. We may wake up in the dark of night and think about death, but that is an unpleasantry that we are likely to quickly put from our mind. There is always the sleeping pill to deaden the issue.

Perhaps we would have fewer drug problems if we all made active inquiry into the important question of our identity. If the next time we woke up at two in the morning, we meditated on the purpose of our life and how best to worship God, we might come to some personal conclusions that would help us on the path to self understanding. From there we could plan how to relate better to others and to the world. If we came to believe in the importance of ourselves personally as a solution to world problems, we might be more inclined to shoulder our share of the responsibility.

We are faced with problems of environment and armaments before which our present governmental structures seem helpless. The people who make up these governments also have their problems at two o'clock in the morning. They need all the help they can get. To overcome the specters of drugs, environmental abuse, and world destruction is going to take the total dedication of all of us.

There is no more place to run. We are not quite ready to leave the earth for a haven in outer space prepared for us by an ever-provident God. It would not do to take our same old egos to a new planet. Being who we are, we would carry our own seeds of destruction with us. We must make our transformations here and now on our own very precious earth! Our daily *business as usual* must include building a respectful relationship with the spiritual elements of our individual beings and the spiritual possibilities of our earth. Covenant and consensus, as processes that may help in building these relationships, become very important in our present and also for our future.

Covenant and consensus have to do with people, and how they can achieve order in the world. Achieving and maintaining order has always been a problem with humanity. How do we bring into operation the great government that will rule all people justly? Much of the success of a government has depended on the wisdom of a particular ruler. There has been the notion that one prime leader is necessary, and the rest of us are to follow. In ancient Egypt the people believed that the pharaoh led them with the wisdom given him by his god, and that the pharaoh alone was selected to know how to rule. Later rulers accepted the idea of advisors to assist in wise governance of the people. The people were still considered to be followers, like sheep who had no reasoning minds of their own.

Perhaps we are fortunate enough to have reached a new stage in the life of the earth. We may no longer need authoritative leadership that we are expected to follow subserviently. With mass education possible, people can learn how to use their own capabilities, and can govern themselves. The masses of today have enough education and knowledge of local and world events, so that they can see clearly when the chosen leaders make grievous mistakes. We can see through the power plays to find the common humanity in those who strive to guide the nations. The people of today may be ready to accept the responsibility that once was the sole proprietorship of the pharaoh. We must examine the possibility that the God who created all, is able to work through the people that she/he created, so that they can achieve loving order on the earth.

1.2 NEBUCHADNEZZAR'S DREAM OF THE AGES

As we are concerned today with the forms of government that

control us, and the various means of maintaining order in our society, so have previous generations thought deeply on these matters. There is an early folk tale found in different cultures that encapsulates the worries of collective humankind regarding the continuous rule of kingdom after kingdom. There seems to be a belief that after some calamitous future, there will come an end to governance by kings, and that some other type of rule will take place on the earth. This notion can be found in Holy Scriptures in the second chapter of *The Book of Daniel* where the vision of Nebuchadnezzar is described. King Nebuchadnezzar refused to tell his sages what he had dreamed, but irrationally demanded of them an interpretation. When they admitted that they were helpless without knowing the dream, he ordered all Babylonian sages put to death. Daniel, as a Jewish sage in Babylonia, came under this death sentence, and was able to stay the mass execution of sages, by relating what the king had dreamed and the meaning of it.

He told the king that his dream was of a great statue. The golden head of this statue was interpreted to be the reign of Nebuchadnezzar, and the less valuable metals of silver, bronze, and iron in the body of the statue represented following stages of the government. The feet were made of potter's clay. These dynasties of power were destroyed by a small stone that grew into a mountain which filled the whole earth. Thus Daniel praised the king as being the golden head, and comforted him, and postponed the troubles of the kingdom (and of the earth) off onto future generations.

We may look at this performance, and marvel at the imagination and wisdom of Daniel, but on closer scrutiny, we are also obliged to marvel at the communication of ideas and the allegorical worry about governmental problems, that intertwined in the folk stories of the early Near East world. These queries about the suitability and justness of governments must have been carried in the hearts of the common people, and brought to expression in various places. The story about Daniel and Nebuchadnezzar supposedly took place some time after the Jews were carried away to Babylon, perhaps in the fifth century BCE. The tale may really have stemmed from a dream of Nebuchadnezzar, or it may be an example of story teller's art designed to carry a moral to the listeners. Again, it may illustrate thought transference where similar original ideas come to people in different locations, as stories on this theme are found in

The ages of the earth are pictured here
in this great statue that you see
O Nebuchadnezzar. Your age is gold.
Its leaders walk familiarly with spirits
believe in dreams, believe in goodness.
You are the crown of human effort,
the earth working, making itself known
in the speech of mankind.

Those rulers who come after you, O King
try to preserve the structures you established.
Silver sinews ripple silver arms.
A silver heart beats in the silver breast.
This second age is less than yours.
Men put the God of all creation
respectfully, in silver boxes
measuring it out to fellow men.

A new age comes - belly of bronze
men's appetites rampage and sicken -
and thighs of bronze, an alloy age
that bows before both God and science
faith and reason, church and state.

The sturdy legs uphold these opposites
in binding culture. Rulers here
seek power, and worship alloy idols.

Iron enters in. Man has no need for
philosophic thoughts or noble deeds.
Weapons and wrath resettle him
to potter's clay, an aggregate of iron and sod.

Yet good comes from this | crumbling frame, O King.
The stone thrown | at the statue's feet
enlarges upwards to a | glorious   mountain.
The land responds to | care by gentle hands.

THE AGES FORETOLD: AN INTERPRETATION OF DANIEL 2:31-45

other cultures. It might be a result of listening to wandering min-
strels, or have been picked up from trades people carrying wares
from Greece. Whatever its origins, it is proof that our ancestors
meditated with grave concern on power, leadership, and order.

Tales relating to this dream of Nebuchadnezzar have been
incorporated in other folk stories. It deserves to be noted that three
centuries earlier in Greece, similar comparisons of metals and eras
took place. We all have heard of Homer and his hero Odysseus.
Shortly after Homer, another man called Hesiod composed a fable
called *The Ages of The World* which related his thoughts on the
problem of order in human history. Hesiod was immersed in the
Greek culture of gods and goddesses. His story was that the immor-
tals on Mount Olympus first created a golden race, who lived like
gods without sorrow, suffering, or aging. Their lives were filled with
happiness and peace. Being mortal, they had to die, but their dying
was easy, like sleep, and in death they became good spirits, acting like
our present day guardian angels.

The next experiment of the Olympians was a silver race,
which seemed to reflect a decline due to intermarriage. The children
required parental protection for a hundred years, and they had
trouble getting along with each other.

The bronze race was created by the chief Greek god, Zeus,
and they liked to make war. Hesiod might have had historical
knowledge of a previous age where armor and household implements were made of bronze. These groups destroyed each other and
passed on to Hades, leaving no names.

Just before the time in which Hesiod lived, were the times
related by Homer. In order to give honor to the heroes that Homer
sang about, Hesiod called the age just before his, the age of the hero-
men or demi-gods. Homer had described them so profusely, that
Hesiod esteemed them as next to the gods. He had Zeus removing
these heroes upon their death to the Isles of the Blessed, along the
shore of Oceanus, where they enjoyed fruits that could be harvested
three times a year.

Lastly, in Hesiod's own time, Zeus made the fifth race, called
the race of iron, which seemed to be a mixture of both good and evil.
This race, Hesiod could describe realistically, as he had day to day
contact with them. They are pretty much like us.

This myth of the ages had comparable themes in countries to

the east of Nebuchadnezzar. The religious group of Jains preserve the myth of the ages in India. In this myth metals are not used, but the state of the world deteriorates as time progresses. Each age has a given color. The first age is the age of light, and there are no diseases, no passion, and no war. Passing to the red age, there is a reduction in justice and piety. In the yellow age passion and disease appear. The final age is black, and plague, hunger, and fear are rampant.

The same type of story is written down in China about 200 BCE, and uses the symbolism of five important elements. In the time of the Yellow Emperor, there were many earth worms and mole crickets, and the forces of the soil of earth were in the ascendancy. Coming along after the yellow era, the founder of the Hsia dynasty proclaimed the force of the element wood, and chose green as his color. The founder of the Shang dynasty used the color white, and the element metal. The Chou dynasty chose red and the element fire. The next dynasty replaced fire with the element of water, which is a reasonable way to put out a fire, and chose black as the color[1] which is a good description of how things look, after they have been in a fire, and doused. It seems that early thinkers all over the world were concerned with the problem of governmental order and changes in leadership styles.

1.3 THE MYTH OF THE AGES & ORDER IN THE SKIES

Some with creative imagination took the story of the ages and related it to what goes on up in the physical heavens. Every 2200 years the vernal equinox traverses one twelfth of the Zodiac, or band of twelve constellations. Back in 2800 BCE it entered the part of the Zodiac with the bull figure.[2] Religious professionals used this event in their worship symbolism. The Near East was inundated with bull worship. We even have the monotheistic Israelis putting up a golden calf in the desert wastes as it seemed their own invisible God had forsaken them.

About the time of the carrying away to Babylon, circa 600 BCE, the vernal equinox entered the sign of the ram. Bulls went out of style, and those who sought political power, such as Alexander the Great, prayed before the ram-headed Jupiter-Amon. This brings us back to *The Book of Daniel*, chapter 8, in which is described the vision of the ram and the he-goat, a power struggle which was to take place in the near future.

For us in these later centuries the vernal equinox has shifted again, and we have a song lauding the Age of Aquarius. We are so overcome with a multitude of communication information, that we do not seem to have the time to attach religious symbolism to this Zodiac figure. Our forebears may have already done this for us. Different countries have had different traditions for the Zodiac symbols, and the writings of men have many varied forecasts for what will come to pass. If we could digest all these pieces of information, we might learn a lot about what humans dread and hope for in earth's future, and we also might learn a lot about ourselves.

From our vantage point today, we can look back across the previous fabled ages and marvel at the wide distribution of common knowledge, in spite of long distances and lack of modern communication facilities. We also can marvel at the ability of early authors to twist and polish old tales and to give them bright new meanings, with which to reshape and renew dying forms of worship or of governance. All these stories make us realize that for the time of its sojourn here, humankind has been very concerned with the problems of governance and order. Also evidenced is the human wish for a time of fulfillment and a fear that the final age will be one of despair.

As all peoples have been created by the same God, it might be necessary for different races to go through similar stages or processes before coming to more fulfilled understandings. How many of the legends of the past speak of the weapons of war and power plays, rather than of cooperative ventures and the gentleness of parents with their children! A God who created an earth out of love, and described it as *good*, as in Genesis, surely must have felt dismay as the violent bronze age, gave way to the iron age with superior spears and consequent butchery. What must God feel today, as humanity arrogantly stands ready to demolish our earth?

It may be wrong to expect a future time when all will be just so and perfectly fine for the human race. Such an event would imply an end or a ceasing for the necessity of the process of becoming. We get our fulfillment from working within the process. If we are to believe in a God of order, who does not flinch before his/her virulently behaving creation, then we may believe that this God will allow that creation the freedom for the ultimate in power plays and destruction. What is worst in humanity may be necessary, to make that same humanity see what is truly for their good. God allowing creation to wreak disaster, is likely to precede God's saving hand working through that same creation.

Where do we find that saving hand? It is up to all of us to analyze what needs changing. In the description of Nebuchadnezzar's dream, invisible and insignificant people at the foot of the statue may have been the ones that caused the hurtling stone that debunked the whole structure and made a mountain that filled the whole earth. A mountain contains many particles forming one vast whole. A statue represents authority and power. Where can we find a way to govern that can consolidate and unite all peoples with the impartially of a mountain?

1.4 AN UNDERSTANDING OF COVENANT

There are many possible forms of government that have never been tried. Those in power seem to want to stick with the power structures the way they have always known them. Most of our governmental forms arose out the needs of small land holders to defend their properties against encroachers, and are the result of competitive societies. As the world approaches the need for greater understanding among peoples, we might consider community structures built on more cooperative methods, such as *covenant* and *consensus*. The human cooperates with God through *covenant*; he cooperates with others through *consensus*.

A covenant is a solemn compact between two parties. It may be of a legal or of a religious nature. The covenant spoken of here is to be considered as a covenant between the individual and his foremost ethical belief or ideal. Each individual has in his heart some prime object of his devotion that represents the best that he is able to be, or the maximum good that he can imagine. We might describe this covenant as an agreement between the human and God. If the person making the covenant is an atheist, the covenant becomes more of a pledge to simply perform at his maximum. The individual in covenant is still a very fallible human being, but one who is headed in a certain direction, one who is determined to become a fulfilled person. His fundamental options are to support what is best in himself and in others. There is to be no elitism in this covenant. Each is to esteem others as equally accepted by God.

There are two parts to every covenant. If a person makes a pledge to God and believes in the existence of that God, there seems to be a response on the part of God. If the atheist makes a pledge to be the best that he can, there seems to be a response from others around him, and even from the natural world that he inhabits.

When you get two covenanted individuals together, they often respond to each other, inspire each other, and build each other up. This reinforcement makes it necessary to define another word, *solidarity*. When two covenanted people support each other, and desire each other's fulfillment, then they can be said to be in *solidarity* with each other. The term *solidarity* in Pope John Paul's encyclical *Sollicitudo Rei Socialis* is used to describe a firm and persevering determination to commit oneself to the common good, the good of each and all and of the natural world.[3]

All this talk about covenantal pledge may sound idealistically positive. The optimists among us might be quick to project that if the earth were delivered into the hands of such dedicated and covenanted people, any form of government would be successful, but this is not the case. As we are fallible human beings, a well-run world may not necessarily be in our future. We have the choice to covenant in both positive and negative directions. Consequently, in our covenanting we can be well-meaning but misguided.

Those who govern nations today are often covenanted individuals committed to the good of the majority of those under their jurisdiction. People observing a certain method of governance, come to decisions about its appropriateness, because they have different enculturations. What is seen as oppression by some, is seen by others as altruistic. The leader may firmly believe that what he is doing, is for the good of the governed. As an extreme example, we could describe Hitler as a covenanted person dedicated to certain ideals. He had people on his staff in solidarity with him. They visualized a super earth run by a master race. Unfortunately their fundamental options did not include the good of all people. In order to have a viable government, we obviously need more than the two positive qualities of covenant and solidarity.

1.5 AN UNDERSTANDING OF CONSENSUS

At first glance, consensus can be taken to mean that a group of people have the same opinion. If all of us on earth held the same opinion, it would be a rather dull earth. Would that be a reasonable price to pay for world peace, a bunch of automatons mouthing "yes, yes" to a leader saying platitudes? God declared in *Genesis 1* that God had made a *good* earth, even though the people created to dwell in Eden had differences of opinion. Peace must mean something different to God than monotonous conformity.

How we all search for peace! What really is peace? Is it the absence of motion? Is it the stillness of death? Somehow I don't think God intended peace to mean absolute stillness. Peace is a word which can be equated with action. It might be described as actions that we continually must take, in order to live together in harmony.

Harmony is a good word to use when talking about peace. Peace does not come when we all believe the same thing. That is rather a definition of monotony. Do we enjoy the playing of a piano when someone taps the same note over and over? Isn't our enjoyment of music greater when many notes and instruments blend together? Peace might be better described as unity in diversity, as the harmony that comes about through blending many tones and themes constructively.

In the same manner, consensus does not mean unanimous agreement. Consensus is more of a harmonizing situation. If we speak of the person in covenant having the desire to do God's will in sincerity, then we can speak of those in consensus as also desiring to do God's will, even though they are in disagreement with the other parties in their consensus group. Consensus might be spoken of as a walking together in the same direction,[4] even though going by different paths. There is also the notion that one must have toleration for the other person; one must see that the different path is perhaps the right path for the other. In our search for the just world we must all start where we are, in some particular cultural setting, but we must maintain a broadened vision.

To work for justice in our own particular environment, using the principles of covenant and consensus, would require trust in one another and open communication with one another. For consensus in any matter, it is necessary for those involved to sit down together in a consensus circle and hear each other out. When we have all listened intently to one another's beliefs and have come to greater understandings on mutual problems, then a covenanted people can better decide in which direction to move.

1.6 AN INVITATION

This book is an invitation for you to join with me and others in an experimental consensus circle. Perhaps you have never participated in such a circle. The best method of attempting to come to consensus on any given topic is to have about twenty people sitting in a circle, so that everyone can see the expressions and reactions of each of the other participants. Everyone gets his chance to speak concisely on a given subject, and while he is speaking, no one interrupts him. No one gets a second turn to talk until everyone else has either spoken, or declined his turn. No one is allowed to speak too long, because others are waiting. No one criticizes the other members of the circle, or puts himself down. Everyone is respected and given opportunity to express himself.

There is no leader for this group. The group appoints one of its members to facilitate the process. This member states the topic that is to be discussed, and ideally he should not feel too strongly one way or the other about the topic. Then he is in a good position to call for a moment of silent reflection with an attempt at understanding, if he observes dissonance arising in the group.

Consensus operates well when the people who are gathered together are informed and serious about the chosen topic. If reactions with another group are being discussed, it would be wise to get members of this other group to participate. Many great ideas can come out of community discussions where everyone is listened to and the participants affirm one another. As many hands make light work, so do many minds come up with better ideas than any single mind working by itself.

When a topic is chosen, good ideas spring up if positive suggestions are emphasized. It is self-defeating to down grade a suggestion or to say that certain actions will not work. As much as possible, the positive must be emphasized, and peoples' capabilities must not be underestimated.

When people come to a consensus circle to work together on a subject, we find that positive results come from positive people. Circle members must be committed to what they truly feel is best for their group or best for humanity. We might describe them as covenanted individuals. They have made a promise to themselves or to God to attempt to be the best they can be. Thus people in covenant and consensus, should be able to run the world in a more creative manner, than those governments who either work dictatorially, or those who merely support the majority position of the citizens without considering vital needs of minorities.

Going back to my proposition of forming a consensus group on the subject matter of this book, I am assuming that all who read this book are covenanted individuals with some questions and some answers about the problems of the world. Consequently, if we seriously considered the structures which are the discussion of this book, we could come up with creative ideas on how to improve our world system. We might even improve our relationship with the God who created this world.

The topic I should like to open up for consensus discussion is one of worldwide dimensions. I observe that governments often seem to be more of a problem for people than a boon to those they govern. The subject I have chosen is: How can governmental structures be improved; specifically, how could we use the principles of covenant and consensus in order to benefit the people of our world?

Good ideas seem to come when people are face to face and committed to the subject which is being aired. Unfortunately the consensus circle to which I am inviting you is not of such high caliber. I am going to give my ideas on this topic, and will only get your reactions from a distance, if you care to respond. The more people who contribute their ideas on the subject, the better will be humankind's chances for improving their collective lot. I invite you to listen to my ideas, but in order to achieve maximum output from our consensus circle, I request that you carefully weigh my belief statements and temper them with your own covenanted and creative thought.

1.7 SELF-PRESERVATION, COMPETITION, AND COOPERATION

Humankind is an amazing race. Each of us is the product of a long genetic line extending back to our legendary first ancestors, Adam and Eve. In some marvelous manner we come from God's creativity, with who knows what inherent possibilities! We have reached where we are today through a process of competition with others and also through cooperation with others.

Competition can be seen in the young child's urge to live. He will fight his siblings for the attention of his mother who represents to him nourishment and comfort. Yet he will cooperate with his mother in her demands, as he sees that correct behavior furthers his own personal well being. At some point he will also learn that his own good depends on cooperation with his siblings and with other people in his enlarging world.

The mature individual emerges out of this *me first* attitude, being pleasant with others as he realizes that you catch more flies with honey than you do with vinegar. In this dramatic process of becoming an adult, sympathy for and understanding of the other often rub off onto us in our intertwining lives.

From a necessity for some sort of order in the helter-skelter of living, people shaped different types of viable community out of this mixture of egocentric personalities. Frequently this community grew naturally and directly out of what was at hand. The family community tended to give authority to the father who from earliest times usually possessed the physical strength to enforce his will on the other members. Groups of these fathers would band together to protect themselves and their families against other groupings of similarly self-seeking and family-protecting fathers. Across the whole earth people collected in communities, usually choosing or accepting a leader to direct them in whatever activities they felt promoted the good of the group.

It seemed that individual people survived better in the environment of earth if they were self-seeking and gathered in supportive groups. These groups survived who consolidated for the purpose of aggrandizing their group or increasing their territory. Competition between groups became the order of the day, and still is much in evidence in our present social structures.

Inside these aggrandizing groups, modes of cooperation were developed. Sometimes this cooperation was a blatant yielding to the authority of the group leader. Slaves learned their place. The lowly fawned before royalty and hierarchy. Caste systems developed. In a more positive manner some societies had communal leadership. Others accepted the wisdom of judges or prophets. All were looking for self preservation for their group.

Today we have nation states and applaud nationalism, many being willing to die for a particular flag or form of government. There are religious groupings, sometimes self serving and elitist. The generally approved practice in both church and state is to have a strong leader who affirms the primacy of one's select society. People often seem to believe that self preservation demands that their community compete with and overcome some other community that they imagine might somehow harm them. Thus we manufacture racial prejudice, religious intolerance, and wars between countries.

Apparently, this is the way the world runs. But it doesn't have to run this way. It might operate better in some other fashion, with some procedure which no one has yet tried. As we look around us, we find that the communities to which we have trusted ourselves, are letting us starve, are killing us with weapons, are not caring properly for us and the earth.

The purpose of this book is to open up possibilities for new modes of community living. It is to urge the world community to govern itself by covenant and consensus. As we are egocentric individuals, self preservation and competition would still be in order. As we are citizens of one convergent earth, cooperation and understanding of the other, would be a necessity. In a community using covenant and consensus, each individual would use his free choice to assist in the building of the group.

The individual has massive potential. The community, as made up of individuals, can be an even more surprising entity. It is a difficult thing for one human being to forgive the wrong done to him by another, yet often we see reconciliation and forgiveness that astound us. Groups, too, can forgive. People on opposing sides in bloody wars, can set the past aside, and create new structures. Only because of the resiliency of humankind, have we lasted so long.

With our human inventiveness and freedom, we should have the courage to try new methods of interaction with one another. Perhaps we do not need governors, kings, priests, teachers, bosses, or authorities lording it over us. Using the collected wisdom of the ages, it is conceivable that we could make up our own guiding regulations and laws for our own particular group. Differing cultures could continue their unique practices without fear of displeasure from other groups.

With our world becoming so interrelated, we must have new ways to worship the one God of all the earth. Perhaps we do not need temples or Gothic cathedrals, or church prelates. Confining God to a structure or an individual may encourage us to think of God's sphere of influence as limited to one particular temple or one particular religious leader. With the communication of ethical standards spreading over the earth, our individual consciousnesses are more open to the spiritual wisdom which can dwell everywhere and anywhere and in anybody.

With the promising possibilities of television, we may no longer need the authoritative school structures which we inherited from the Romans. It may not be necessary to segregate teen agers into one difficult to manage group in a "high school" area. We must not standardize the students' education, but let them formulate their own inclinations and enlarge their horizons through discussion groups and experiential learning, which can help them to exercise their own individual abilities. Television could be structured to give a variety of supporting courses. In order to build a better society, those covenanted individuals charged with organizing such inspiring television would be dedicated to character building rather than materialism.

Television is relatively new on the scene, and like most human inventions, can be a problem or a blessing to our present age. It is there as a challenge for us, and, please God, we will rise up and meet the challenge. There are also problems in our writhing world today that seem to have been with us from time immemorial. We power grab; we act from fear; we mistreat our children. Will we profit from looking carefully at our past errors, or will we continue to have the same agonies over and over?

If covenanted people meet in consensus circles, and discuss wise measures of governance, we may discover new methods of creating order in our world. We may come to better understandings of God and of others. Under the consensus process, we may find that some feel that God is a God of power and that God's will is accomplished by his working through powerful leaders. Others may affirm that it is more probable that God is a God of love, and that only the compassionate aid in God's processes. In order to investigate how God's people should comport themselves to be on the pathway towards good government and a Utopian society, we must try to understand what God is like. Therefore our next step will be to discuss a possible God-system based on consideration and kindness.

2

THE WAY

OF

THE ETERNAL GOD

2.1 THE EARTH AS BORN OF CONFLICT

Looking out from our small portion of terra firma, we see the vastness of created things from an all-too-human perspective. God is so large, and we are so small. We hold reverently in our minds that in the beginning God created the heavens and the earth (Genesis 1:1). God saw all God had made, and indeed it was very good (Genesis 1:31). We are commanded, "Be holy, for I am holy!" (Leviticus 19:2). The immensity of God and the universe can easily disturb us, and we may become discouraged, believing that we can never hope to perform in anything that comes close to imitating a Godly manner.

In order to become holy or Godly, it is necessary to have an idea of what holiness is, and what God is like. It is difficult for the smallness of us to understand, even partially, the bigness of God. Even the wisest ones among us, after prolonged meditation and discussion, can only generalize and point off in the distance. Ineligible as I am to write on the subject, I shall try to make a rough sketch of the scene as I see it, viewed from the inside of one monad on planet earth. I shall set down possible relationships among God, humankind, and creation. You may disagree with these, and you are invited to decide upon your own set of relationships, and to use that as the basis for accepting or rejecting the remaining ideas that I set down here. Only if we can come up with a reasonable way that God might "act", can we hope to imitate God's actions, and to have any sort of success at being "holy".

Our approach to any problem is conditioned by the assumptions we bring to it. For example, the biblical God has promised the land to those who would follow his injunctions. If we assume that God is, above all, a compassionate God, then we might interpret this to mean that God has given humankind the earth to share compassionately with one another. On the other hand, we might assume that there is a very special relationship between ourselves and this compassionate God, and that God's love is given only to us and not to our enemies. Then we would be justified in concluding that our enemies did not deserve a peaceful spot of land to call their own. Since many assumptions pertain to our relationship with God, we need to step way back, and see that relationship in the broad context of creation and the nature of God.

We must marvel at the physical and mental components of God's ultimate construction, the human being, who displays such interesting propensities for both good and evil. In looking realistically at ourselves, one of our major ruminations should be to reflect on what kind of a God would set up this type of situation, of human beings on a round globe. Comparing this minute planet we inhabit with the vastness of surrounding space, there is a certain difficulty in imagining an infinite being forming this finite entity, our world, and our seemingly finite selves.

This creation of God's was no mild and peaceful process. If the heavens declare the glory and splendor of God (Psalm 19:1), we must look at them and also see the turmoil, the tremendous explosions, the upheaval and the entropy of their construction. Stars are born and die, in order to rise again like phoenix from their ashes. We must not fail to see the black holes that go into nowhere for infinity. All this reflects the mysterious hand that continues to infuse and to create this riotous masterpiece.

God and the human look at this stupendous organism and both proclaim it good and marvelous. God looked on this work, and said it was good (Genesis 1:31). Man professes to see God-guided order in the firmament which shows God's handiwork (Psalm 19:1). How any one can see order in all this hurtling of stars and meteorites with consequent possibilities of collision, is a marvel in itself. But how often in our knowledge has our sun had a major collision? We do not know for sure of any such dramatic, earth shaking, and heaven shaking occurrence, unless it was such an event that spawned our

THE WAYS OF GOD ARE REFLECTED IN GOD'S CREATION

solar system. The seeming stability of this solar system gives us confidence in God's protective care. We dwell in a certain kind of security, an equilibrium that we see as a safe place. Looking at the earth from a God's-eye viewpoint, we have a wonderful environment in which the human race can grow to maturity. The heavens may be akin to Fourth of July fireworks on a magnificent scale, but outer space does not molest us. We are treated to a distant view of star explosions and to near-by wonders such as comets. Occasionally a large meteor may drop in, but on the whole, the universe allows us plenty of room in which to develop. From that perspective one could conclude that our God is a providential God for the entire human species.

2.2 DIFFERENT CONCEPTS OF GOD

God didn't just create the earth and retire to his throne room and forget about us. He penetrates our individual consciousnesses, and invites our thanks and our worship. We attempt to visualize God and to thank God, but we each are constrained to do it in our own way. Due to the many distinctive cultures represented on our earth, we come up with different ideas of God and also with varying notions of what God expects of us. Abraham thought of God in a slightly different manner than did his son Isaac. The God-idea of Jacob combined the learnings of his two thoughtful ancestors, with Jacob's own experiences. Thus we have the God of the Jewish people often described as the God of Abraham, the God of Isaac, and the God of Jacob. The God-idea profits from the knowledge of both the ancestors and the group. Our God-concepts today are formulated from previous wisdom down through the ages, and also from our reactions to our present culture. Yet we can combine all this knowledge, and still admit our abysmal ignorance of God's plan and God's purposes for us.

In our culture today we are not usually in the mode where we ask our neighbor with openness what he thinks God is like. However, if we are to even begin to understand the nature of our world wide God, it is necessary to seek and sort through humankind's many actions and reactions, and also to attempt to see through the eyes of others who are of different times, cultures, and religious beliefs. Some of these others have very strange thoughts about the being who is in control, and whom they choose to worship. We should be prepared to be startled.

While observing the justice and punishment systems of our society and other structures that have been formed which encourage both the person's humanness and inhumanness to others, I came across an individual who professed the religion of Satanism. I asked him about his worship, and he assured me that Satan was a friendly and obliging master. If he prayed to this being, he would be given material needs and power. With these gifts, he would then be able to help his needy friends. With generosity, he offered to allow me in the circle of this worship, promising that this being was kind to all who came. Several reservations made me unable to accept his hospitable offer. One prime draw back was the man's feeling that he had to carve a pentagonal symbol on his flesh. It seemed that a being who demanded mutilation, in order to be worshiped properly, might not be my kind of God.

Then I thought about Father Abraham and how his God required that all the males of his household come under the knife of circumcision. There was even a question in Abraham's mind as to whether or not his God required the sacrifice of an infant son. Many people put their trust in a jealous God who demands strict adherence to proscribed behavior accompanied with many placating offerings.

When I considered what Satan was willing to do for his friend today, I came to the conclusion that Abraham, the friend of God, didn't really get much more. Abraham worshiped God in order that he might have his material needs filled and that he might have power. Abraham's power consisted in having the gift of land to pass on to those he loved and had hopes for, namely his descendents. As it was necessary in this scenario to have descendents, Abraham's God also supplied progeny to Abraham.

Many of us today worship God for what we can get out of God. As long as God fills our needs and answers our prayers, we are faithful to our worship. Often if there is some sort of a calamity in our personal lives, we become angry with God. We shout, "God, I hate you for doing this to me!" We shake our fist at God and refuse to have anything more to do with religion. Our God has failed us. We do not hear that Abraham's God ever failed Abraham, and Abraham has become for us a shining example of faith. My acquaintance, the Satanist, is comfortable with the relationship he has with the being he worships. Is there so much difference between his faith, and the faith of Abraham? All of us construct our God from the cultural elements that surround us. My acquaintance had been rejected by society, and he could not come up with a more appropriate image of power that would protect his weakness, and be in opposition to his persecuters. In like manner all peoples throughout the ages worship a God who is relevant for them. We have to start imagining God from where we're at. Certainly, none of us can claim to be fully acquainted with the Being that is the ground for all being. Most of us start by recognizing a power beyond ourselves, and want to keep on the *good side* of that power. Often we believe that this *power* is interested in our welfare, and is against our enemies.

We must marvel at the faith of Abraham, coming as he did from a multi-god culture, where each city-state had its own most powerful deity. Leaving his father's house, and going into an unknown land, he needed a God who would protect him. Perhaps at that point of time, there in the mind of Abraham, was the birth of our present ideas of a personal God who walked beside the human and guided his footsteps. This God began as a small-time God of a sheep grazing country, in a time when the Near East was thought to be all the known world. As humankind's horizons broadened, ideas of God enlarged to include God's sovereignty over all the earth.

Abraham had to think often about the wishes of his new friend. Did his friend believe in child sacrifice, like the lesser gods worshipped by his contemporaries? Abraham had no Bible and no church. He held the community together with the covenant of circumcision, another idea that was employed in the culture of his day. Abraham's God enabled Abraham to overcome his enemies and to rescue his nephew Lot. Did Abraham believe that his God hated those enemies? Did he feel that the enemies were children or creations of a different god?

The God of Isaac also came from the culture of the time of Abraham. With Isaac there was no question of sacrificing small children to appease an unstable character in the heavens. Still this God seemed to enjoy being praised and noticed and thanked for the first fruits of the land. This gentler notion of God may have been instilled by his mother Sarah. God according to Isaac, seems to be a more caring God, and assists in finding his devotee a suitable wife. God may care for Isaac, but God is still very formidable, not a being to mess around with. If Isaac is to pass God's caring concern on to his sons, it is a very serious matter. Thus his worship of God included bestowing blessings which gave the recipient a special relationship with God.

Isaac's son Jacob evidently acquired the cultural heritage that spoke of a God that was concerned with following through on appropriately conferred blessings. It became very necessary for Jacob to be the recipient of a particular liturgical formula. In his youth Jacob is not too concerned with the thought of God's caring love for other people. The God of Jacob would show favoritism to whomever manuevered themselves into the way of a heartfelt blessing. Jacob pictured God as someone who permitted you to use deceit, in order to acquire power. This God allowed Jacob to ignore the needs of the other, even when the other was his own blood brother.

Fortunately, Jacob grew up, and as he grew older, he changed, and as he changed, his notion of God changed. In his youth he saw himself as the ruler over his brother. In his maturity he believed in a God that allowed him and his brother to live in the land as equals. This change of religious belief was not accomplished without agony. We are told of Jacob wrestling with God (Genesis 32:23-32) and that ever after, Jacob walked with a limp.

Could it be that during his wrestling match, Jacob was given new insight on the validity of blessings and on a person's true relationship with God? In his youth Jacob believed that a father's blessing was efficacious for passing on every material good; he believed this so heartily that he behaved dishonestly to gain this blessing. In his age his eyes were opened as to the weakness of any blessing, without appropriate kindness and forgiveness. We are not told in the Bible story that Jacob lorded it over Esau. We are told that each brother found a suitable territory, and that they lived together without altercation (Genesis 36:6-8). Could we learn something here by comparing the immature Jacob to the immaturity of many people today? Should any of us believe that God's blessing of a secure land, is only for us?

This altercation of Jacob with his God may have signalled a change of direction for the whole human race. In our growth as a species, we evolved selfishly. Those who survived to reproduce were those individuals who thought, "Me first." Those who were gentle and gave way before aggression, died out rapidly. Competition was the name of the game. Jacob had come to a point in his life where continued competition was liable to mean non-survival. He had to learn a new game called cooperation. In our present nuclear age, the whole world has to learn this new game, or our species may destroy itself.

The ideas of God enshrined in the minds of Jacob and Esau came out of the times and culture in which they lived. Our ideas of God are also culturally conceived. Conversely, how we feel about social customs is directly affected by how we feel about God. Culture gives us suggestions about God; we nurture and reflect on these, and then we plow these ideas and ideals back into our culture. If our God is a warrior God fighting to maintain his superiority in the heavens, we will develop notions of vengeance and use strict disciplinary measures to enforce authority. When circumstances or maturity lead us to more loving notions of God, we will consider these refinements in our hearts, and perhaps change our society accordingly.

Each individual in his time, can ponder on the heritage of prior cultures, and also learn lessons from his present culture, in order to come up with his own personal God formulation. Paul, in bringing new God concepts to the Athenians (Acts 17:23-34), attempted to give them fresh insights about the being they worshipped called the Unknown God. Of course, God is unknown to all of us, but as people meet together and compare notes on how God seems to them, they can grow together in their understandings. Paul quoted the trusted Greek scholars, Epimenides (In God we live, move, and exist.) and Aratus (We are all God's children.) to his Athenian listeners. Then he proposed his own enlarged belief in Jesus as the carrier of God's word. By Paul's efforts, belief in the saving God of the Jews was spread through the Graeco-Roman world, and the God vision of humanity was broadened.

Likewise for us in our age, there is a need for broadening our concept of God and God's activities. Let us look within ourselves, and try to express what sort of God is relevant for the future which we hope for. We manufacture our particular God portrait from our individual outlook on what we believe to be the virtues and disadvantages of our present society. It may be influenced by how we see our religious beliefs furthering effective community. As we come from the same time period and similar culture, and as humankind has a tendency to create the God image needed for its historical period, there may be similarities between our beliefs. As we all have our individual differences, our God concepts will have their variations.

The model which follows is proposed as one possible starting point for our discussion of the renewal of the earth. Of course these pseudo-theological comments are not the final word for all times and for all places. Having been formed in a Judaeo-Christian milieu, it is natural for me to speak from that viewpoint. As we communicate with those of other faiths, our ideas grow, but continue to spring from our roots. In having to do with God, theology *becomes* as the concept of God *becomes*; people's ideas change and are broadened as they interact with others, and as the world spins onward.

2.3 EVOLUTION

Our ideas of a *special relationship* to God depend on our perspective of the entire creation, and how we fit into that total drama. We see ourselves and our earth as the product of millions of years of development. What does that tell us about our journey and our God?

The only way we come to know anything about the unknowable God is through his creation and primarily through ourselves, through humankind. Humankind exists. We agree that we have the quality of being. Anticipating death, we find this being to be temporary and finite. As our material knowledge of our being is unable to go before our conception or after our death, we assume that we have a beginning and an ending. Thus, it seems that we are finite. From this possibly finite viewpoint, we observe certain processes in action, and come to corresponding conclusions about life and death, good and evil, and what deeds might be appropriate to influence the process. We ask ourselves, "What is the purpose of life; what should we do?" With the rich young man of Matthew 19:16, we wonder, "Master, what good deed must I do to possess eternal life?" Eternal life becomes an important thing, a specific *good* that we egotistically wish to possess.

The evolving human seems to contain a seemingly selfish streak that enables him to exist in the material world, and to seek for some future existence in a spiritual realm. This egoism may be necessary for the development of whatever plans God has for us. We must respect ourselves and seek for the good of ourselves, if we are to have empathy for others.

If we accept as fact that humanity is due to the natural selection of the fittest genes to cope with the environment, then we must also admit to the fact that as the human progresses across the stage of history, he also naturally selects the fittest institutions and ideas that will assist him to survive in this world. These ideas and institutions need not be perfect, and are going to change with evolving problems. As the centuries move to wherever time is leading us, the needs of our religious, governmental, economic, and legal structures slowly change in both our individual and communal perceptions.

In thinking of biological creation and evolution, we first need to explain the urge to evolve. There seems to be an ongoing change from the simple to the more complex life form. The odds for life developing from non-life are very low. The odds for a world that supports life, to come into being out of the rubble of star explosions, are very low. This urge to complexity under such low probabilities, gives us reason to argue for a Controlling Omniscience, which inspirits the lowly atom with the drive to unite. We choose to believe that this omniscience created a cosmos to love, drawing it from energies within, and inspiriting it on a path that fulfills certain purposes. If this creation were a random happening, it seems that we would not have this urge to move forward, or a hope for the future.

The fact that we have choices in making our way towards the future, displays the whole process of evolution. Different forms of life evolved, and those which were the most adaptable, survived. In our daily lives we make choices, and those that seem to lead onward to something positive, we encourage. Those that lead us backward, we take note of, and make resolutions not to repeat them (or plot how to conceal them). Here we have the origin of the idea of good and evil. We have this desire to go in the direction of the good. It must be that our very genes are inspirited with this thrust to fulfilled life. It seems that this thrust exists, not just in the individual, but in the gathered community. We have a collective dream of perfection; we speak of a future when all will be justice and peace.

We compare the good we hope for, with the imperfection we see around us. We use the words, *good* and *evil*, to describe the different degrees of progress or retrogression. We can compare good and evil as we compare shades of light and darkness. We can see the shades only by comparison. If there were total darkness (absolute evil), we couldn't see at all. Total light would also be blinding. It seems that varying shades of gray, is the fertile ground where humanity exists. We do our work in the shades of gray, and we try to maximize the light and minimize the darkness. Our thrust is toward the ideal, toward the absolute light. Is this blinding light the goal of humanity, or is there another reason for our existence? Perhaps the goal of a Utopia is unrealistic for humanity; more important might be the way we walk toward the possibly unobtainable goal. It seems that the plan of our God might be that we participate somehow in the creative process, which remains forever unfinished.

2.4 ENERGY OF THE EARTH

There are energies that flow through the world. Some we can evaluate, and some we have no means of measuring. We are familiar with the power of electricity. Electrons flow along a wire, and if the receiving object is properly designed, we will observe an animation. Other energies are not confined to wires and travel through air, as radio waves, or even penetrate solids, as x-rays. It seems reasonable to believe that space may be crowded with energies, all set in place by a purposeful God.

It is plausible to believe that as everything has been created by God, each atom is somehow inspired by God. Every material aspect of creation has its corresponding non-material charges. The scientist priest, Teilhard de Chardin, termed this psychical aspect of matter, the *with-in*.[1] He associated this energy which he saw working throughout the earth, with God's evolutionary thrust. He expected all these energies to help to lead us up to the Omega Point, or apex of fulfillment for humanity, a seemingly finite solution for a finite earth.

Teilhard's notion of *with-in* can have many variations. It may be a very simple attachment to the elementary molecule, or it may be a vitalized concentrated energy like the human soul. In the prehistoric sea, electric sparks from lightning jostled the non-vital *with-in* of chemical elements and sea water, changing them to vitalized plankton. There is a difference between the *with-in* of the growing tree and the *with-in* of the crafted table. There seem to be as many diverse types of *with-in* as there are designs of the material. We meditate in awe on the *with-in* of the total material globe we call the earth. There are those who hold the Gaia theory that the earth is in some sense alive. Teilhard considered the concentrated thought layer of all humanity and visualized it as a noosphere of loving energy gradually growing and encircling the world.

We cannot measure the energy of this noosphere. Our space scientists have not yet invented the cameras to photograph this energy of our earth. However, we can observe that living things, and particularly the human being, possess a large potential for empathy, caring love, kindness, and constructive action. The spiritual energy that this represents obviously exists, and flows from many in this world to many others,- often at great distances. People feel the joys and the suffering of others; they act to spiritually unite themselves with the other; and they devote their lives to the common good. Strange psychic power is manifested in times of great national stress:- a nation prays, spirits are raised, hope soars, and miracles occur. The Hebrews are led through the sea. A Joan of Arc unites her countrymen. These examples speak to a force beyond our ken, which seems to be constantly at work in humankind. Some people might call this force, God. Some might say it is Holy Spirit. Some might term it energy that is initiated by God. Some might feel that it is simply the way that things work in a universe that has happened by chance.

It is clear, nevertheless, that the human spirit is capable of being activated and marshalled to great effect. There apparently is a great reservoir of spiritual energy within the human heart, that is not always, yet frequently, tapped for the momentous creation of good. This phenomena is observed in many individuals, and, even more dramatically, in the occasional consensus for good among peoples.

2.5 ORIGIN AND CONTINUITY OF THE HUMAN AND THE SOLAR SYSTEM

Individuals, tribes, and nations rightfully hold that they have special relationships to their creator. The nature of that relationship, however, depends on the perspective one has of the totality of God's creation, and our place within it. That perspective shifts as we learn more and more about the realities of space, the universe, and the tiny craft we call earth. We have a role, perhaps a crucial role, in an incredibly vast birthing process.

We think of our world as a closed finite system. We also see our solar system, large as it may be, as a finite unit. However, we cannot comprehend the bounds of the universe, so we describe it as infinite. We also describe God as infinite. We are related to God; our earth is related to the infinite universe. The infinite and continuous God is somehow connected to our finite and non-continuous world. These unexplainable energies that go along with our visible created earth, must be our tie-in with the eternal. Somehow, we are all part of God's never-ending system.

Our particular spot in the vastness of space, this sun with its family of planets, was born four and a half billion years ago. To this star, our sun, we can relate the story of Genesis,- in the beginning of comprehensible time, God created this solar system and this earth; but Genesis says nothing about God's beginning, or the beginning of the complex flow of matter and energy, of which we are such a small and finite part, when considered materially.

If we take our eyes off the fact of our physical death, we may see a new aspect of our importance. We are both matter and energy. In some form we shall go on forever. Our material substance does not totally vanish when we die. It may change into other substances. If we think about it, we can see that we undergo transformation, not only at the moment of death, but all through our lives. Our spiritual energies also fluctuate. When our physical bodies decay into other forms of life, people often remember the kind ideas we had when our thinking minds were with them; some of our spiritual good remains behind us. Thus, what is our being has its ebb and flow, both spiritually and physically.

The total universe has its ebb and flow. All matter and energy pulse in a vast process. Scientists predict that our sun will cool and our solar system will degenerate. The material aspects of our solar system will scatter, perhaps, to form new stars. Its spiritual *within* may be incorporated in new star systems, or may somehow be

united with the energy of the Being that guides the whole astounding
infinite process. It is within this wonderful system that the human
species has developed. We expect that all this is somehow the plan
of God. This total creation, therefore, which of course includes *all*
peoples of the earth and humanoids of other star systems, is the
object of God's love and the working area for God's process.

2.6 THE NON-BEGINNING OF THE UNIVERSE

Our provincial view of space has often been accompanied by a
provincial view of time, as well. We tend to think of our current time,
or at least our own recorded history, as the only important time. For
the future, we look forward to a definitive completion, or fulfillment
of our hopes. The special relationship to God,- the *promise* of God,
is anticipated in real time. However, time, too, may be much larger
than any of us has imagined. We already realize that it has taken
millions of years of evolution to fashion the human minds of today.
Even our notion of the beginning of time, with the advent of creation, may prove to be provincial and limiting to our concepts.
Sometimes, just hypothesizing a broader model of reality helps.

It may be unrealistic to believe that we should have a finite
universe with a beginning, hooked up to a system of an infinite God.
Our material universe may not have happened at some point in time.
It may be a continuous creative process that goes on forever (as God
goes on forever. God may be its *With-in.*) The universe may have its
physical singularities where it collapses into black holes, but it also
has its points of regeneration. We cannot comprehend its galactic
oscillations. It is hard to push our minds back to infinity, but we can
see in our everyday time frame, that there is a transfer between
matter and energy. We have a tree because it gets light energy from
the sun. When the tree decays, its particles decompose and have the
potential to give energy to the soil. Do all these processes wind down
to entropy? As our sun gets cooler and cooler, our solar system as we
know it, will perish. Like the decaying tree, earth's dust will feed back
into new solar systems. Will the whole universe run down? It hasn't
yet. It seems to be in pretty good working order.

There is the belief that God always was, and it is possible to
picture God as pure non-material First Cause. We say that God is
love, yet a non-material First Cause cannot be love, in isolation, as

love requires an object. Some explain this apparent contradiction by saying that God is Trinity, and thus could love the other aspects of Godself. This sounds a bit narcissistic. Another explanation is that God could love a creation that did not yet exist by foreknowledge,- that we existed in the mind of God, and consequently God knew about us and could love us.

It seems unnecessary to postulate an instant of time for the creation of the universe, when it is just as easy to suppose that this ebb and flow of energies in which we exist, always was and always will be. Thus God always had this *other* to love, if we visualize this *other* as the material aspect of God's continuous creative process, rather than as a creation back at some point in time.

With this continuous system it is more reasonable to consider God to be Infinite Love, as God consequently always had an object to love. Instead of finitizing God by calling God "Trinity" we might recognize God as Community consisting of Godhead in union with matter and energy. Being bound by our earthly considerations, we might see matter as being represented by the possibilities of God in the material. We might see energy as Holy Spirit, or the *with-in* attached to this matter. This matter, energy, and God as the instigator of the process, keeping all in flux, may always have existed.

These conjectures may miss the mark. However, to simply admit their possibility, and our necessary ignorance, serves to free us from provincial interpretations of God's promise. The universality of God's love throughout space, embracing all peoples within its infinite vastness, can also be seen in God's continuous creation. The fulfillment of God's promise, therefore, is not limited to a particular place of our choosing, and also not in a particular phase of our comprehension. In the light of the grandeur of God's creation, and his infinite love, we can expect his promise to be similarly universal in both space and time.

2.7 THE DIMINISHMENT OF GOD

Older myths about God, particularly from the ancient Greeks and Romans, emphasized the power of God and the exercise of that power. Many associated concepts of the warlord nature of God followed. That image tends to give the spoils to the victor or the good, and to punish the loser or the transgressor. On the other hand, there is the even stronger image of the all loving God that steadfastly wills human fulfillment. In this perspective, the God-inspired attributes of compassion and a willingness to sacrifice for another are dominant.

When a mother pours out love to her child, the mother is not diminished by that outpouring. Knowledge, too, can be shared without loss to the giver. On the other hand, a mother is ready to sacrifice worldly possessions and pleasures for the good of her child. The Old Testament has a strong flavor of sacrificial offerings to God as a symbol of readiness to give of one's self for another. Jesus, too, emphasized by his suffering and death, the nobility of personal diminishment for another. What does this tell us about God? Considering that God may likewise exhibit an empathetic love which fosters giving and even sacrifice for another, one might illustrate the nature of God in the following manner.

In our hypothetical presentation of the universe, God always had this community of love with matter and energy, and somehow supports it and regenerates it, as the universe continues to be in good operation. In continually renewing the material aspect of creation, God has nothing other than Godself with which to uphold it. We consider God to be total love. If we love another human being, even imperfectly, we are willing to give of ourselves for that person. A mother may give her life for her child. If God totally loves us, God is willing to be diminished for us.

Admitting that we do not understand the Mystery that is God, we will conjecture that this Mystery is perhaps comparable to a type of energy that we will term *God-energy*. If *God-energy* represents total love, then God was (and is) (and will be) willing to give of God's self to God's creation. We are accustomed to think of this in terms of God's spirit, or *the holy spirit* present in the depths of each person. Total love, it seems, would be willing to give of itself, in this way, even if that meant, in some sense, a diminishment of God for the universe. Cyclically, God-energy could be transformed into the material universe.

In order to illuminate the idea of this flow of God's love, consider for a moment an extreme case. If at any time this were a total transformation of God-energy into the material and spiritual of the universe, then we might believe with the Buddhists in a God of

Absolute Nothingness. If we were to consider that all the material and spiritual goods of the universe have come from a God who has been totally diminished for this purpose, we would be left with a point of transfer, the point of absolute nothingness, through which all things are given to the universe, and back to which all loving energies from the universe, gravitate. These energies from the universe, upon touching this Point, could return immediately to the service of love throughout the universe.

It may not be necessary to believe in a God who is merely a Point of Transfer. God is infinite, and although it is hard to imagine, we can take an infinite amount away from an infinite quantity, and may still possibly have an infinite amount left. God may keep putting an infinite amount of God-energy into the material aspect of the universe, and still contain in Godself, an infinite amount of God-energy. It may be mathematically impossible to totally diminish God. We sense this in our contemplation of God. God is with us, but is also Mystery apart from us. God is immanent in the universe, yet transcends the universe.

Another objection to a totally diminished God comes about by making the comparison of God to a wise parent. The wise parent knows that it often is not in the best interests of the child to give the child everything. If you want your child to grow mentally, morally, and emotionally, you give the child freedom to operate, but don't force yourself upon him. God may remain aloof, so that we may be fulfilled.

In this hypothetical model, whether as Point of Transfer or Surplus God-Energy, we see God immanent in the world, imparting some essence of the Godhead within the creation, and particularly within the peoples of the world. We see Love-Energy as an integral part of the universal creation process. We see God continually giving of that essence for the fulfillment of all persons. Though the model is imperfect, perhaps the underlying concept has validity. And if we can perceive the essence of God to be granted, and potentially active, in all persons, then we cannot fail to be motivated to emulate and support that process. That nature of God calls for a reflection of that giving nature in ourselves. It calls for our own caring love, with compassion, and with a willingness to diminish ourselves, when appropriate, for the good of all of God's creation.

2.8 THE PURPOSE OF HUMANITY

We have been looking at the upper side of the process, at the relationship of God and the universe. In order to come to greater understanding, let us speculate further on what possible role humanity plays in God's plan. Perhaps God loves us in order that we may return God's love. God supports us in order that God may be nourished by us. We are not made without possibilities of redeeming service. It may be that we are created in God's *image* in order that our human energy may nourish God-energy. It may not be that we are merely created for an ecstatic personal or community rapture, with the comfortable feeling that we will enjoy the reward of a distant heaven. Our best services to this God-energy may be in the *here and now*.

Feelings and their expression are very important to our material being. Their effects go beyond the past and present time, and beyond our present space. Our willful reactions and suppressions of feelings can affect the whole way of the world. They can enhance how we move amidst the material. If we look at a stranger's face and have a feeling of instant dislike because it reminds us of something embittering, then we can willfully change our feelings, and pray for the good of the stranger, and for peace for ourselves to accept whatever embittered us. This does something positive to the energy that is running loose in the world, and to the energy that is warped within ourselves. Re-settling the intangible energy within ourselves, can change our whole physical being. We can greet the stranger, sending out subtle signals of friendship and positive vibrations, which will somehow affect his physical being. Our willful energies can nourish incomprehensible realities.

In our humanness, therefore, we can create the sustenance God uses to replenish an essence of Godself. The Hebrews believed that the blood of sacrificial animals would cleanse them from sin. As they believed it, it was so. The material signs helped in the manufacture of positive attitudes. Jesus, in his life and death ennobled the world. As he showed us total love in the willing diminishment of himself for others, those who believe in him motivate themselves to live in like manner. By this way, they seek salvation. Salvation might therefore be defined as the adequate manufacture of God-energy. We are a successful world if, in spite of whatever material and spiritual frustration we have, we manufacture a good quantity of God-energy and thus are privileged to cooperate in the loving process which is God.

If our purpose here is to produce God-energy (in order to return this quantity to the Godhead or Point of Redistribution, so that it may be spread out again to those in need), we should analyze the different ways we can accomplish this. A human being can act certain ways in everyday life, for the furtherance of love. In living in harmony with God's plan, and in prayer, one can create energy that goes back to God-energy. We can observe the ripple effect of a generous deed. It activates similar generosity in the hearts of others. Better known names for such God-energy include empathy, caring love, kindness, forgiveness, healing, justice, and freedom. In everyday life, we have the opportunity to increase or to decrease these precious commodities. We add or subtract from the common wealth of the world community in these matters.

God's promise, the fulfillment of humankind, must relate to this over-riding purpose of humanity. We succeed only to the extent that we are part of that divine plan for the universe. Fulfillment comes only in being and living so as to contribute our spiritual energy to God's loving creation process, which embraces all of God's space and time. We implement God's promise as we become the people of God, the holy people, integrating the essence of God unto ourselves, and recognizing that essence in all others. In practice this can only be done by generating God-energy with forgiveness, justice, empathy, love, and kindness for all.

In death, too, when the human soul is freed from the body, a tremendous energy may be released to return to Godhead. Both our life and our death can contribute to the flow of love. The Great Shepherd cares for the sheep tenderly, because we were designed with certain potentials, and in our proper living, we contribute to the purposes laid in place by this design.[2] The Great Shepherd gently guides our souls, for in our life and death, they may profusely contribute to the well being of the whole flock.

2.9 THE PLACE OF EVIL IN THE UNIVERSE

There is a lot to be said for freedom of choice. It is a gift from God. If we were made to behave in a perfect manner, there would be no

merit for us in this perfection. It is our conscious choice to love that
builds God-energy throughout the earth. Sometimes our choices are
poor in their energy value. We make a choice according to what we
think is good for us, when we should have considered what was good
for both ourselves and another person, or even what was good for
the whole world. We forget that we are only a part of God's precious
universe. We try to optimize the good in a very limited sphere of
space and time. The continuing challenge is to be ever aware of
God's total creative process, and to strive to optimize the good in all
the space and time we can comprehend.

Our leaders build larger and more powerful weapons, because they think they are protecting our people; the ultimate result
of their choice is to destroy other people. They think they are
building love and security for themselves and their country, but they
are confused. They confuse God's universal plan to be their myopic
provincial plan. However, their confusion enables others to see the
necessity for different choices that truly do lead to the manufacturing of love among all nations. From a different perspective, other
peoples learn from the bitter experience of myopic leaders. Gradually, a wider view prevails among more and more peoples. In the
process, great harm may be done to other individuals and other nations.

There is some small consolation in the belief that many
persons have been inspired to loving counter-actions, and this
energy is not lost. In the awful event that we totally destroy our world
in the process of building better weapons, one can hope that the
accumulated God-energy may be available to create spirit anew,-
even possibly in new worlds millions of light years away. In any event,
it's OK for the universe to be swirling with creative and destructive
powers. This is the sign of the caring presence of a process God. This
God gave us freedom, and to properly exercise freedom, there must
be options for us to select.

Dame Julian of Norwich inquires, "Lord, what do you do
about sin?"[3] God replies that he doesn't blame us, that he is not
angry because we sin. Sin is a process that goes along with learning
to love. We only become experts in love through the method of trial
and error. If we make no moves, test no situations, God will spue us
out of his mouth (Revelation 3:16). Sin, from heaven's viewpoint,

may often be wounds of honor; it is the way we all grow.

Goodness is not moral obedience to law, but the innate spirit of all that is, exercising the process of choice, of overcoming error. The structure of reality (what God operates) is good; the structure of society (the operation of humankind) is full of error, but we need that error to give us room to grow. "The Lord allows both weal and woe" (Isaiah 45:7). We learn from our woes and attempt to structure our society to lessen these woes. If we keep plowing through our ever present errors, living through our weaknesses, we will look back and see that each *sin* or *despair* was potentially a turning point, a spot of resolution and renewed responsibility, a point of glory, a new beginning, an instant when we were privileged to manufacture love energy.

In this model of God, God is not a God of wrath. If we feel wrath or annoyance because of error, ours or another's, we must not say that it is God's wrath. It is our wrath, our annoyance. God allows us to feel wrath and annoyance, that we might better see the error of our ways, and strike out into new and better directions. Many of us want to punish the other person when he *sins*. Pointing our finger at another, makes us feel just. God's justice isn't like that. God's justice leads to creative improvement, though it may come through difficulty and pain. This pain, which can be seen in the optimum in the pain of Christ on the cross, is the pain of all of us, of all the universe, the agony of our decisions to be in the process with God, the terrible writhing of our wills to act in accordance with the larger joy that can be our fulfillment.

To speak disparagingly of another's wrong doing, is to cut down on the manufacture of love. The first sin mentioned in the Garden of Eden story is the sin of finger pointing.[4] The human pointed a finger at the helpmate. The helpmate blamed the serpent or social custom. They each had the choice to build up or to tear down, and they chose the sleaziest alternative.

Similarly, in many conflicts, we are tempted to see only the sin of the other. Then we self-righteously meet barbarity with equal barbarity, and enlarge the wrong-choosing on both sides of the issue. The abandonment of empathy, caring love, and kindness, in addressing our so-called *enemy*, likewise abandons the path to personal and community fulfillment. Such decisions to hurt the other can be a kind

of suicide that destroys our reason for being. They prevent the possibility of realizing God's promise,- humankind's fulfillment in contributing spiritual energy to God's loving creative process. Only in
turning towards forgiveness, and in recognizing our enemies as
children of God, can we regain possibilities of fulfillment.

2.10   LOVE AS A PRODUCT OF CREATIVE COMMUNITY

Ever since humankind passed over the threshold of reflection, it has
realized that there is something important about community, and
about relationship with the neighbor. We have devised laws to help
sort out these relationships, frequently slipping into the pitfall of
obeying the law, rather than implementing the purpose for which the
law was made. The Mosaic Code was designed for the furtherance of
love of God and love of neighbor. Harsh rulers used these and many
other sets of laws to solidify their position, and to control the
populace, as is still done today. Prophets spoke of the importance of
love and dreamed of the idealized community where the lion and the
lamb would lie down together in solidarity.

    Jesus analyzed the problems of his time, drew from the
Jewish heritage, and proposed a community where each would treat
his neighbor as he himself wished to be treated. If we inquire as to the
best way to create love in a community, we learn from Jesus that it
does not come from humble acceptance of authority. We are told
that we are to think for ourselves creatively, and not to acquiesce to
any man's authoritative guidance. "Call no man *father*!" (Matthew
23:9). We are admonished that "the great ones of the earth exercise
authority," but that in the loving community of neighbors, there will
be a different mode of operation. Those who have greater gifts will
use those gifts to serve the weaker and the poorer. Justice and
respect for the dignity of all, as God's common children, must
prevail.

    Besides lightly dismissing his words on authority, our com-
munities today neglect another important emphasis in Jesus' teaching, the quality of forgiveness. In forgiveness of another, we do not
necessarily go crawling to the person who harmed us and gently
accept his wrong doing. We try to correct him and we pray for his
fulfillment. We use our minds creatively to enhance both our own

self-esteem and his self-esteem. We do not act as a door mat, but as a door way, through which transformative energy can flow. Each of us must remember that we are just as human as the one who wronged us. We must keep in mind our common purpose to increase God-energy. We must always be seeking creative ways to produce love in cooperative community.

2.11 HOW THE SYSTEM MIGHT WORK

In our attempts to imagine what God is like and what God might want from us, we have tried to free ourselves from the constraining ideas set up by earlier civilizations with different needs. Hopefully, our outlook has broadened outwards from belief in a territorial God of tribalism and national preference who protected us at the expense of all others. We are able to look today at the broad sweep of the universe and the possible flows of love energy that this creation can exhibit. We considered the purpose of humanity as the participants in this continuing creative process. From this perspective we viewed the universalism of God's love in space and time. In a corresponding hypothetical model of a process God in action with a continuously creating universe, the energy we manufacture as loving human beings returns to God and is redistributed as God sees fit. We create this energy when we live with compassion, forgiveness, and justice, and when we pray for all the creations of God in this world, and also when we pray for all that God supports in being, everywhere in the universe.

We ourselves possess spiritual energies by virtue of being material aspects of God's universe. From the lowly mosquito to the possibility of advanced life in other star systems, we recognize in all nature an energy that comes from God and is attached to living creatures. We also recognize that all chemical and physical structures, including the various parts of the atom, possess transferable and bonding energy. All this is conceived and structured by a vast knowledgeable Mystery beyond us that our human minds have been given the desire to seek. When we consider the possibilities of life after this human life as we know it, let us remember that our God is a living God, and that energy that comes from God will somehow be returned to God for redistribution. The wise God will certainly know how to redistribute those energies to best advantage. Our purpose is not so much to selfishly preserve ourselves or our egos for whatever modes of resurrection are possible, as to be the creators of energy to sustain God's process. Behold how the energies produced by the prophets, by Jesus, and by the great spiritual leaders of the East, have upheld humankind for thousands of years!

We should rejoice that God gives each one of us the opportunity to become a part of that fabulous energy process! God is not a static being against which we measure our short comings. God is a totally loving reality, absolutely self giving and forgiving. We are presented with the opportunity to replenish God's diminishment, in our choosing to become the dream that God has for us. The love that we manufacture and channel back to God is returned to us. Only by accepting God's generous invitation, and living in order to augment love, forgiveness, and justice, can we find true fulfillment. Only in this way can we obtain the promise of our fulfillment that is inherent in God's loving creation. God invites humanity to be in full partnership!

I have proposed this love-energy model of God, because if we are to solve social problems, it is necessary to set down background information that may assist us in our reasoning. Only if we have a certain understanding of the place we are coming from, can we make intelligent decisions about the places we hope to go. Only if we decide, each for himself, what a holy God is like, will we be able to obey the command to be holy.

3

THE WAY

OF

THE FINITE HUMAN

3.1 CREATED BY GOD

Whether we believe in instantaneous creationalism, a slow evolvement, or a continuing process throughout the universe, each of us is created by God and is unique. This earthly uniqueness of each of us today may have taken millennia. We are the product of genes, some of whose structures may have been put in place before the human being took up thinking as an avocation. Each and every one of us had our beginnings in the beginnings of the earth, hence the name Adam, meaning *of the earth*. Evolutionists believe that the genes we carry around with us that mastermind our body characteristics, owe their shape to chemical combinations which devolved from antedating life forms covering the span from pre-history to the relative present. Creationalists think that God as all-wise and all-powerful bestowed life on our original parents through instantaneous crafting of these marvelous genes.

All of us on this earth, coming from that original gift of life, are in reality related as being creations of the same creator. How can one claim a special relationship with this creator God, without admitting to God's equal love for every human being God created? It seems that the entire human community should be destined to live cooperatively, indeed, lovingly, as ultimatively we have all sprung from the same creative hand. Respecting the dignity and the rights of each other, understanding the needs of each other, and seeking the common good, are the aspects of the world-wide communal life to which we are all called.

3.2 FLOW OF LIFE MODEL OF BEING

Our faith holds that a flow of life was initiated by God in the process of creation. Humankind were appointed caretakers of this flow, in God saying to them, "Be fruitful, multiply, fill the earth and conquer it. Be masters of the fish of the sea, the birds of heaven, and all living animals on the earth" (Genesis 1:28). This mastery and conquering does not imply ruthless extermination, but concerned care by human beings for the earth's ecosystem, so that it may serve their needs. It speaks of cooperation between human beings and their environment for the optimum survival of both.

In fulfilling the injunction to multiply, human beings are expected to use reason and responsibility. It is easy to see that over multiplication of the human species cannot be supported effectively upon a finite earth. In the event that the heavens become open to human colonization, we will still be expected to use our reason in deciding how much humanity a well developed universe can support. God's dream for humanity on earth visualizes enough humanity per square mile, to allow each human to rest peacefully under his own fig tree (Micah 4:4). God's dream does not seem to contain starvation through overpopulation.

We can visualize life as a stream flowing from God, and ourselves as participants in that flow. We feel in our collective consciousness that it is wrong for us to hamper this physical flow that originates and is upheld by God. We say that it is wrong for us to destroy life. However, we as individuals, and various components of our society, have many different perceptions of this physical life, and many different interpretations of what constitutes destruction of life. What is *wrong* for you may be *just right* for me. The wrongness of a choice depends on many factors. When we say, "It is wrong for us to destroy life," we qualify the statement and set down exceptions. These exceptions are usually agreed upon by a consensus of at least a portion of our society. For example, culture says that it is allright to destroy animal life, if we are using the animal for nourishment, and if animal protection laws are properly observed. On the other hand, our culture condemns the torture of animals. There is no consensus on some treatment of animals; for instance, our culture is undecided on animal experimentation. However, because we have the approval of our society, is obviously no guarantee that our destruction of life is moral or in harmony with God's plan for the flow of life. Pogroms, infanticide, genocide, slavery, inquisitions, racial injustice, and many other forms of intolerance, all have been approved by one society or another.

When it comes to adult human life, society says it is permissible to take another human life in self defense. American society is undecided as to capital punishment, the taking of an adult life when the person is convicted of a certain crime. Society is also undecided about euthanasia, inducing death painlessly as a relief from suffering. Thus when considering adult human life, we see that there is a question as to whether or not it is totally wrong to interrupt the flow of physical life initiated by God, under varying circumstances. There may be reasons to cut the flow at one point in order to increase it at another. Often in considering life, we seem to be guided by the principle that you must not take, what you do not have the power to restore.

As we go from consideration of the adult human to the animal, we seem to have acknowledgement of this *restoration* principle. The shepherd can use the sheep of his flock for food, because he has power to set in motion factors that will produce more sheep. Thus his action in killing the sheep is not detrimental in some larger view. He is using the sheep to further his family's life, and he is able to produce more sheep to replace the one used. Looking at this situation and considering God's flow of life, we see that the total flow has been furthered, even though a component was interrupted. Societies have often taken such a position, wherein the total flow of life takes precedence over any individual component (or individual life). That this can be a dangerous rationalization was evidenced by the acceptance of the *final solution* of the Nazis, in the near extermination of the Jews, for the supposed benefit of the Third Reich.

Abortionists, too, may argue (like the shepherd) that the human flock will be replaced by others, and that the society is somehow better off because of the abortion. Frequently, the argument is that the abortions are a lesser evil than the starvation which might take place if there were more mouths to feed. Another example is the infamous killing and cannibalism of ship wreck survivors, in order that the other survivors might live. In these examples of the destruction of physical life, the extreme position seems rational to its proponents.

With the turmoil over abortion legislation, much thought has been given to the question of when a human life begins. If we go back to our picture of life as the flow of a vast river churning against obstacles, then we can examine these obstacles, some obvious and some less obtrusive, and see how humankind interrupts the flow. The disruption of any section of this flow, pinpoints the necessity for a moral choice by either or both, the individual and collective humanity. With this river model we can perhaps build a framework from which to consider the relative seriousness of humankind's interruption of any particular section of this flow of life. We also might be able to see possibilities of maximizing or of minimizing this total flow of life process.

3.3 THE IMPLEMENTATION AND DEGRADATION OF LIFE THROUGH SEX

It is necessary, when considering the total world picture, the purpose of human life, and humanity's relationship to the infinite, to look at everything from the broadest viewpoint possible. Each human unit can only start on this vast project from within his or her own particular consciousness. Fortunately we can enlarge this base by our capacity to consult with others, and our ability to coordinate their information with our own.

We can relate to others, not just in the present, but to those in the past and in the future. We can look backwards in time, and investigate the consciousness of previous cultures. We should have no need to feel that our culture is the best expression of whatever has happened on earth. Likewise, as we project forward, individually or collectively, we tend to have great hopes for the future, and our culture today is presumably not the best example of what can occur in all time. Our own particular consciousness may end, but we assume that other similar consciousnesses will exist in the future, that can relate our ideas to their own particular cross-section of time.

Sex, as having to do with the initiation of new physical life, is one quality that we use in relation to others, and that we also consider ethically and religiously. At this point in history it seems that most people tend to consider the sexual urge from a very limited personal viewpoint. It does not enter the everyday mind to think about the sexual urges of our ancestors, in spite of the fact that we wouldn't be here without the presence of such phenomena. We also don't think back to the importance of sex in early religions. Our religions today lean towards not mixing sex with worship, or even making of sex an anti-religious symbol or calling it an out-and-out sin.

Primitive religions, as more basic, recognized the importance of sex in daily life. They knew they wouldn't be there themselves unless their parents had exercised this gift of the gods. The gods that they worshipped were very knowledgeable about sexual needs, and often required their adherents to keep temple virgins around, just in case a god or his proponents needed to fulfill a godly urge to reproduce. Many societies, including the Australian aborigines, and African tribes, had puberty rites which included a form of circumcision. It was natural to associate this with pleas for divine blessing, fertility, and good lives for the offspring. In all this, there was a strong consciousness of respect for life, as part of God's creative process.

Our ancestors felt that sex was given to them as a means to populate the community, so that there would be people who could properly worship the local god who reigned. Today when there is so much worry about over-population, we feel less of a need to have sex with the object of producing people. We also seem to have forgotten the idea that the God who reigns needs people to worship in his or her temple. Hence, we must have new explanations of the purposes of sex to satisfy the unspoken queries of our mass consciousness.

Further deteriorization of the concern to bring children into the world, to either worship God or to populate the community, is evidenced by our present high divorce rate and the problem of abortion. People marry for various reasons, some of which have to do with raising children, but sex, both inside and outside of marriage, can be had without any noble purpose in mind. Sex was established by God as part of an overall creative plan. Marriage was put in place to presumably further this plan. Today marriage is seen by many as a cultural legalism that makes a puzzling sex act honorable, or as a convenient way to keep sexual urges under control. It is not seen by many in the population as a dedicated and secure community in which to bring up children.

Often the flow of life is considered mainly from the female viewpoint. We are told that the female should have something to say about her life as opposed to the life of an infant that may be forming inside her womb. Our culture does not emphasize that this life is there due to the action of a male in using his gift of sperm either thoughtlessly or purposefully. Early peoples did not know that the infant in the womb had forty six chromosomes, twenty three of which came from the sperm of one parent, and the other twenty three from the egg of the other parent. They seemed to know intuitively that each parent had a distinct part in the flow of life. Our early forebears said by their family and community preserving actions, that they believed the sexual urge was given to them so that they might continue the community, as that was the will of the unknown they worshipped.

We of the scientific world of today might come to the same type of conclusion, yet broaden it with new insights available to us. We could enlarge our community group to include the whole earth. If we believe that our sexual urge is given to us so that we might bring to fruition the whole human race, it would emphasize the further need in our day, for a responsible sex act. Every participant in a sex act, whether alone or with another, is to consider this act in the light of building his own personality, encouraging the partner's growth, or looking on the possibility of a third person, yet to come, out of this act. This is no time to scratch, just because you itch. We are taught to be ashamed of our irresponsible acts, as thoughtlessness can drag us away from positive goals. We are to view each sexual act against the backdrop of fulfillment of the entire population, present and future.

We don't want to give the impression that our ancestors had more stable sexual attitudes, for if we look back for the faults of previous generations, we can certainly find them. There often was a narrow provincialism to keep sex within the bounds of the community, which could foster intertribal warfare, and the selfish promotion of the tribe to the disadvantage, disrespect, and destruction of outsiders. A warped emphasis on sex has been one of the ways patriarchal powers have had to keep women in stereotypical positions. This same attitude has prevented men from taking their rightful place as the equally nurturing parent. If men of all eras had been able to devote 50 per cent of their time to being concerned fathers, they would have imbibed more forgiving and less warlike attitudes. Early religions and our own Judaeo-Christian faith had insights on the rhythms of life for individuals, and for families, that we have evidently lost. Hopefully, in our day and age, we will recover the best portion of these insights and gain new ones that we can pass on to future generations.

3.4 FLOW OF LOVE MODEL

In considering the flow of life, we must give thought to God's purpose in initiating life. It seems that we were not put here to reproduce and to decay like vegetation. We have hope that we are more important to God's mysterious plans than the grass of the field or the fish of the sea. We were put here, not just to live, but to love. We can't talk about the flow of life, without also talking about the flow of love. The flow of life has to do with animation or activity, and the flow of love is the essential humanization of that activity. The flow of life has to do with animation of the body; the flow of love has to do with animation of the soul. We proposed in chapter two that love is the purpose of this creation by God, but in order to love, humankind must be given freedom by God to build or to destroy, and choices that may lead in either direction. Love that is forced or automated, is not love. Love is a free decision by each individual.

The flow of life was initiated by God. The flow of love is kept in operation through the response of humankind, collectively and individually, in cooperation with God. Humankind can accept responsibility for producing this flow of love, or it can selfishly turn its back on the environment with its needs, and show no empathy or concern for other humans. The flow of life, as a physical dimension, has its corresponding spiritual dimension, the flow of love. Physical births are the means to spiritual birth,- to the growth of empathy, forgiveness, caring love, kindness, freedom, and justice. The human being is privileged to engage in furthering this remarkable God-like spiritual flow.

This flow of love, the essential aspect of an on-going creation, is like the flow of life in being subject to human whim, and can be impeded or diminished in many ways. For example, violence to any human being is contrary to love, and seems in opposition to the creation plan of God. The detached observance of violence is also contrary to love. Violence tends to be an abandonment of any pledge to live in covenant with God. To illuminate the qualities that must underlie our covenantal basis with God, let's consider some extreme cases of violence to others in this world.

People are very important in God's scheme, first because they are loved by God, and second, because they are the means of expression of God's love, as they can love each other. They can be like God in this loving of each other. If they do not create this love, but choose to destroy each other, then just in their attitude of destruction, they have not shown forth the God that they are capable of imaging. Human beings constantly have the choice to further life and love, or to set up road blocks to this flow. If human beings are not loving, then we block and minimize the very flow that we should encourage and maximize. If a nation builds up armaments, and thinks to assert itself over its neighbor, or enlarges its own economy while bleeding dry another country, then that country is not being loving, and even before blowing each other off the face of the earth, such nations have destroyed the God within them by their attitude, and hampered the flow of love.

This may be why we are advised to "boast not of chariots, and not of horses, but to boast about the name of the Lord our God" (Psalm 20:7). If we keep God's love in our hearts, we won't find weapons necessary. We have learned also from present day psychology that when we are loving to one another, neither side feels threatened. We don't need pistols to keep order, but we do need love. Love is very important to promote positive communication among human beings. Armaments make it unnecessary for us to be loving and kind. Guns are made for the express purpose of killing people, and consequently end both the flow of life and the flow of love.

Can we say something similar for capital punishment in which a unique individual is destroyed by his fellow human beings? The executed is not used as nourishment for other higher life forms. Nothing ennobling is accomplished by his physical death. Those who execute him are somehow less, by this retaliatory action. Proponents of capital punishment may argue that this man's death is a sign that forces others who are meditating murder, to desist, but capital punishment as a deterrent to others is not an established fact. There is no demonstrable benefit to society by the killing, over other less violent solutions such as permanent incarceration. On the other hand, the destruction of the physical life also involves the termination of any possibility of further spiritual growth in that person. His potential to think creatively and to love is destroyed. That possibility, and the possibility of enkindling the spark of God that lies hidden within him, were not extinguished by his crime. The immanence of God in the universe was not necessarily eliminated by the crime or the conviction. Primarily, the killing expresses the anger of society, and the desire for revenge. Capital punishment, therefore, seems more like a blockage to the flows of life and love, than a furtherance of the stream.

If we consider the making of chemical, biological, and nuclear weapons and the human ability to destroy life on the earth, we have an example of human beings collectively ending all possibilities of love. This seems to be a much more serious situation than that of one human being ending a life in the womb, and yet they have something in common. These two examples, one of collectively ending life on earth, and the other of individually ending a fetal life, both have something to do with denying God's love for other people. If we deprived God of this total creation through our senseless nuclear explosiveness, God would have nothing left to love, and thus could not be love here on earth. This quality of love as pertaining to God, would not be allowed expression here. In a smaller but similar way, the termination of life in the womb is also a termination of the love stream which that human potentially could contribute to God's plan.

These illustrations of physical violence, however, are only the most evident obstacles to the flow of love. Mental and psychological violence are more prevalent, and often more destructive. The denials of self respect, dignity, personal freedom, or justice to any human are likewise violations of God's will, and interruptions to his plan for humankind. Communities as well as individuals are called to further the flow of love. All too often, we see that there are nations which firmly believe they are justified in the military subjugation of others, or the economic exploitation of others, in order that their nation might prosper. Compassion, forgiveness, cooperation, and mutual support among dissimilar communities (rather than confrontational politics and disfranchisement) further the flow of love, and are basic elements necessary for a world order of covenant and consensus.

3.5 PHYSICAL FLOWS VERSUS SPIRITUAL FLOWS

Physical sufficiency, as given in the flow of life, is only the start of God's dream for the fulfillment of humanity. To live fully, in the promise of our creator, is to live humanely. The capabilities given to the human species, to love, to forgive, to be free, to exercise justice, to be compassionate,- these lead to our fulfillment. They character- ize the covenanted individual life and the consentaneous communal life into which we are urged. Each person has an individual respon- sibility to maximize the flows of life and love in his particular center of existence, and humanity has a collective responsibility to be caretakers of God's creation.

We finite humans have a certain difficulty in judging as to whether or not physical life should be encouraged or enhanced over possible spiritual good that we cannot see with our eyes. We shrink from sickness, and fail to recognize the spiritual uplift that may arise out of physical pain. We may see as a present evil what can be recognized later as part of God's plan for our fulfilled lives. When we have difficulty judging what is good for ourselves, how can we judge another who has his own ideas as how to further the flow of life and love?

In our soul searching and in our inquiries into individual behavior or group activity, the issue must be assessed in the light of God's universal love, God's immanence in the total world, and the plan of God for the flow of loving spirit. Basic questions must be pressed, such as: Is the sacredness of life understood? Is the sacred- ness of the physical life, and the sacredness of a fulfilled spiritual life for each individual understood? Is it understood that we are all part of God's universal creation, all objects of God's love, all carrying that hidden spark of God within us, and all destined to play our role in the furtherance of love here on this earth? Have the participants suffi- ciently stretched their capabilities for empathy, caring love, and kindness? We can apply these questions to every type of human activity.

God's promise is the fulfillment of humankind as they con- tribute their aggregate spiritual energy to God's loving creation process. That enrichment of the spiritual flow of life, in empathy, caring love, and kindness, is the primary reason for being. Therefore, the purpose of procreation and its flow of physical life, is to provide the carrier of this spiritual process. There is the view, however, that maximizing the spiritual growth is not necessarily synonymous with maximizing the physical growth. Maximizing the growth of the primary flow,- the spiritual, may require responsible regulation of the physical flow.

Sex mores are classic examples of spiritual versus physical because of the obviousness of the flow of life component. The religious celibates, for example, believe that the non-use, and consequent waste, of sperm and eggs is justified by the devotion of their life energies to the spiritual well-being of others. The diminishment of the physical life flow, in this case, is the opportunity for the enhancement of the spiritual life flow.

Each couple, in childbearing, similarly withholds the flow of life to some degree. Acting freely, the loving couple must assess their environment and their capabilities. Instead of the maximum thirty or so children, physically possible, they have the number of children they think they can raise properly. In so doing, they "waste" the precious sperm of the male and the eggs of the female. According to God's broader plans, proper lives are fulfilled lives with consequent growth in consciousness, where empathy, caring love and kindness exist among the couple and their offspring. This noble and holy result is the execution of the couple's covenant with each other,- a reflection of their corresponding covenant with God, for the furtherance of the flow of physical and spiritual life. To live that covenant, with finite energy, time, and resources, does require parental decisions on how many children can be handled properly.

The sexual act itself deserves to be considered very carefully by each individual. So often sex is degraded for the commercialization of women, and to help participants overcome a sense of inferiority or incapability. Rather, first and foremost, it must be understood as God's gift, intended for the furtherance of the flow of life, both physical life and the spiritual life that is thence made possible. It is an element of our covenant with God to progressively grow humankind in God's image. The sexual act, evidently, also furthers conjugal love, in a divorce-ridden world. Particularly when the couple retains a consciousness of their covenant to each other and to their God, the sex act furthers the primary purpose of life,- the flow of spiritual life, involving forgiveness, spiritual unity, empathy, caring love, and kindness. It is thus a wonderful gift from God, to be employed in loving consensus, and spiritual nurturing, with co-responsibility, self control, and respect for the God-given nature of both parties.

Some would say, further, that this flow of spiritual life in the couple's sex act, particularly involving their spiritual union, in love and forgiveness, is a vital part of their covenant, to each other, and their God, with or without the plan of immediate offspring. This argues for the value of that spiritual union, in the sex act, even when the act itself is not open to procreation (as with rhythm, contraception, or age). Though the answers are not clear, the important thing is that people are more willing to ask the difficult questions, and focus on the spiritual side of the process, even when the asking seems counter to established culture. Standing aside from culture and accepted practices, thoughtful persons ask, "If we can approve celibacy for the good of the greater community (even though the sperm or the egg are thereby *wasted*), should we not be able to accept a sex act that doesn't have the union of sperm and egg as its outcome?" If non-production of children by married couples, at a particular time, is carefully weighed by them to be in the best interests of the community, should not the act be judged in terms of the spiritual life flow thus created?

Still others would say that we should also consider the value of the spiritual flow of life, even in the case of a stable, single partner, homosexual relationship. Is it possible that God's plan for the growth of spiritual union, empathy, caring love, and kindness, can be fulfilled in such a bonding?

Favoring a spiritual flow of life, without furthering the physical flow of life, is the kind of decision that requires mind-expanding awareness. Whenever we come so close to obvious participation in God's plan for humanity, we are reminded of the awesomeness of God's creation, and our potential role in that plan. It would seem that, in cases of a justified "waste of sperm and egg", whether by celibacy, decisions on the number of children, avoiding conception during the sex act, or even stable homosexual marriages, basic questions again surface. "Are we sufficiently stretching our capacities for empathy, caring love, and kindness?" "Are we maximizing the good, to the best of our ability, in all the space and time we can comprehend?" "Are we living fully according to our covenant with God for the cooperative fulfillment of humankind?" "Is our course the best one we can choose, to meet all these objectives?" These are subjective, difficult questions, that only the individual can answer. They are also the kind of question that humankind is uniquely gifted to address. It is, perhaps, by struggling to use that unique capability, as individuals, that we each grow in personhood, and grow closer to God.

3.6 THE RESPONSIBLE HUMAN

The awesomeness of God's creation, the grand purpose of human-kind's fulfillment, and our role in the flow of spiritual entities, are factors that must impress us as we examine our relationships with God and others. We were created to be responsible people, respon-sible for God's earth, and every person on it. Each of us is responsible to decide what is best for the earth, as God is immanent in all of God's creation and thus can be found in each God-directed heart. We have the capability to respond constructively. Each act that we perform is part of that response. Each act in our daily lives that affects the flow of life and love in others,- their growth in dignity, freedom, and love, their growth as full persons, and full children of God, is part of our response to the call to live in covenant.

We are responsible to the neighbor and the foreigner, to the old and to the very, very young. We are responsible to what is great and to what is small. Without the smallness of the sperm, and its interaction with the egg, life would be interrupted. After the union of sperm and egg, human life is not complete. Our purpose, or God's purpose, may not be completed in the fetus, in the baby, in the young child, or even in the adult. If human fulfillment is a possible criteria for the achievement of God's purpose, some of us may need a stage in purgatory for further refining. The process is not completed in the individual, but in the loving interaction of the individual with other members of the community, and in the individual's and society's relationship to God. A humanity that has no positive relationship with God, or which has nothing to do with love, seems to have no idea of the purpose of the flow of life, and apparently loses its own sense of purpose. Our society today shows its irreverence for life in the various ways it interrupts this flow.

A responsible sex act must be considered in light of the whole of God's creation. Surely God's plan is for us to continue to use this gift, for purposes of offspring, and for expressing our love and support for one another. In a world where many people are undergoing malnutrition, we must consider the timing of sex, so as not to be guilty of either over population or abortion. A proper and responsible sex act would eliminate the necessity for abortion and for the argument about when human life or consciousness begins. It also would end the frightening idea of a woman's right to choose on the life or death of her baby. It would put the right to choose in the proper place, on the responsible shoulders of two people who are discussing the possibility of engaging in a sexual act. This would insure that there were no unwanted children, and consequently would be less of a disastrous situation if two "partners" felt compelled to split up an arrangement.

Today sex is still a gift from the creator God, and to live nobly in this earthly environment, we must use this gift very carefully and responsibly. Irresponsible sex acts can make us fall prey to disease; poor judgments on our part can steer us into present and future disabling directions.

Often in our feelings of helplessness brought on by our total societal situation, we reject this call to responsibility. We narrow our vision. Our priorities become skewed, and we don't want to worry about when life begins, or about the totality of life, or about who is ending life. We find it much easier to simply say what is wrong with those who hold opposing opinions. To cover our own inadequacies, we are content to point fingers at pro-life or pro-choice people.

In a similar way, we refuse to see the injustices done by our nation. We refuse to face up to the terrible fact that as a nation who is building arms and profiting from their sale, our national attitude is that of an accomplice to a killer. With the arms escalations, moreover, are we not increasing the possibilities of killing off the entire world? We are not going along with the flow of life and the flow of love from God. We may instead be sliding blindly to destruction. Only by constantly broadening our vision, and striving to see the universality of God's plan for spiritual growth, can we avoid such blindness.

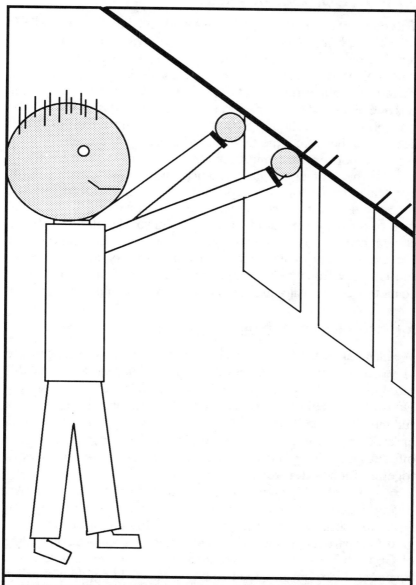

THE SEXUALLY RESPONSIBLE PERSON IS THE ONE
WHO IS READY TO LOVE, FEED, AND WASH THE
DIAPERS OF ANY HUMAN BEING HE MAY PRODUCE

3.7 PLACE OF EVIL IN THE HUMAN

This concept of the flow of life, and dead end due to blindness and selfishness, brings to mind the concept of evil. Perhaps we could redefine evil as a blockage to the flow of life and the flow of love. It is not going with the flow; it is making choices that go nowhere. Evil is a failure to make a contribution, or an impediment to contribution. It is one of the rocks in our figurative river of life. It is choosing to be *ir*-responsible. It is choosing to blind oneself to the outcome of one's actions, as they affect the flow of spiritual, empathetic life.

Abortion, for example, may be considered an evil, but it may also be the agonizing pain that encourages our society to think, ponder, and move together to further God's justice. Abortion can be the prod that helps us consider our own personal selfishness in the face of an over-populated world; the drawbacks of the abortion choice force us to consider our attitudes towards the total flow of life. So, too, we can make an opportunity of every failure, once we see its reality. Recognizing the prior narrowness of our vision, we can be motivated to boldly launch ourselves to higher empathetic ground.

3.8 COVENANTAL POSSIBILITIES

We have taken a quick look back and speculated on the importance of sex to our far away ancestors who also had to deal with this puzzling phenomena and probably understood it better than we do. Do we today feel that there is anything sacred about sex, or is it a rudimentary appendage that we put up with, because it has a certain entertainment value? Whatever our opinion, we must incorporate our sexual attitude into our covenantal action if we are to work together for a better world.

To live by a covenant can mean a very wide variety of things. Living by a covenant with God is to orient our lives in harmony with God's will, so as to lead to the fulfillment of God's promise to human-kind. Our part of a covenant with God depends greatly on our image of God. Only by our corresponding actions do we complete the covenant. If we imagine God to be power wielding, domineering, and expecting instant obedience, then our part of the covenant would naturally be in support of that mode of behavior. If, on the other hand, our image of God is of a loving creator, then the covenant with God can mean a striving for a perpetual awareness of God's universal love, and living to further God's plan by enhancing God-energy here and now. If God seeks the fulfillment of human-kind by our participation in that creation, then empathy, caring love, and kindness become our part of the covenant. The important parts of the covenant are, first of all, the existence of God's helpful immanence in our lives, offering the grace of love, and secondly, the decisions and actions we take to respond to that offer and to use our talents to help create further love.

To live by the covenant means living totally by the covenant. It cannot be that one part of our lives is covenantal and another part is not. Our private lives, our intimate lives, our business lives, our actions in public and foreign affairs, all must be covenantal. Other-wise our covenant is a sham. Unfortunately, we frequently compart-mentalize our lives, and in so doing we can easily abandon the cove-nant.

Each of us variant monads is able to form a select covenantal relationship, pledging to make optimum choices for himself and for his world view. His choices may frequently come into conflict with those of some other individual who sees progress in the world from a different viewpoint. Individuals or groups who are at loggerheads with one another, each believing they represent what is best for the earth, must somehow find a place of agreement, as they derive from the same God. They should be able to come to consensus as to basic truths, and should make decisions as to what aspects of society have caused secondary degrading effects. Then instead of fighting each other, they can perhaps work together to relieve deficiencies.

3.9 ARE WE WILLING TO COVENANT?

It is all very well to set up a God-system, and describe it ethereally as a flow of love, but the average human being doesn't seem to acqui-esce to his incorporation in such a flow. We frequently find ourselves nodding partial agreement to nebulous statements that God is a Spirit and must be worshipped in Spirit and in truth, but in actuality we physical entities don't appear to have much to do with Spirit. We ignore or downplay our spiritual potential. We find it difficult to translate our natural needs to eat, drink, procreate, and control others, with spiritual finesse. Most of us are not thinking of spiritual ways to fulfill our lives and the lives of others, but of our own practical egotistical material needs. We do not concentrate on Utopia, because we are too occupied in the business of everyday living. It does not occur to us that we may have the inner resources to change our situation, each other, or the world.

Is it possible for the earthy individuals that we are, to combine together, and direct unified energies into a positive spiritual direction? We are vastly insulted if someone describes us as "animals." We do not want the capabilities present in the human species to be underestimated. We know that we are superior to the animals in that we can act creatively in the present, look back to the past, and plan ahead to the future. This active, planning life, with its inner and outer energies comes from somewhere. It seems reasonable to suppose that it is going somewhere. Our catapulting earth with its precious cargo of humanity, is operating in time, and is making some sort of history. What part should we be playing in this stupendous act? What should we be doing about the great unknown quantity we call God? Humankind has a vast potential for supporting the processes of the earth and for achieving the continuation of love. Our purpose for being has to do with life and the furtherance of life and love. Collectively and individually, what is humankind doing about this?

Collectively, under our various governments, we continue to respond after the manner of patriarchal power structures. Our religious, economic, and political bodies continue to function in the same manner as did the militaristic city-states of Ancient Greece. Our children are brought up to be competitive both in grades and in sports, and those with less obvious talents end up discouraged, the prey to low self-esteem. Competition is emphasized in our educational processes, rather than cooperation and questioning creativity.

Individually, those of previous times who questioned the system, and tried to search out spiritual reasons for our being, were often dispatched precipitously by others who feared losing control. In Ancient Greece, Socrates was forced to drink poison hemlock because he asked too many questions. Creative thinkers through the ages have been crucified, burned at the stake, or condemned as witches. Today, we still have examples of creativity being squelched. Church theologians are asked to be silent. Women in certain areas of Africa are forbidden to plant trees. Why do those who have power, whether it be religious, political, or economic, want to keep that control? Why can't they share their wealth with the economically deprived, and expand their narrow perceptions by listening to opposing viewpoints? Why must they possess the most ornate houses, and the largest cars? In order to need so much show on the outside, they must feel some need to cover up for the smallness of what is inside in the spirit.

Thus, individually, many of us show by our actions that we do not have faith in earth's natural processes, but trust only in the structures we have made of money and power. We do not learn from the past. We do not plan for a future world where our children's children will grow up in a society of harmony and cooperation. Unquestioning, we go with the flows of our present culture and society, accepting as standards for truth, the pronouncements of whomever is in power at the moment. Our theory seems to be that if we align ourselves with the powers that be, then we, too, will be taken care of properly. We eat our fill, with hardly a thought for the starving. We scatter our leftovers along the highways. We use our built-in urge to reproduce, without recourse to restraint, as if all we were here for was to do just what we felt like doing. Everyday life plummets along, day after confusing day, and we feel that we have to rush along with it in order to keep the whole incomprehensible mess going. Life often seems like a tangled and frightening jungle. However, even in a jungle, there is the opportunity to pause and reflect.

Our reflections might be on the following themes. Should we continue on indefinitely with our present modes of operation? Are there changes we could make, individually or collectively? Should we in the United States continue our present system of electing leadership? Along with leadership often comes the opportunity for graft. Those we elect accept campaign funds from, and pass government funding to a select few of their constituents, often ignoring vital needs of the less influential. Those allowed to hold office or excercise control in a political, economic, educational, or governmental situation should be those who have proved their worth by being gentle and understanding with all humanity.

On the individual plane the using of money or goods for oneself should be seen as possibly causing the deprivation of the other. The rapid destruction of resources should be recognized as a drawback to cooperative society rather than as an asset or a right of the present first world society. We can only claim rights to what we are able to replace. Fastening an economic handicap on the poor of the third world, by shackling them with a debt entered into with their dictatorial governments, is a massive injustice. We must ask ourselves if there is any connection between the interest which we accumulate on our investments, and the lack of resources available for third world children. From a governmental standpoint many first world countries could assist in easing the debt burdens of poorer nations by reducing their own budget deficits and eliminating protectionist trade policies. Unfortunately, the United States government continues to spend debilitatingly on the military as usual, a custom which is becoming ingrained in the American psyche. They do not believe the adage, "Those who take up the sword will perish by it."

Collectively and individually, we must think through the different options that we have, and then covenant with ourselves to further our positive purposes. Above all we should keep in mind that the greatest gift of life is having the opportunity to love and do for each other in order to build both the self and the other to fulfillment.

4

THE WAY

OF

HOLY COMMUNITY

4.1 DEFINING HOLY COMMUNITY

In considering the individual monad, we find that it is equipped to have a distinct relationship with its creator. If we so desire, each of us is able to enter into a covenantal agreement with the force that formed us. When we take into consideration groupings of human monads, we may also have a vaster purpose, so we must further consider the relationships possible among all living monads. There must be some obvious ways that monads can work together to extend the common good and increase love energy.

In this cooperative community or just society, we would expect to find responsible people making a contribution to the flow of spiritual, empathetic, loving life. Different monads would have different individual capacities. Some might be on the low end of the spectrum and contribute only to their own well being. Others might be on the high end helping to make a better life for all people. In combination they would be able to generate goodness throughout their society.

Shall we return to the examples left to us by our forebears and their structures of community order? Early peoples, like people today, had problems, problem solvers, and those who gave up when the going got rough. We have discussed how members of primitive religions had a very keen respect for the male organ of reproduction and recognized their creative powers as a sacred gift from God. This gift of life was passed from parent to child, and thus a person was considered immortal in his progeny. The rite of circumcision was often connected with dedication to God. This operation, combined with an announcement of covenant, was frequently done at puberty to impress the candidate with the responsibilities of his coming manhood.

Different faiths today continue to practice circumcision, but usually shortly after birth, so that the candidate won't be too discomfited. Unfortunately, this omits the emphasis on responsibility present in cultures that reserved this sign for the teen-ager. Consequently in most of today's culture, we find a fun-and-games attitude towards sex, and lack the notion that the sex organs are a special life-giving gift from the creator. Instead of thinking of sex as a precious gift, to be cherished and used to further community life, sex frequently becomes illicit and abortive. Our present social organizations seem unable to handle this fundamental aspect of humanity.

Down through the centuries, people have banded together into social groupings in order to cooperate in problem solving, to implement the flow of life, and to decrease what is negative and nonconstructive. What characteristics are needed for optimum operation of such a group? Is it necessary for it to be war-like or elitist? Many of these communities were fashioned by people who had a certain notion of God. Some groups had a nature God, who could control the lightning. Other groups had a warrior God who would lead them out to battle. As religious communities grew, they would fall into practicing elitism. They would believe that if God was for their group, God would naturally be against those outside the group. Often their *New Jerusalem* type communities were inclined to have all the gates closed against the outsiders.

With this notion of closure, can we ever believe that there is such a thing as *Holy Community*, a collection of individuals who strive to see God's justice flowing freely through *ALL* the earth? Humankind has been inclined to build walls around his cities and his castles. His bridges are likely to be drawbridges over moats. His temples and churches have thick walls and solid locked doors. With exclusion of the other, comes reaction from the other. To exclude is to invite violence. To exclude is a stoppage of the flow of God's justice and love. The exclusive society is thus very unlikely to be a just society.

Going to the Bible to see what wisdom can be gleaned about holy community, we find that we are warned that we must "be holy, for I, Yahweh your God, am holy" (Leviticus 19:2). In our search for the Holy Community that is open to others, it would be appropriate to find a good definition of the word *holy*. It evidently does not mean self-righteous, for we often find that the self righteous are very exclusive and condemnatory. It is their particular pleasure to point out and castigate the "sinner". There is little room in their hearts to try to understand the other, as they are so busy trying to assure themselves of their own proper behavior. It is good to have self-respect, but you cannot have true self-respect without respect for others. The self-righteous often have a notion of a punishing God that condemns human actions, rather than of a just God who understands the people he/she created and who wants their fulfillment.

True holiness consists in conformity to the nature and will of God. This is the individual responsibility of each of us. In imitation of God the holy community should be the community that strives for the fulfillment of all peoples. It should be a group that can come to consensus on what the will of God is, for their particular community. It should be a structure which is designed to maintain the flow of life and the flow of love in the community group and throughout the earth. Therefore, its members should try to understand those who are outside the group, as God gives us God's example of total understanding of the other. We have postulated that God's nature is love, and thus all members of the group should be sure to treat everyone, both in the group and outside the group, with empathy and kindness, without exception.

4.2 OUR FINITE EARTH AS OUR PLACE TO GROW

What have we done with this space that God created for us? God and the human both agree that this earth was pretty good to start with. It seems that it should be difficult to mistreat such a large quantity as our globe. However, there are ebbs and flows that take place on the earth, similar to the motions and gyrations of the heavens. This dynamic process is evidently God's way of doing things. There are forces and counter forces, and as they exist side by side, they hold peoples, their environment, and their social structures in some sort of an equilibrium. That equilibrium point, however, constantly evolves.

For awhile there wasn't much on earth but rocks and moisture in a fairly static state, but some little element of change crept in, and the earth's crust grew and developed. Deep down in things there is this little element that acts, that moves slowly, that urges all things on to increasing complexity and consciousness. That inner force has evolved, until we, as human spirit, have the ability to recognize it as inspired by the spirit of God. While it acts, all things continue to be held in equilibrium, from above, by some sort of power. Perhaps we are seeing here God immanent in the creation, and the power from above, God transcendent to the creation. Not all advances or changes, however, are permanent or part of the main stream. The process also includes life structures that cannot adapt successfully, and thus wither and fade away. The vanishing of the dinosaurs is an example. We would hope to also rid the world of certain viruses. Totalitarian government might also be an example of a structure that is dying out.

From the earth being only rocks, it progressed to an ability to support worms, and then to the capability of hosting dinosaurs. At some point for unknown reasons, the dinosaurs disappeared from the scene. Perhaps they developed too well on planet earth. They may have multiplied profusely, and earth couldn't produce enough green growing trees to feed them. As the dinosaurs ate all the trees and destroyed their nurturing ecology, the earth's envelope changed, and became desert for awhile. If this is a true scenario, we must forgive the dinosaurs for not noticing their destructive act. They had very small brains, and so couldn't use intelligent freedom of choice to take care of their situation. God must have concluded that the globe needed to be populated with a more intelligent and less greedy animal. Nature rolled back into equilibrium and the earth produced humankind. Will this smaller and, hopefully, wiser creature be able to succeed where the mighty dinosaur failed? Will he be able to form intelligent consentaneous communities that will take care of the earth?

The earth today still seems to be in a precarious state of equilibrium. We can see how humankind upsets that state in certain cases. If gypsy moths invade the environment, humankind sprays poisons around which weaken the birds' reproductive capacity. Therefore at the next invasion of gypsy moths (which usually only destroy unhealthy trees), there are fewer birds to hold down the increasing moth population. Humankind has upset the balance of nature, and in his ignorance (and the secondary desire of the marketplace to sell more pesticides and make money), he applies destructive chemicals in a thoughtless manner.

We can see an even greater threat to the earth's equilibrium in the physical and political consideration of nuclear power. Some communities in the earth see opportunities for more fulfilled living with nuclear power to run machines. Others, objecting to the problem of nuclear waste, attempt to keep a balance by advocating water, wind, and sun power for electricity, and sanely emphasize the dangers of radioactivity when nuclear energy chances to get out of control. Thus, the physical survival of the earth, as well as the quality of life, increasingly depends on present human awareness of the future consequences to all peoples. It depends on the concerted thoughts and actions of those living today, to insure a tomorrow.

4.3 THE HUMAN IN EQUILIBRIUM

When we look inside humanity itself, we see a similar shifting of equilibrium. We sometimes call this equilibrium the choice between good and evil; people choose what they perceive to be the greater *good* or the lesser *evil* as they compare the alternatives available at a certain time. When God has created such order held together by such marvelous balances in the great outer universe, should not God also be expected to dynamically control excesses in the interior of the human? Should we not expect that the more violent excesses would be self correcting, so that we would evolve to better moral standards?

Looking at the historical picture, we observe different ways that humans have devised to maintain personal equilibrium. Early humankind acted in unity with the earth's balance of nature in producing crops to feed themselves, and they multiplied their numbers so as to take better advantage of the earth's resources. In most cultures women were gradually designated as having an inferior status in the scheme of things, yet held families and societies together in spite of this inconvenient labeling. The male who was usually the dominant member of the family, often strove for personal security by pledging himself to serve a valiant leader.

Humankind rarely went against natural desires in order to gain equilibrium, but in giving allegiance to another person, the human being had to renounce some personal freedom to maintain a secure balance. Women tolerated secondary status in order to enhance the well being of the family. Those designated as slaves were advised to be obedient to their masters, and were often able to achieve interior peace by accepting this servitude gracefully. Individuals strove within their cultures for optimum life for themselves and their families.

Other odd life styles were tried as a result of pressing community problems. The monk or ascetic came into acceptance during the Babylonian Captivity, as those of the Hebrew ruling class were made eunuchs by their captors.[1] Asceticism gained in popularity as the world became more secularized. Many followed St. Anthony to the desert, to meditate in private without worldly distractions, when Constantine's acceptance of Christianity brought pomp and power to what had been a persecuted faith.

There are very few places today where the human can escape the world to meditate and to renew equilibrium. Often this running from the world seems like a cop-out instead of a retreat to pray for the world's well being. Perhaps today a completely isolated monasticism is not very feasible. There is more need to serve the oppressed, than to retreat from the world and have a nice, cozy feeling by oneself. One should find God in one's fellow human being, rather than freeing oneself of responsibility for the fellow human by meditating in the desert. Teilhard de Chardin affirms that, "The saint, the Christian saint, as we now understand him and look for him, will not be the man who is the most successful in escaping from matter and mastering it completely; he will be the man who seeks to make all his powers - gold, love, or freedom - transcend themselves and co-operate in the consummation of Christ, and who so realizes for us the ideal of the faithful servant of evolution."[2]

Thus, individual humankind seeks a special kind of equilibrium. We do not seek escape from trial, but rather seek at least a temporary mastery of it. The powerful energies that sometimes threaten to engulf us must be harnessed and steered into productive channels. Yet, the challenge and the trial do not end, and we find ourselves in a continuing struggle to maintain our tenuous equilibrium, battling against the tide of disrupting energies. We speak of a well-balanced person, meaning one who sets and follows reasonable priorities in his life. Often this individual perseveres on such a course as a result of overcoming fears and challenges. Other individuals may not be so fortunate, and after being knocked off balance once, may find it very difficult to climb back into equilibrium again.

No one achieves and maintains perfection. We only attempt to walk in pre-decided pathways. We have the freedom of choice to propose our fundamental options, yet with so many of us rattling around together like marbles in a shaken bowl, we frequently find ourselves off course. However, we seem to be inspirited with a seed of God (or a spark of God's image) that we are encouraged to develop and bring to fruition. We may speak of this as an inherent urge to birth God in our being. This seems to be an evolutionary thrust that lies within us. It is normal for the human being to go in this positive direction unless others of us human beings hurt and warp his outlook so cruelly that he is turned away from this great design. He may be frustrated into participating in actions, such as drug abuse or disease-associated promiscuous homosexuality, that may lead to an evolutionary dead end.

As we respond to this inner urge for harmony with our creator, our struggle for a better equilibrium is buttressed by a sense of community with our God. Reaching for that added strength, then leads us to search out the question of how we can best align ourselves with the divine plan for our own fulfillment. If we are to make a commitment to that plan, or make a covenant with our creator to that effect, we need a clear idea of what constitutes that divine plan.

Some of those who worship think that love for God is shown best through prayer and praise, or through burnt offering. Does God need our prayer and praise? The prophet states that our burnt offerings and religious festivals can offend God (Amos 5:21-23). What kind of love are we speaking of, when we ask how man loves God? The Greeks speak of three types of love: *filios* or brotherly love, *eros* or passionate love, and *agape* which is the love that is willing to sacrifice oneself for the other. These are the three kinds of love with which we relate to God. As God out there is a nebulous sort of being, the best way to show that we are willing to give of ourselves, is to give of ourselves to our neighbor. Perhaps the great commandment is saying to us, love God and love man, in what may be a typical Hebrew repetition for emphasis. "You shall love the Lord your God with all your heart, and all your soul, and all your strength, and your neighbor as yourself" (Matthew 22:37-39). These two loves may be set side by side in order to clarify the meaning of how to love God.

A common conclusion is that we love God by giving of

ourselves (direction, energy, time, resources) through service to others. Our greatest gift to God is to respond to his love by becoming as fully conscious of the other as we can, using empathy, caring love, and kindness. Our loving response fulfills both us and the other, and also fulfills God's loving plan for us. By our example, we also further the growth of empathy, caring love, and kindness in others, and so promote the growth of the community as God intended it. By myriads of such gifts, we participate in the growth of consciousness in the world, and hence in the birth of God's Spirit in the world.

4.4 PROBLEMS OF THE HUMAN ELEMENT IN COMBINATION

In order to maintain equilibrium upon the earth, individually and collectively, humankind has formed various natural units. These units could reflect economic needs, educational needs, needs of order, and desire to properly worship or placate the unknown. As we continue our investigation of the scriptures, we find that God believed that it was not good for the human to be alone (Genesis 2:18) and encouraged him to have a helpmate. Being inventive, different religious and cultural groups have found many ways to structure this community of helpmates, so as to assure themselves of security and power. They have also proposed ways to dissolve or prevent combinations that were not going to be successful. Success, of course has been a very subjective quality, but a fundamental consideration would seem to be success in increasing the empathy, caring love, and kindness between the helpmates and those other persons that they affect.

The Bible gives multiple guides for forming the ideal community. Genesis 1-4 gives us the community of the family where two people are advised to give each other mutual support and consideration, and to accept responsibility for the care of their environment and the behavior of their offspring. When one of the offspring, Cain, behaves so violently that he can no longer be considered a member of the group, he is turned out of the family, much as some banish the recalcitrant teen-ager out of their homes today. In each difficult case, those involved must ask whether their actions are for the long term good of all concerned, or merely punitive.

From the family unit, humankind advanced to larger aggregates of humanity, in the economic, governmental, and theocratic spheres. Sometimes the motivation for this has been all for the basic purposes of greater personal security. In other cases, there is a strong motivation for the spirtual well being of the members of the community. In all cases, it seems, the security of the group can easily become the dominant motivation, even to the point of drastically reducing the spiritual well being of the group.

The ideal theocratic community in which all community efforts are oriented to the fulfillment of God's plan, is a dream that has never been fully actualized. Many groups have striven for security and national progress, binding themselves together under the leadership of their deity or of his representative. This was one of the aims of the early Hebrews. One of their offshoots, the Essene community, looked for an even deeper relationship with God through physical and mental purification. Even in such cases, one might ask whether the motivation was not, in part, the selfish pursuit of personal advantage and long term security. In more recent times, we have the dedication of the Japanese people to their so-called God-Emperor, who was to lead them to military and economic dominance. A little later, we witnessed the devotion of a deeply religious group to their charismatic leader at Jonestown, and the disastrous consequences of their blind obedience when his establishment was threatened.[3]

When we consider either theocratic or non-theocratic communities, we can observe a wide range of governments in present day nation-states. Physical security, economic growth, and spiritual well being (concerning factors like empathy, caring love, and kindness) are treated with different emphasis. Often, the latter is sacrificed in favor of the former. The total well-being, involving all these factors, apparently is very difficult to maintain. It is very impressive that the same dictatorial power models which seem to be very ineffective for the promotion of the well being of the total community, are employed over and over with poor results. In many cases, the cumulative buildup of power results in less and less participation of the masses of people in the determination of their own fate. Leaders intent on power are usually unwilling to risk a governmental process which carefully listens to the voice of the common people, both minorities and majorities.

4.5 THE COVENANT OF THE RAINBOW

Can we learn how to better take care of our earth, from studying groups that have existed in historical time? We have biblical examples of covenanted people living together in small faith communities. The people did not act through consensus, but obeyed patriarchal authorities. As communities grew and multiplied in the Near East, it became necessary to establish and enforce tribal regulations in order to insure the well-being of the tribe. Matters involving extra-tribal relations were usually settled by conflict, justice being considered to be with the victor. We have not advanced too far beyond this point in our relations between nations today.

Some community regulations leaned heavily on accepted cultural behavior and historical factors, while others seemed to derive from what might be called God's moral laws. For instance, an important consideration for the period of time immediately after the biblical flood was that the earth be repopulated. Holy Scripture tells us that when Noah descended from the Ark, he was told to "Be fruitful, multiply and fill the earth" (Genesis 9:1). This injunction was vital for that era, but might be considered as already fulfilled in the nations of India and China today, and could be easily discarded as no longer relevant.

On the moral side, Noah, like Adam and Eve, is instructed to care properly for his environment, with particular attention to the life that is represented by blood. "He who sheds man's blood, shall have his blood shed by man, for in the image of God man was made"(Genesis 9:6). There is nothing to state that this was not an international law, and God seems to feel that it holds for the whole earth, as he sets his rainbow in the sky as a sign to all generations. However, humankind seems to prefer to think that people in other nations are fair game for any kind of weapon that they may invent to shed one another's blood. Whenever we see the rainbow in the sky, we can think of the collective guilt we all share, those of us who make the weapons, those of us who fire the weapons, and those of us who are content to live as guilty by-standers in a community that legislates the shipments of armaments around God's globe.

Instead of seeing this law of Noah as a preventive injunction, humankind has held it up as a justification for further shedding of blood. We are told that this law requires us to give capital punish-

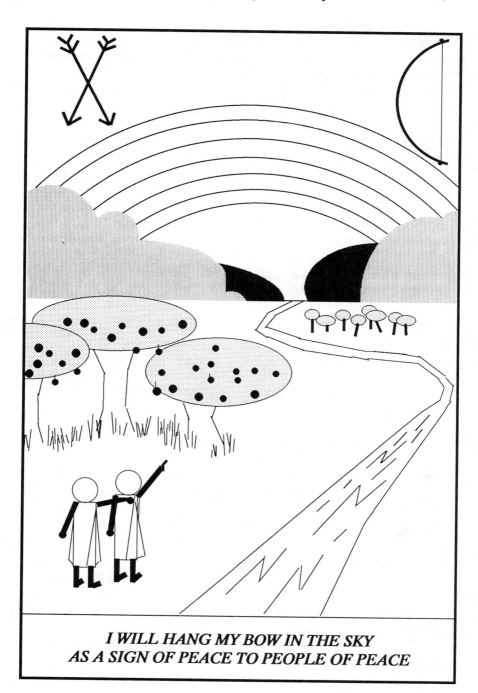

I WILL HANG MY BOW IN THE SKY
AS A SIGN OF PEACE TO PEOPLE OF PEACE

ment to the murderer. If this were so, we would have to give capital punishment to the man who killed the murderer, and then we would have to give capital punishment to the man who killed the man who killed the murderer, and so on, ad infinitum, until we were left with one remaining human being with no one left to execute him.

When God commands not to kill, he is speaking to the hangman as well as to everyone else in the community. Jesus, defending the adulterous woman advises that only the one without sin should cast the first stone (John 8:7). Governmental bodies can not legalize sinlessness in this regard. When God commands not to shed blood, other men cannot dispense us of our responsibilities. Even the person employed by the corrections department to pull the switch on the electric chair feels this incongruity. He frequently comes to his job through a devious route and wears a mask when he performs the deadly act, so that the community will not discover his identity and respond with distaste.

It is a long time from the days of Noah to our own age, and it seems that presentday humankind in the development of the ideal community, neglects the wisdom in Noah's pronouncements. Many today do not seem to feel the urge to respect human life by considering the appropriate population size for maximum good of the earth's people. Governments do not concern themselves with the need to preserve the life blood of humanity in nations other than their own, but send weaponry wherever they can make a sale or believe it diplomatic to encourage agitation.

In the days of Noah laws were not considered to be as binding as we conceive of them today. Laws were given for guidelines to improve relationships among human beings in the community. The Laws of Noah are given in the covenant setting. They are not only to improve relationships among human beings, but to improve the relationship between God and the human. If the human being keeps in mind this agreement that God has with him, then the human will also have in mind what God said at the covenantal meeting, and will operate in a positive manner with his fellow human. The early covenanted human was not so much striving to keep rules and regulations, as he was eager to remain in a covenantal relationship with heaven. The rainbow, as a sign of God's care, was more important than an exact interpretation of a law.

Today we look back at the Covenant of the Rainbow and we

see only God's side of the covenant. We chortle happily, "God will never destroy the earth by water again!" We fail to remember that every covenant has two sides. Man's part, in this covenant, is to properly care for the earth. Today the human is doing a sorry job of caring for the earth, so God has every right to dismiss God's side of the bargain. God would be totally justified in flooding us out of existence. Perhaps in destroying our protective atmosphere with pollutants, we encourage our own self-destruction, and assist God in carrying out the negative part of the covenant.

4.6 ABRAHAM AND THE BLESSING OF THE LAND

Scripture also tells us of God's covenant with Abraham and his tribal group. Abraham did not have the Bible to read or even the Ten Commandments to follow, but his relationship with God was so satisfying that he was known as the *friend of God*. This friendship was solidified in covenantal form. As all of Abraham's household *belonged* in this relationship, they were signed with the community sign of circumcision. Through this sign they became bonded to God and to one another.

There were also those in the community who could not undergo this bonding sign. Abraham's household included both men and women. As the women were not expected to be circumcised, they were included as property of the man. Some of the women coming out of this circumcision community attempted to assert their rights by the lesser known operation of female circumcision. Circumcised, or not, the women were a viable part of the community, and their opinions were heard. It seems likely that a degree of community consensus was practiced.

The environment was not left out of this relationship between God and Abraham. In this covenant the many heirs of Abraham are promised the land *if* they abide in friendship with God and with one another. We will all be given our share of the earth, if we are willing to share the earth and care for the earth in concert with all of our fellow humans.

Being creatures sprung from the earth, it often seems that we are in tune with some particular spot on her vast surface, and that if we leave that spot, we become disoriented. As a fish has problems when he is removed from his environment, the water, so we have

problems adjusting to the tunes of a new space. We are bound up
with our pieces of land, with our countries, with the cultures that
have sprung from our territories, and with the structures that have
grown out of our societies.

We must give credit to Abraham, that when the monotheistic God called him to come from his father's house, and go to a new
land, Abraham left his old culture, and his old gods, and trusted
himself to the care of this unknown God who had invited him. So
much of what is positive in our individual and communal heritage today, is due to Abraham's willingness to step out, and to be in
covenant with this God who was generous with beautiful stretches of
pasture.

The earth that God made for us, is full of wonderful variety,
and we grow and delight in its fertile environments. Yet it often
seems that we who dwell upon the earth are not given equal shares
of its bounty. What is the cause of this seeming favoritism?

God's dream for all creatures is for their joy and fulfillment.
With God so anxious to love and care for all of us, what has gone
wrong? Is it fair for me to stand on a hillside and to thank God for a
gentle winding river, while a woman in Brazil swats at flies in a
corrugated shack covered with dust? God wants a peaceful home for
her. She is a child of the same earth that nurtures me. Is my *more*
really so much more? Is she perhaps blessed with deeper love in her
heart, as she has greater understanding of what it is to be without?
Her birthright as a child of earth is to have and grow in the soil of
earth. Who am I to say that I have grown better or that I am wiser,
because I have a larger, seemingly safer plot of earth?

As communication across the earth increases, the woman in
Brazil and myself can compare our cultures and hopefully discover
what each of us lacks, that will make for greater fulfillment for both
of us. We may be able to help each other to realize our potentials.
Perhaps she is more in tune with her spot of nature than I am with
mine. Perhaps her daily actions contribute more to the total growth
of humanity than do my more self-centered, land-centered reflections. In her own way, she is building her world. I like to think that I,
too, have a part in bettering the earth. If she and I could reach out
from our separate homesites and bridge the gaps between our life
styles, we might find that we could work together effectively for
greater world understanding. If we each have a personal covenant

with God, we will surely be able to work together in cooperative consensus.

4.7 WE CAN CHOOSE TO WORK TOGETHER

With the increase in worldwide communications, people from different nations are able to establish new links with each other. The potential of a united humankind is staggering. When people cooperate, they can perform wonders. The pyramids were built by human beings under forced cooperation. Our country became a model for the world when its citizens organized in freedom to work for the common good. We have all been inspired by the sight of a graceful bridge reaching from shore to shore. Many are thrilled by the team work visible in a football or basketball game. What shall we build, here on this, our earth? What dream needs fulfilling? If we humans try, there's no telling what we might accomplish!

One thing humanity is blessed with, individually, is freedom of choice. Though many of us are hampered by culture and location, we have a certain ability to choose what we wish to become. We can set goals for ourselves. If we try to reach these goals individually, we may be fortunate enough to achieve what we desire unless another individual, or group, or institution chooses to oppose our path. Then we may be forced to modify our goals in order to respect the needs or requirements of the other.

If individuals or nations form into community groups that wish to accomplish a stated objective, they often inspire each other to greater energy inputs, that speed their successes. If each individual or nation works separately, without consulting the other's wishes, they often run into road blocks set up by those whom they excluded, who may simply be peeved because they were not consulted. As each is searching for personal freedom and personal security, there is always the suspicion that the one who is working alone may be using unethical means to secure gain. Sometimes our elitist actions cause our own downfall. The individual or nation may wake up one morning to find out that what was believed to be rightful property is no longer secure, as an excluded group was allowed to become overburdened. We must be responsible for the needs of all the others on earth, if we are to take proper care of ourselves and of our own safe spots.

As our stock market rises and falls and we bid on debt burdens of other countries, as our private automobiles pollute the air and use up finite resources, as we eat and drink excessively, our national safety demands that we keep in mind the starving in other countries and also the hungry and homeless in our own land. If we are not concerned for these have-nots, they will not only be forced to allow their own environments to turn into slums, but their lack will creep insidiously into our environments. Our culture will sink to include all the most unethical attitudes caused by their poverty.

Speaking plainly, these selfish and family-centered concerns for our own security and the pleasantness of our neighborhoods, have very little to do with God's justice and righteousness, but are only a common sense regard for our personal safety and the safety of our immediate descendants. For our own selfish good, it is wise to give of our material wealth to the poor, so that they will not be jealous of us, and terrorize us.

However, God's true justice has much higher and broader motives than care for the well being of our immediate family and selfish monetary concerns. It pleads that we respect the other who has not, and supply his needs, as he is our fellow human being and a marvelous creation like ourselves. God's righteousness asks that we give food to the hungry beggar standing on the street corner, because we empathize with the agonizing cramps in his stomach. Our own selfish need for security, and thus common sense, suggests that we give to him, so that he will not come to rob us in the dark of night. God's justice asks more than fear of the other from us; it asks us to have empathy for the other. With our freedom we can choose to have empathy or we can choose to shut out the other from our thoughts.

Some of us use our freedom to totally exclude the other, and to squelch his protests with legal forms or arms, as one chains a hungry animal. Some of us partially recognize the other, and allow a few crumbs to fall in his direction, as to dogs under a dining table. If we are to be truly ethical, we must make generous room at the table for our fellow human beings. For optimum constructive purposes we must unite with both those who have and those who have not.

In unity there is strength. What shall we do with our united abilities? Shall we build clean cities free of drugs and their accompanying crime? Shall we encourage small organic farms? Do we want to lift the threat of nuclear holocaust from our world? In choosing our objectives, we must remember to consult with all others who will be affected by our actions, to respect the freedom of those others, and to invite those others to participate constructively in the task.

4.8 BIRTHRIGHT, BLESSING, COVENANT, AND CHOICE

There were others who wanted the land in Abraham's time, and various chieftains were willing to fight for property rights. When a group of these others kidnapped Abraham's nephew Lot, Abraham used force to secure his holdings. There was no process of open consultation with the others or a consensus meeting to identify needs. There was no possibility of communication from a safe distance, in order to clarify problems.

Hopefully, with communication so easily available, we creatures of the present will choose in freedom to generously share this blessing of earth with one another. Hopefully, we will all be able to work together. The time for elitism of races or nations is past. We are all of the same creator from the same dust of earth. We are all on the same evolutionary trek, dreaming of the same unreachable Utopia where everyone will be secure from all fear. Thus one group cannot enforce its will on another, or ignore the needs of another, without damning the whole process.

In many places in the world today we see upheaval due to one group or individual selfishly putting its needs above another. Situations like this have been in process for millennia. The story of two antagonist brothers, Jacob and Esau, is told in Genesis 25 through 36. There is much to be learned from this story. Down through the centuries, many have sought to justify Jacob, as destined from the womb to be the favored son. One of the probable purposes of the original story may have been to question the whole concept of primogeniture. Later-day rabbis sought frantically for some way to excuse the outright lies of our now-revered father Jacob. When this story was first related, it was probably not told to justify Jacob, or to give land rights to the Holy Land. Its purpose was to make the listeners think ethical thoughts, and come to appropriate decisions. The story flows along in the following manner (Genesis 25:19-33).

Esau and Jacob were twins and Esau was the first born. Esau

was a happy-go-lucky type who enjoyed working hard and hunting. Jacob seemed more introspect and had difficulty with the inheritance customs of the times that gave the prime inheritance to the first born, and required those younger to serve the elder. These customs enabled a person to pass down a herding area in its totality, and to designate one specific individual to head up the tribe. If the area were split up, then there would be factions warring over herding rights. The custom served a worthwhile purpose, but it must have been very annoying to Jacob who might easily have been the first twin to come out of Rebecca's womb.

Jacob evidently felt his insignificance as the younger, and looked for an opportunity to change his position. Esau, secure in his place as the elder, didn't worry too much about the situation. One day coming in exhausted and hungry, Esau was tempted to jokingly give away his birthright to Jacob for a plate of soup which he felt he needed immediately (Genesis 25:29-34). Jacob was astute enough to insist that Esau give him his oath on the matter. There must have been a family argument about the value of this religiously important oath in such a flimsy situation. It seems the mother sided with Jacob as she had already had a message from God that the elder twin should serve the younger (Genesis 25:23). The father sided with social custom, evidently not believing his wife's revelation, and continued to feel that Esau should receive the rights of primogeniture. Perhaps the father was displeased with Jacob's lack of hospitality to Esau. To share one's bread with the hungry was one of the prime teachings of that time and area, and is still an ethical requirement today.

When the father Isaac was old and blind, he called his son Esau to him and bade him make ready to receive the blessing of the first born (Genesis 27). Esau was to go out hunting and prepare a stew for the festive meal. The mother Rebecca overheard, and summoned the other son Jacob to also prepare a stew. As Esau was hairy, Rebecca covered Jacob's arms with lamb skin in order to confuse Isaac's sense of touch. Jacob deceitfully received the blessing that the father actually believed should go to the other son.

The blessing that Jacob received is the blessing for a fortunate farmer and herder who would be the chieftan of his tribe (Genesis 27:27-29). "Yes, the smell of my son is like the smell of a fertile field blessed by Yahweh. May God give you the dew from heaven, and the richness of earth, abundance of grain and wine! May nations serve you and peoples bow down before you! Be master of your brothers; may the sons of your mother bow down before you! Cursed be he who curses you; blessed be he who blesses you!"

When Esau returned successfully from the hunt with his father's meal prepared, there was no blessing left for him. His brother Jacob had received all that the herding community deemed most worthwhile. Because of this misplaced blessing and his cultural beliefs in its validity, Esau would be required to serve his younger brother. The father Isaac searched his mind for what was left to give to his deprived son (Genesis 27:39-40). "Far from the richness of the earth shall be your dwelling place, far from the dew that falls from heaven. You shall live by your sword, and you shall serve your brother. But when you win your freedom, you shall shake his yoke from your neck."

One way of looking at this second blessing could be to say that Esau was given the rights of the city dweller or of a soldier, who was required to live under power structures or with economic barriers. He was given a life dependent on proper trade and security relations with the farmer and herder. In early times the city dweller could employ his talents in creativity, economics, and politics, only if those dwelling in the countryside were stable and able to produce a surplus of food for all to exist on. On their part the farmers in the countryside depended on friendly soldiers to protect them from harassment of other tribes who wanted to farm their territory. At some point in time the social and economic structures formed by the city dwelling community or the camps of the soldiery became relatively independent of the farming community. The figurative Esau was able to shake off the yoke of the figurative Jacob.

Returning to our story, we find that Esau became very angry at Jacob. He determined to kill his brother, yet one noble thought stayed his hand. He did not want to make his beloved father unhappy. He would wait to kill Jacob, after his father died, so as not to distress this beloved parent. The parents sent Jacob away, to keep him secure from the justifiable wrath of his brother Esau.

Jacob traveled out of harm's reach, and learned further lessons of life at the residence of his uncle Laban. His quick wittedness may at times have looked like pure chicanery, but all the time Jacob must have been coming to grips with his ethical beliefs and growing in his understanding of God and man. He is described as wrestling physically with God (Genesis 32:23-32) shortly before he returns homeward to renew his relationship with Esau.

When the time came, for the adult Jacob to meet with his estranged brother, we are told that Esau assembled four hundred horsemen (Genesis 33:1), and through this show of power, the brothers ironed out their differences peacefully, pledging their respect for one another. The wonderful gift of forgiveness given by the man Esau who had been deeply wronged, to his brother Jacob, is an often neglected high point of this story.

One of Jacob's descendants, King Solomon, used interpretations from this story to justify rule of the Jews over Esau's descendants, or the country of Edom (I Kings 11:14-17). This sort of mindset, which spoke of the elitist rights of Jacob, stayed with the Jews for centuries, and is with us today. The fact that later on the yoke of Jacob is again removed and the tribe of Esau comes out from under the oppression of the tribe of Judah (II Kings 8:20), is pretty much forgotten. People remember only what they want to remember, and often use knowledge obtained, only for the purposes of maintaining power.

It is interesting to note that the Edomites were finally incorporated into the tribe of Judah in the Maccabaean era (I Maccabees 5:65). John Hyrcanus compelled them to be circumcised, and thus they had partial recognition as Jews. The Herods who reigned under Rome in the time of Christ were of Edomite stock, so there was a remnant of resentment against them due to previous ancestor action. But at that point in history there was no longer any Jacob-versus-Esau conflict. They had become one tribe.

Obadiah's prophecy on the relationship between Jacob and Esau affirms their brotherhood (Obadiah 1:10, 12), and speaks to God's continued governance over the nations. Edom is described as violating a basic human relationship in blinding its eyes to the agony of its brother Judah, the descendent of Jacob, in Judah's dire need. Such an action could cause it to forfeit its right to a future.[4] In like manner, any nation that denies the equality and brotherhood of humanity will forfeit its right to live in God's future.

Time has passed and the Esau-type soldier/city-dwellers and their governmental structures seem to have eclipsed the importance of the farmer. In our world today we might look at the peasant, and think that this Jacob type blessed by the sun and dew, is playing a sorry second fiddle to the Esau city dweller to whom we are indebted for art work, educational systems, manufacturing, world trade, debtor nations, environmental distress, police forces, prisons, and nuclear armaments. Yet is the Esau type blinding its eyes to the basic needs of those who depend on Mother Earth, and even destroying the earth itself? We must remember the message of Obadiah,- "Those who deserve a future are those who make the Lord's future, their future." The land is given to those who care for it, and who do God's justice.

Looking at the *togetherness* of the two individuals in Rebecca's womb, we might conclude that in spite of cultural customs of primogeniture, God finds these two types of humanity equal in his sight. The world belongs to all of us, and we are to speak out when our rights are violated by another's selfishness, we are to attempt to forgive that same selfishness, and we must all try to get along in the world that God made for us all. Esau and Jacob found it in their hearts to live peaceably in appropriate sections of God's land. Surely, through consensus and consultation, we people of a later day can find ways to share God's resources of land and water.

4.9 THE TEN COMMANDMENTS AS AN APPROACH TO THE IDEAL COMMUNITY

The descendants of Jacob,- Moses and the people he led, made a covenant with their God on Mount Sinai. The guidelines that accompanied this covenant have become an accepted legal code for many community groups which have not often considered what the code meant for the people of its own age.

In this legal code during the time of Moses, no punishments are stipulated, only encouragement is given:- Do these things that it may be well with you in the land God has given you. It is assumed that if one strives to maintain positive relationships with God and man, all will be well.

Failure to maintain these good relationships was known as "missing the mark". Later on in the history of the tribe, we find (through the Book of Deuteronomy) that the community devised a system of payments due for those who could not maintain good relationships. Gradually a notion of sin slid quietly upon the scene, and it became apparent that some people were considered to be less capable of "keeping the law" than other people. Some people were "righteous" and others were "sinners".

We maintain this notion of good and evil people down to the present time, in spite of up-to-date knowledge of psychiatry and our understanding of the influences of genes and culture. We demand payment of a person for his *sins*, and refuse to recognize that these *sins* are not so much his but belong to all of us. They rise out of the frustrations perpetuated by our culture and are indulged in by random members of that culture.

Our expectations of payment for sin have likewise changed with passing time. When the Hebrews made their covenant with God at Sinai, they agreed consentaneously to strive for good relations among themselves and with their God. If someone did not live up to this agreement, he himself was the reason for the breakup of the relationship. If he wished to depart from the tribe, it was his own doing. If he wished not to follow Israel's God, it was his choice. He ended the relationship. If he had a change of heart and wished to return, God was willing to accept him back freely. However, those people he may have wronged were not quite as God-like in readmitting him to the tribal community. There were certain formalities to be gone through and restitution to be made that was necessary if all were to live in God's justice.

Today we think very little of an offender's eventual return to society. We do not require monetary or physical restitution for crimes committed. Our main purpose in today's prison system is to keep the relationship between the person and his community severed. His punishment is given in time, not in goods. Time is a way to keep a person in isolation from the community. It also keeps the person from entering into a new community with new relationships. The prison system, as it is organized in many present day countries, is a place that maintains breakage of relationships, and teaches the incarcerated isolation and frustration. The Ten Commandments did not envisage a prison system. They were established as a norm to help tribespeople maintain good relationships with one another.

4.10 THE CIRCUMCISED HEART

The Bible mentions other types of covenantal action. Instead of a physical cutting of flesh as in circumcision to demonstrate an agreement to serve God, Hebrew prophets suggested that the sign was less important than the true relationship. The circumcized heart was the covenanted heart. One who had such a heart would be loving and kind with his neighbor, and would keep the justice of his God clearly in mind (Deuteronomy 10:12-22).

The prophets also suggested regulations for improving relationships between human beings by establishing practices for the Jublilee Year (Leviticus 25:8-22). These regulations can be seen by some as highly impractical, and a threat to the acquisitive. They may have been designed to make sure that the same families would always own the land. They also were put in place to service the oppressed, and those who fell upon hard times. Certainly the regulation to let the land have its rest every seventh year would prolong the fertility of the soil. If these regulations were entered into and understood by covenanting members of a consentaneous community, they could easily lead to a community in which individuals supported each other with consideration and affirmative aid in time of need.

The Law of Love proclaimed by Jesus was the natural outcome of these many Jewish attempts at loving community. Noah and Abraham, as responsible patriarchal fathers, were concerned with building a covenanted cohesive tribal group in their piece of earth. Esau and Jacob, in the settlement of their differences, clearly loved each other. The owner of the circumcised heart was a person who wanted what was good for his fellow human beings. With the advent of Jesus Christ, the dream for loving community grew to worldwide proportions.

The early Christian communities had "all things in common." Every member of the community had his part to play in supporting the community, and was in turn supported by others. Each individual was respected for how he or she perceived the Holy Spirit of God speaking within. Gradually, what the majority of the group decided was the truth, became the accepted TRUTH, and authoritative fathers were set in place to enforce this supposed truth. There was no room for differences, and minority beliefs were deemed to be heretical.

This body of supposed truth had very little to do with the Law of Love. In its operation and enforcement through exclusionism and inquisition, it often ran contrary to the Law of Love. The *majority* or the *authority* was again in control, and they felt that there was no need for consensus with the minorities. Those on the seat of power (like the ancient Egyptian kings) often seemed to think that the Holy Spirit spoke only to them. In our search for a loving sense of order, we had retrogressed pitifully.

4.11 COOPERATION AND COMPETITION AMONG GROUPS

Humankind evolved in a competitive manner. Usually the land went to the strong. Esau and Jacob saw beyond this folly, and cooperated to share God's gift of the earth. Our competitive genes urging us to survival are firmly fixed in our psyches. They are tied in with our respect for life, our own life. If we are to also give credence to the seed of God's love in us that urges us to participate in the flow of love in the universe, we will individually direct our psyches towards cooperation with others and to the forming of loving communities. As a body has many parts, each person must be expected to do his job for the group in order for the main group to operate successfully (I Corinthians 12:12-26). However, each person in the group will show optimum performance only if there is a competitive aspect to his job. That aspect may be nothing more than a desire to act in a near perfect manner or to see oneself as righteous. It may be giving your own person self-respect.

Individuals need the drives to both competition and cooperation to exist. Communities also should be based on both competition and cooperation. Groups form out of cultural, economic, and governmental interests. These group formations may or may not be in opposition to other groups. We may have two groups on two separate nearby islands each forming their own governments to each keep order on their own island. These two separate groups may cooperate with each other in keeping their common water clean or in supplying transportation to the mainland. They also may compete with each other over fishing rights, or battle each other to death if a member of one group violates the rights of a member of the other group.

Groups operating in consensus can make the same types of choices as individuals. They can consentaneously endorse actions leading to the flows of life and love, or they can choose the opposite.

Groups that give up their rights to an authority or a majority of their members are not making full use of all the God directed energy that exists within that group. To operate at its maximum, competitively and cooperatively, the consentaneous soul of the group must be given full freedom.

It is difficult to listen to every individual in a national group, yet there are some places in the world today where leaders are giving a reflective ear to what the common people are saying. People are more willing to express their national competitive spirit in sports stadiums, than on battlefields. They display cooperation with disaster victims of other lands. In the economic give and take between nations we find that competition plays a more important part than cooperation, but that both are certainly required in order to maintain a sense of equilibrium. As the authorities and majorities listen to the needs of others and respond cooperatively, our group competitive urge may be reduced to the need to display the greatest kindness and consideration to minority or oppressed groups.

4.12 THE NECESSARY PROPS FOR THE STAGE

If all the world's a stage, and human beings singularly or collectively strut across it, what are the props that we find on the stage? When giving a play, the cast always acts against a certain back drop. Humanity has created an exciting back drop of culture, custom, and social structures. Often this background overshadows the players. We need only to look at the specter of atomic energy, to realize that our human abilities to provide God's justice have not kept up with our scientific abilities to provide weaponry to enforce various human notions. Our ideas of loving concern are handicapped by social constructs and laws of previous generations that we seem almost helpless to rectify. The back drop of the stage has developed a commanding presence of its own, and has put in place certain competitive norms that contain glosses of elitism that often lead to desperate wounding of one group or individual by another.

If some of those players on the stage find themselves in conflict with the social regulations that have been put in place in their society, they may be required to experience the prison milieu or even death, for their non-conformity. Today's world has led them to have certain thoughts about their relationship to God and to other people, yet the structures of yesterday's world rise up and arrogantly confront them. What is wrong with yesterday's structures? Isn't the God of Abraham still a usable God for us humans of today? Don't the Ten Commandments still apply?

Today's structures have been built on the God-inspired ideas of yesterday. Each new direction for an established structure was conceived as a possible pathway to greater utility, even to greater holiness. Being human we can't foresee where our designs will lead. When it becomes our turn to bend and shape, like those before us, we search diligently for positive corrections. Often our intentions are misinterpreted by those who dwell beside us and by those who follow.

Whether it be an individual, or a group of individuals forming a society, the essential concepts for justice are: the realization of God's universal creation, the potential immanence of God in every person, and the continuing process of creation that involves all of humankind. When we see this continuing process to be the growth of consciousness- empathy, caring love, kindness, forgiveness, and freedom for all of God's children- only then will there be a possibility of a just society.

We find that we have individuals with opposing ideas who refuse to listen to one another; they cannot seem to weigh their argument in the scale of God's flow of life and flow of love. We likewise have communities of people who find it easier to exclude than to sit in an open minded meeting and come to consensus on a heated issue. There is usually some *both-gain* solution that is possible in all situations. God is willing to help us work through our differences and gives us the freedom to use the gifts of covenant and consensus responsibly. To use responsibility, to think things through, both individually and collectively, is to be a positive part of the God process.

5

THE WAY

OF

THE NEW JERUSALEM
AS OPPOSED TO
THAT OF BABYLON

5.1 THE FIG TREE

The fig tree is a symbol of prosperity for Biblical authors. When God
is pictured as angry at Israel, he allows the locusts to destroy their fig
trees (Amos 4:9). The great promise of God in Micah 4:1-4 describes
future good times as a man being able to sit under his own fig tree.
This whole promise is worth repeating and investigating more thoroughly.

> *In the days to come*
> *the mountain of the Temple of Yahweh*
> *will be put on top of the mountains*
> *and be lifted higher than the hills.*
> *The peoples will stream to it,*
> *nations without number will come to it;*
> *and they will say,*
> *"Come, let us go up to the mountain of Yahweh,*
> *to the Temple of the God of Jacob*
> *so that he may teach us his ways*
> *and we may walk in his paths;*
> *since from Zion the Law will go out,*
> *and the oracle of Yahweh from Jerusalem."*

He will wield authority over many peoples
and arbitrate for mighty nations;
they will hammer their swords into plowshares,
their spears into sickles.
Nation will not lift sword against nation,
there will be no more training for war.
Each man will sit under his vine and his fig tree,
with no one to trouble him.
The mouth of Yahweh Sabaoth has spoken it.

Micah 4:1-4 Version of Jerusalem Bible

It is wonderful to look forward to a future where humankind will undertake peaceful actions. It is a soothing blessing just to think how the spirit of God may work in people so that arbitration can take place between those in conflict. Is it really possible that there will be a time when there is no more training for war! When we look at Ireland and Israel and Cambodia, we must try to believe that some-day their pressured citizens will sit happily in their gardens and will not cause trouble for each other.

Not only in the writings of the prophets does God promise good times to those who do God's will, but also in the Book of Genesis are many interesting stories that help us to believe that God wants us to love and care for each other. The author of the book of Genesis sets out very neatly for us what are some of the problems of her time. The reader is presented with a situation and must make an evaluation of that situation. We have already investigated the story of Jacob and Esau and the social custom of primogeniture. It is only recently that Europe has started to give up primogeniture, where the first son inherited the title, the second went into the priesthood, the third joined the army, and the last went to America. Our conclusion was that in spite of social structures, those with circumcised hearts should be able to get along in the land together.

A second social situation described in Genesis 34 has to do with relationships among men and women. Jacob and Leah had a daughter Dinah, and Shechem, a young man from a different cul-ture, fell in love with her and raped her. He asked his chieftan father Hamor to procure him Dinah's hand in marriage. Jacob agreed to this marriage as long as Shechem and the other males in Hamor's

*I will make rivers flow among barren hills (Isaiah 41:18)
and each shall sit in peace among his own vineyards and
fig trees, and no one will make him afraid (Micah 4:4).*

tribe received the mark of circumcision, which they willingly did. Hamor, Shechem, and their relatives seemed like very agreeable people. They may have had circumcised or covenanted hearts, but Jacob's sons did not recognize this quality. They were more interested in the religiously correct circumcision of the male organ. Consequently, Levi and Simeon, Jacob's sons, ruined the whole situation. What could have been a joyous wedding celebration and a bonding of two disparate communities, turned into a slaughter by the self-righteous. When the men of Hamor's tribe were still weak from the circumcision operation, these two entered the town and killed them all, presumably to avenge their sister's rape. Because of this thoughtless incident, Jacob had to take all his family and move to another territory. No one comments on how Dinah felt, having her lover killed and being ordered back home by her ruthless brothers. The name Dinah means *judgment*. Women, even today, are seldom asked for their judgment. This story bringing to our attention the problems of rape and mixed marriages, may have been related to the rape of Tamar, an incident in the reign of David described in II Samuel 13.

A third story (Genesis 4) describes graphically what happens when the brothers Cain and Abel, children of the same loving parents, don't get along. Cain, the farmer, kills Abel, the sheepherder. One aspect brought into play here is the question of punishment for murder. It also brings to the fore the social situation of herder versus farmer. Again, this story was apropos in David's time when Absolom was charged with the murder of his brother Amnon (II Samuel 13:23-37) as an appropriate teaching that covered over the names of the culprit and the assasinated.

We might conclude from these situations spoken of in Genesis, that there is not too much reason for Micah's hope for the peaceful person under the fig tree. If only the sons of Jacob were more concerned with circumcised hearts! If only they allowed their sister freedom to make her own judgments! If only Cain and Abel could have shared the land like Esau and Jacob! If only the social structures we put in place would reflect the love that God has for all individuals! To realize the dream of the time of the fig tree, what should the world be like? Women do not need to be shackled and sequestered. They have the ability to make wise judgments. Brothers do not have to battle each other, but should support one another's needs in love. To dwell in comfort under the fig tree, we must each care for our own bodies, yet remain understanding and respectful of the needs of other individuals and groups.

5.2 THE CITY OF BABYLON

Having described some of the community concepts present in the Hebrew scriptures, we shall step forward in time and try to relate those structures to where we are today, and even to future ages. From the idea of women as mindless property, and notions of opposing groups such as herder versus farmer or city dweller versus country dweller, the Bible progresses to the idea of the good city and the evil city. These latter ideas were fashioned at the time of the carrying away of the Jews to Babylon. Of course the evil city was given the name of Babylon, and the city of hope became Jerusalem.

A later day writing, The Book of Revelation (chapters 17 and 18), gives us the characteristics of the evil city. Many of this book's descriptive phrases are taken from the Old Testament. This haunt of devils and loathesome birds (Revelation 18:2) is described picturesquely in Isaiah 34:11-12. That her sins reach up to heaven is spoken of by Jeremiah 51:9. The fact that kings and merchants mourn over this fallen city when she is cast into the sea, makes one suspect that she represents structures that enhance the wealth of the powerful.

Augustine writes in his *City of God* of both the celestial city and the secular city. The two "have been formed by two loves; the earthly by the love of self, even to the contempt of God; the heavenly by the love of God, even to the contempt of self."[1] Augustine was a dualist and saw things as black or white. For him, those who served God could have no compromise with secular laws and purposes. One was either for God or against God. People could make choices one way or the other, and there was no room for variation in between. His model may have served for his time, but the model of God we hold today is much broader.

Instead of thinking of the two cities as a group of good people versus a group of evil people, the two cities may be interpreted more liberally as variant social structures that have been formed by the good intent of the community. Well meaning people put in place structures that they hope will be beneficial. Time passes and defects appear in these structures. Other people point out the defects and attempt a restructuring.

For the purpose of effective functioning, communities would put in place customs that helped to keep their society orderly. The secondary place of women is one example.   Another outdated custom is primogeniture. Generations that followed the institution of such a custom might find reason to disagree with its wisdom. In the case of primogeniture, let us suppose the first born son was mentally deficient. It does not seem wise to allow such a person to rule over others. However, institutions established take on a life of their own, and one might be forced to have an idiot in charge, due to social conformity.

If we consider the people that must follow along and obey these customs, we must admit that they are not being evil when they install an idiot as ruler of the tribe, or when they burn their wives who don't pay up on their dowery. They are using what they believe to be wise community regulations, to further the life of the community. If we look at social structures today and find that due to economic custom, many people are obscenely rich, while others working through the same structures are desperately poor, we must not blame the people so much as we blame the structures that are set in place by previous generations (and upheld by us legalists in our generation).

We may interpret Babylon as social structures that at one time kept equilibrium among people, but which now have become burdensome to those they once served. The city of hope which is called Jerusalem (Revelation 21) may represent the future society with renewed structures which reflect new possibilities of human fulfillment under God. These two cities, Babylon and Jerusalem, do not necessarily represent an elitest group of Jews as opposed to evil strangers. Jerusalem can represent the hope for all peoples. Babylon, as a structure useful to past generations, is mourned over, but no longer useful for God's purposes. Perhaps Babylon is a necessary step on the way to a New Jerusalem. The Jews carried away to Babylon could certainly see more clearly how they should have behaved in Jerusalem. Can our society today, carried off to a figurative Babylon of nuclear weapons and drug overdoses, see more clearly the vision of the city of hope?

Babylon and Jerusalem may also represent cultures that conform to the opposing characteristics of competition and cooperation. We evolved and survive as individuals because we are self-centered and competitive. The aggressive and alert caveman would live longer than the amenable. Self concern is inbred. Now that there are so many of us, aggressiveness becomes a less desirable characteristic. If we are to survive as a species, we will have to learn how to be unselfish. We must overcome our tendencies that have served us so well; we will have to restrain our sexual and aggressive appetites out of concern for the race. All peoples will have to cooperate or perish. Competition has brought us to where we are. Competition may lead to nations destroying each other. The methods employed by New Jerusalem will have to combine cooperation with understanding. The types of competition to be allowed will have to be related to the fulfillment found in creativity or the challenge found in being loving and kind to one another.

The cities or communities which are like Babylon are built on groups ruthlessly competing with one another to rise to the top of the pile. These groups all being made up of persons, they do not need much alteration in order to be transformed into New Jerusalems. The one thing necessary is a change of heart of the people. Groups need to understand the others who dwell in their midst. Then competition gives way easily to cooperation.

5.3 THE CHOSEN ONES

Those Jews who lived in captivity in Babylon, retained their Jewish religious identity, and some of them returned to the city of Jerusalem to rebuild what they believed was their heritage. Some of those who stayed behind remembered their Jewish beliefs, but others became encultured as Babylonians, accepting the religion and social structures of Babylonia.

In scriptures when God is reported as being concerned for the Jews, he is certainly guiding those Jews who are in the Babylons of this world as well as those who dwell in Jerusalem. God yearns to also guide and comfort those who forget their heritage, and who are entrapped in the vicissitudes of life. When we consider who are the citizens of Babylon and Jerusalem, we find that Jews and non-Jews inhabit both places, and that God is willing to be present with all.

When the creator God who runs the universe promises to be with those created, it is hard to believe that any particular person (either man or woman) would be excluded. The themes of the Bible are a lot broader than narrow elitism. If we find anything which we can associate with separatism in a Biblical quote, we must examine it carefully and search out a fuller meaning. Often the Psalms are taken to express God's favoritism for Israel and for David. Instead of stopping God's love at one man, David, or limiting the God who created the earth to love of one country, we must enlarge our perceptions of God.

David represents a certain phase in the history and purpose of the Jewish people. He is chosen to lead a group of human beings in a specific territory who have ethical beliefs that seem to please the God of the Universe. As long as they follow their particular version of God's justice, they will be able to dwell peaceably in the land. Furthermore, it is their duty to bring the message of God's justice to all the nations.

Though some might interpret many of the loving words of God in the Bible to mean that God is on the side of the Jews as opposed to the Jews' enemies, or that God loves the well behaved fundamentalist much more than those who have homosexual leanings, a much broader meaning is available. For maximum empathy among peoples, the true Jew may be interpreted as anyone who yearns for the Messianic times when God's love and justice are available to all. This person God supports and upholds. The fundamental option of this person is united in action with the God who moves the whole creation towards Omega, towards the time when justice and love keep our eratic world situations in endurable equilibrium.

Who is the true Jew or Jewess? Historical background on the true or rightful descendant of Abraham is that he takes his name from the name given to Jacob during his wrestling match with God (Genesis 32:29). After Jacob, the supplanter and deceiver of his brother Esau, had an all night confrontation with the Almighty, God changed his name to Israel. This incident pinpoints the beginning of the tribe of Israel, which name means approximately *may God show his strength*. It also implies a new purpose in the ways of Jacob. He turns from what seems like the deceit of others for his own personal gain, to acceptance of others and to trust in God's care. He grows from competition to cooperation. This new purpose is what merits him a change of name. God's strength is shown in the *true Jew* or in the true servant of God anywhere on earth, when that person shows empathy, caring love, and kindness towards another human being.

In wrestling with God, Jacob must have argued persuasively for the human's position. We all like to justify our actions, and Jacob was evidently very able in maneuvering other people for his advantage. If we look at the average person in the world today, it surely might appear that God created the human to be self-centered and competitive. In Jacob's time, people were likewise thinking of what would best benefit them. Thus Jacob could easily justify his crafty actions in his dealings with both his brother Esau and his father-in-law Laban. In his careful observance of genetics, Jacob was able to secure the best of Laban's herds (Genesis 30). He could justify this for he certainly needed abundance if he was to take care of his wives and children. He likewise could justify depriving his brother Esau of both birthright and blessing, as necessary for his own survival and perhaps the survival of future generations. After the wrestling, it appeared that Jacob's outlook was broadened, and that he was willing to see the good in cooperation, and to have respect for the other individuals involved.

In Psalm 147 we see that the God who rules the heavens (verse 4-5) is the God who is in tune with the humble (verse 6). The strength of the military means nothing to him (verse 10), and those who rely on his love (verse 11) are precious to him. How then should we interpret verses 19 and 20, "He reveals his word to Jacob, his statues and rulings to Israel: he never does this for other nations, he never reveals his rulings to them"? The only way this second part of the Psalm makes any sense is if we understand Jacob to be any righteous humble creation of God. Each of us is capable of being this type of human being. Other nations or groups that are excluded from this knowledge of God, are those people who shut themselves off from his righteousness because they have been excluded and offended by misrepresentations of God. They are not enemies of an elite Jewish nation, but may be those wounded by our inattention. As such it becomes a challenge to those who claim to be God's proponents, to bring these others back into proper fellowship with God. It is up to those favored by God to "reveal God's rulings to them" so that they can become a part of the true spiritual "Israel."

The story of Noah and the ark (Genesis 6 and 7) does not have to be interpreted in an elitist manner. The other men of Noah's time may have been the victim of poor social structures. The story of Noah might seem to be saying,- "Be good, or God will destroy you and your world." We often use the threat of punishment to inspire children (and adults) to more acceptable behavior. Some religious groups even continue to use the concept of burning in Hell, for this supposedly noble purpose of causing correct behavior. However, the primary emphasis in the story of Noah is on Noah's faith. The story encourages its listeners to respond to what seem to be the urgings of God in their hearts. Today God does not advise us to build an ark or a space ship to escape an evil environment. He urges us to accept one another in love, and to build a livable earth together, for ourselves and for our children. Unfortunately, when we criticize or point out imperfections in our social situation, we usually tie in a specific person or group as the reason for the imperfection. We finger point in order to inspire our group to optimum behavior. We find it difficult to separate the sin from the sinner.

The human occupants of Noah's world were destroyed along with their unworthy social structures. Those washed away were not necessarily the world's greatest sinners. They were part of the calamity of the time. God sent his rainbow to remind us that all of us together have possibilities of building a well-structured world. The many colors of the rainbow shade into each other and remind us of what beauty we can create when we humans in our variety compose a unity, especially when that unity is cooperating together to build the earth.

Humans can work together very effectively to change the world. We have many examples of people helping people. Often we find that groups have optimum cooperation, when they are working against another group with opposing opinions. Sometimes the result of such good examples of cooperation is the horrible result of war. Terrorists work well together to harm the innocent. Instead of people cooperating together against another group of people, we should strive to have people working together with those of opposing opinions, to establish justice on the earth. We should have a type of government that is able to consider the needs of all human beings.

Democracy may be going out of date as it creates a certain type of separatism. When we talk about doing the will of the majority, we automatically exclude the minority, who may have very viable reasons for their point of view. Minorities who are forced to conform to the will of the majority may commit overt actions against that majority. Socialist governments pride themselves on taking care of the concerns of their helpless minorities, yet often alienate their more prosperous citizens by ignoring their right to personal gain for their labor. There is a need for consentaneous forms of government that listen to and respect *all* individuals. Rule by majority or by power no longer is of optimum effectiveness. The age of the powerful nation and smaller satellite nations has passed its usefulness. In being non-supportive of the economic needs of poorer nations, the greater nations are slowly destroying themselves.

5.4 THE AGE OF THE CONVERGENT EARTH

As more people populate the earth, and as communication increases among these people, the thoughts of all these people gel into a world covering consciousness. Opinions are exchanged to such a degree that scientists have speculated that there may be some as yet unknown medium for transmission of brain waves. Often two distinct individuals will come up with the same original thought at about the same time without having previously communicated this thought to anyone. If one person publishes a truly creative thought somewhere in the world, it seems to be easier for other people to think along that same line. Not only are we connected in our verbal communications, but somehow in our brain wave patterns. Social enrichment results from cooperative communication, yet at the same time it is not necessary for the individual to become a conforming robot. Each is able to maintain his own unique personality and culture.

This can be seen in the thrust of the major world religions. They remain with their own structures, rites, Holy Books, and laws, yet they converge in their beliefs of one God and empathy for one's fellow human being. We can be unique, and still be united in empathy and consideration for others.

The same can be said for other structures. In this age of the convergent earth perhaps our wayward structures need only slight positive modifications in order for the city of Babylon to vanish and be replaced with the New Jerusalem. Religious structures were frequently put in place to preserve a group's identity. This necessitated placing *the other* outside the group. When we can see that all humanity is God's creation, the city of Jerusalem will be able to exist with its gates open wide.

5.5 TRICKLE DOWN OF GOD'S JUSTICE

Humankind hopes fervently that the day of God's justice will come soon. Where does God's justice come from? It flows through the earth unobserved filling every crack and cranny. God's justice holds all things in equilibrium. We see this verified by observing the balance of nature where when humankind mistreats his environment, disasters follow, such as famine, cancer, or birth defects. In the ultimate mistreatment, we come up with the maximum self-retribution, where humankind misuses nuclear energy and destroys his world. Yet God's voice speaking in the hearts of his created, urges action to prevent this disaster.

There is also a balance maintained by the trickle-down of God's mercy in the economic situation. God's justice opts for the poor, but what happens when man mistreats his fellow man, when the wealthy ignores the cry of the disadvantaged? The punishment is not just for the rich man or woman to wake up in hell and to cry out for the pauper Lazarus to bring him or her a drop of water. The troubled poor of the present living world can cause manifold distress to their rich neighbors.

Let us take for an example the economics of an oil price decline. Certain American investors will take advantage of this situation and will make profits for themselves on the stock market. At the same time they can certainly see that the declining oil prices do have undesirable effects for the poor in Mexico. They can also observe that there are negative effects in our own country in the oil states of Texas and Oklahoma, that suddenly there are a lot of foreclosures, and that joblessness increases, yet they seem to feel that they are helpless to change that situation. They continue to profit from their sale of stock. However, as this is one interconnected world, there comes a point when the banking institutions see that foreclosures aren't making them any money, that Mexico won't be able to pay her debts, and in the near future we may see banks failing as poor nations are not able to pay back their foreign debts. Where does that leave the bankers? They look ahead and see disaster on the horizon. Of course, they have brought it on themselves, but at this point they are anxious to stop the falling oil prices, not because the poor are getting poorer, but because the fact that the poor are getting poorer will deprive them, the privileged, of their wealth. They are likely to go into action behind the scenes to stabilize the economy.

It seems that when the disease strikes our own flesh, we react. Though sometimes slow moving, God's justice does pervade the whole earth. We reap what we sow.

On the economic plane we can see that the greedy business man may organize his life style a bit differently to include enough financial trickle down to keep the whole system in equilibrium. This may not make for perfect justice, but it helps to stablize the situation. Charitable people in the community persuade their governments to make food shipments to starving countries. Because of the competitive urge to make money, forces move in the world, so that the hungry may be fed.

5.6 LAW AND GOVERNMENT AS SERVING GOD'S JUSTICE

There are institutions set up in our world culture that supposedly work for the common good. These institutions may have been set up a long time ago to meet certain needs in early societies. People living in collective groups on the earth found that they were able to exist in a more orderly fashion together if they followed certain codes of law. Herding and farming groups found that if they consistently gave land and chieftan rights to the oldest son, many hereditary disputes could be avoided, and the land would not be broken up into units too small for survival. Organized fighting men became necessary to protect property rights. Slavery entered the scene as a kind way to spare the life of a conquered enemy. The voices and problems of women were systematically ignored. Government became a useful tool for coordinating all these military and economic purposes. People working together and fulfilling their immediate needs, set all these structures in place. Those of us who come after do not question these structures sufficiently, but do our best to conform to them. People have a tendency to attribute these social customs to God's design, when they are merely a temporary human convenience. Primogeniture and slavery are not God's will, but cultural aberrations that facilitated order and prosperity in early communities. Any given law has the possibility of temporality. For instance, United States law supports the tobacco industry monetarily with one hand, and with other later laws recognizes the ability of the cigarette to cause cancer.

Susceptibility to change in society is shown by the new songs that people sing, as generation follows generation. The songs of yesterday do not suit the temperaments of today. Similarly, we should not expect the structures of yesterday to be optimum for the communities of today or of tomorrow. As we sing new songs, we should also use our creative abilities to make new structures for our times!

The human institution which we today term *government* is rarely set in place by those who are under its control. The government often pledges to protect its citizens from every imaginable disaster, yet may be found to bring disaster upon those same citizens. The most noticeable function of governments today may be the ability to tax. We in the United States may disagree violently with how our tax money is used, and question the wisdom of sending arms to other nations. As an institution with a life of its own and archaic forms to be adhered to, the average government takes a long time to hear the voices of its dissenters.

In our search for a worthwhile task that will improve the earth, perhaps one of the dreams we should attempt to bring to fruition, is a government that does not tax, but which is run like a corporation selling services. When we consider the delivery of mail, we find that the United States Post Office seems unable to make money, yet the United Parcel Service is a viable corporation. Another expensive item is a standing army that does not pay its way. If we used our army to rebuild our cities and eliminate potholes in our roads, those thus devoted to constructive purposes, might be less eager to destroy foreign cities and to blow up foreign roads. If we used the soldiery to clean up pollution sites and charged the polluting companies for this purpose, we would save tax money. We also would discourage polluters from polluting. These new ways of employing army personel would require a departure from our centuries old concept of a standing army, yet in these nuclear times the whole concept of *standing army* should be rethought.

The place of government in a nuclear age also needs our

grave consideration and reimplementation. Governments have a very chequered history. People seem to have a notion that they should be governed, that they are safest when they submit themselves to a chosen authority, yet often those chosen to rule escalate our insecurities. As these authorities are all human and fallible, there are always thinking people who are disatisfied with their governments.

We can go to the Bible for some information on early government and the togetherness of tribal people. The Israelis pressed for their prophet Samuel to appoint a king over them. Samuel told them what the outcome would be (I Samuel 8:11-18):- the king would impress their sons into his army; he would take their best fields and give them to his close officials; he would tithe their flocks. They would soon cry out to be rid of this king.

Kingdoms and other forms of government are easy to acquire, but not so easy to dismantle. The earth has tried many forms of government, both in its secular communities and in groups under spiritual guidance. The Bible also gives us the history of a religious rule by the Jewish priesthood. Religious communities frequently outlive governments of nations. Descendents of kings may be killed off, and thus terminate a kingly line. Those who claim to serve the powers of the heavens under a certain structure, pass the authority to rule to others in the community and thus prolong the life of their form of government. Consequently we find the secular government of the Roman Empire partially preserved almost two thousand years later in the hierarchical rule of the Roman pontiff.

Governments of religious bodies take form in the wake of a great religious leader. The church run by Peter's followers differed vastly from the intimate circle of disciples that listened to the Rabbi Jesus. The Muslim way of living has recently been interpreted in more diverse and violent modes than was ever visualized by the God-fearing prophet Mohammed.

In constructing their spheres of influence, religious groups have frequently found themselves at odds with other already established religious communities. They have participated in disputes over forms of worship, innovative ideas, cultural customs, and even argued over earthly territories. Muslims, Jews, and Christians still discuss territorial rights in the Holy Land. The positive influence of *togetherness* in groups is nullified when different groups refuse to cooperate and to share resources, and oppose each other. When nations and religious groups see each other as *the enemy* or as *the heretic,* they destroy the possibilities of *togetherness* in the world as a whole. If we see the needy beggar on the street corner, and we do not even feed him, we are not using common sense for our personal security, and we are certainly not following God's urgings to treat the other as an equal on the human scene.

As we cast our gaze around the earth, we find that there are many faiths with many variations in rites and backgrounds. Yet these faiths seem to believe in one creator God and have the common objectives of concern and empathy for the fellow human being. God seems to prefer variety, yet this variety seems most effective when it displays acceptance of the others' differences. When the various religious groups ignore the differences in their rituals and symbols, and concentrate on doing a good action in the world in unity together, they can accomplish much that is positive.

Thus for optimum operation the various religious communities cannot turn their backs on each other or on world problems and calmly meditate on how to achieve personal sanctity for an elitist type group. The Amish cannot enjoy their Pennsylvania paradise while the Sudanese die of famine. The different groups must unite with one another, and cooperate in action together, in the more pressing need of achieving sanctity for the whole world. Likewise nations and the people in their territories should reconsider outmoded laws and forms that ignore the rights of other nations and the well being of their own minorities, and together restructure these inequalities that work against the common good of all the earth.

5.7 HOPE FOR OUR POLITICAL STRUCTURES

When considering the flow of life and the flow of love in individuals and in communities, it might seem that a flow would take place better in protected channels. This might be true if the channels are carefully constructed to promote maximum flow. However, when making human structures to increase order and promote the common welfare, we frequently find that blocks to flow are often mistakenly set in place. We can look at our own United States' Constitution and observe that the problems of women's rights and slavery have created obvious blockages.

In their finite wisdom, well meaning people can easily cause harm to others. Sometimes when observing the scene, it seems that governments can get in the way of God's justice. When we see our leaders shipping arms to foreign countries, and realize that these arms will be used to kill people like ourselves, we shudder in horror. Yet our government is thinking that it is protecting its citizens by this action.

While observing the United States Secretary of State speaking on a television program saying that he wished to attempt to reinforce American interests, American values, American people, our way of life, I found myself objecting:- This is not the way to achieve peace in the world. If we want to get along with other countries, along with other peoples, we shouldn't maintain an elitest position saying, "Our religion is the right religion; our country is always right!", but we should enter into an empathetic situation with other religions, other countries, and assure them that we feel their value system is as worthy as our value system. If we put down their value system, which comes out of their culture, out of their understandings of the meaning of life on this earth, then we have not given them self respect. We have not built, but we have torn down.

Much positive action is necessary, in order to achieve a peaceful earth. For an individual (or a nation) to gain material security, one may have to give up some personal freedom or make concessions. One may have to become the servant of a ruler, an economic system, a religious community, or a spouse in order to insure protection or support.

This whole idea of someone protecting us is a strange notion. Do we need protection? Does our government fuse up more situations than it defuses? Women and minorities are only recently coming through a period where they have striven to shake off the confining bonds of this *protection* fallacy. When a world situation appears to be getting out of hand, there is always a combustible politician who is willing to stand up and shout, "Follow me! I will protect you." Men have frequently secured the cooperation of women by this macho attitude. In order to allign a female or a wife, a man will frequently tell a woman that he wants to protect her from other men, that he has only her concerns at mind. Often the marriage arrangement is only that this man who thinks he wants to protect a wife, is acquiring a piece of property, the woman, which will serve him and reinforce all his ideas, to his greater glory.

This same *protection* idea was coming from the Secretary of State in his television talk. Seemingly, his only wish was to protect the people. In this protection of people, he maintains a power and authority stance. There is a certain comfort in having power and authority over others. We gain a sense of security in being able to control others. If we are the leader controlling a group of people, or the husband controlling a wife, we have a team. The team is on our side, and we believe that this team agrees with and reinforces our beliefs. We somehow feel that this moral support which we think we are being given, increases our security and safety. It gives us someone on our side, to help us to combat the unknown *other*.

Our beliefs in this respect can lead us into self deception. We may see ourselves as the beloved leader of a benevolent group. We feel that we are right, that as the authority, we know the needs of our team. We come to believe that whoever the opponent is, he is obviously very stupid simply because he is not on our team. We are tempted to conclude that it may be necessary to convince him of his stupidity by a show of force. Such a show of power or authority does nothing to defuse an escalating situation.

Do God's holy people really need a government? Many times it seems that the people of one country are very willing and happy to get along with people from another country. Even if customs differ, people are very interested in the strange customs of other people. They are willing to display friendship and love and to learn about these customs. In the Iran-Iraq war, the people of Iran and Iraq were not really angry at each other. The governments had decided that there was an ideological difference, and that this difference was very important. As a matter of fact, this difference was rather unimportant to the people. Leaders simply wanted to maintain their power in the government framework, and had a certain desire to increase their control. Many of their people didn't care about the ideological aspects of the situation at all, but allowed themselves to be maneuvered into ranting crowds, as they were afraid they would be executed for non-participation.

People in the American government saw an opportunity in the Iran-Iraq case to sell a few arms, and to make some money to support other arms dealings. Arms may promote various psychological effects, but ultimately they do nothing but kill people. After the Iran-

Iraq arms deal, Iran was able to kill a few more Iraquians, and have
a few more of its own soldiers maimed. It is difficult to understand
just what these two countries were fighting about. They were doing
battle in the name of a group of people who really did not want war.
These people didn't want their fellow citizens killed and wounded.
They didn't want arms from America, or any other country. They
didn't want their countries hurling long-range bombs on each other.

Governments have no right to wage war on one another
without the full consent of the people involved. It would be very difficult for any government to get get the full consent of the people for
the purpose of waging a war. Many of these authoritative governments are there only to increase their own power and their own
sense of control. They do not know that they are "poor and little and
blind and weak."

Supposedly, governments rule through the mandate of the
people. We have elections in the United States where we put in the
choice of the majority, but there is usually almost half of the United
States' citizens who do not want these particular candidates to rule.
If governments are to clearly reflect the will of the people, it will be
necessary to revise our government structures. Instead of having
majority rule, we must have collective consensus. The minority must
be given an opportunity to be heard, and to have their program
discussed with government representatives and consequently implemented. When our representative government is working well, it can
inform the public of the wishes of the minority.

The majority must show concern for the wishes of the
minority. The minority must show an equal respect for the wishes of
the majority. We are obliged to hear each other out, and to attempt
to come to a *both-gain* situation. When we really hear each other out,
we learn more about each other, we learn from each other, and we
understand each other. Usually after constructive listening on both
sides, there is a conclusion available that will provide some amount
of good for both parties, because they have learned to understand
each other better.

If individual believers from both the minority and majority
viewpoints were readily heard in our Congress and over our television networks, greater understanding for all would exist in our
nation. This is coming to pass slowly, but surely. If state senators and
assemblypersons able to speak on both sides of the issues, were sent

from knowledgeable discussion groups on the local level, then they would be able to perform in consensus at a government level, on local issues. We could term this type of consentaneous democracy *circular government* because people would get into discussion circles to talk over their problems, and would come up with solutions from these circular discussions. The stated purpose of our leaders would not be to interpret the will of the majority, but to be there to implement the conclusions of the discussions of these circles. This would be a slow process at first, but as people began to better understand circular operation and their part in its development, there would be faster implementation.

Ease in this new manner of governance could come quickly, especially if problems were considered in the light of modern psychology. For instance, the Secretary of State and other leaders would not only understand the needs of the people in their national areas, but they would also understand about their own desires for power, authority, and control. There would be new techniques to consider as to the manner of governing a people who would not be desirous of asserting their elitism at the expense of others in the world. It seems that the duty of a secretary of state for this type of goverance should be to reinforce cultural exchange, and to help the different races and cultures in the world to understand each other better.

We have been discussing the question of control and authority used by governments. There is also the same question in regards to religious institutions, and the problem of the use of authority in the home. We find in the family that when the teen ager is ready to assert his freedom, this is the precise moment when parents clamp down and use the wrong psychology instead of allowing the individual to figure things out for himself or putting him in a situation where he can use his freedom. There is no family consensus process to enhance an agreeable settlement. The state does the same with its younger citizens. Young men are frequently found to go against the flow of society. When this happens, is precisely the time when society clamps down with its multiple legal ensnarlments, and refuses to listen or to try to empathize.

When situations arise where family members or neighbors do not see eye-to-eye, there should be available community resources to encourage open discussion leading to understanding and reconciliation. In communities in New York State there has been initiated a process of mediation of minor disputes. We frequently find that besides one member of a family wanting to control another member of the family, that the landlord will want to control the tenant, and the lover will want to control the beloved, often even after they break up. The tidy neighbor will want to control the untidy person next door. Some of us feel that we must control our neighbors' smoking and drinking habits and their management of their pets. Neighbors are not quite ready to let each person dwell peaceably under his fig tree.

Do governments need to control God's holy people? The policies of any government in any country stand a good chance of bringing the country to ruin, especially when the government leaders have no knowledge of psychology, and little use for ethics. There have been plenty of misguided rulers in the history of the world, and they continue until this day. There are very few governments that are noted for doing God's justice in the land, or for making positive uses of psychology. Our United States' government under Ronald Reagan and Oliver North did not send justice to Nicaragua when it proliferated weapons there that killed innocent civilians. The present Israeli government in ignoring the cry of the non-Jewish dwellers in the land, is certainly not doing God's justice. The English seem rather non-understanding in their struggle to control the Irish. Perhaps it is time to try some other form of government more open to listening to the underprivileged.

5.8 DO GOD'S HOLY PEOPLE NEED THE LAW?

Along with the question of government, it is moot to discuss of what use are legal systems. If we are to make appropriate structures to channel the flows of life and love in our world, should these channels be formed by laws that encourage positive behaviors of citizens towards each other? We have Biblical examples of The Ten Commandments, and Jesus' Law of Love. How much law is necessary for optimum operation of a Holy Community?

In the United States we have multiplied our laws to suit every peculiar situation, and we certainly do need guidelines to drive cars, maintain insurance, and run our businesses. However, there should be an easy recourse for someone who has broken a law. There should be a way for him to explain why he broke that law. There should be a person assigned to discuss this law breaking with him, and the whole situation should be brought before mediation if applicable, before a stricter process is applied. There may be a role for the present day lawyer as a consultant for the unfortunate person who has gone against the regulations. Instead of arguing for the individual's innocence, the lawyer should be trained to do research which would discover where this particular life was over stressed.

It is important that we diagnose the root of a problem. We must find out why a person was led to commit a crime, not just why he is in prison. We must try to understand the psychological and chemical reasons behind an individual's alcohol or drug abuse. Understanding the individual will enable us to give a person rehabilitative help instead of merely warehousing him and then releasing him back into society in a crippled condition. The warehousing method of criminal treatment leads to recidivism, a speedy return to the institution. The disease has not been cured; the person has not been renewed.

There also may be a role for counselors and sociologists, in assisting people in need of concern, help, or advice, before they commit a criminal act. Emergency hot-lines are very useful in this regard. There could be a network of trained citizens, perhaps some who are empathetic because they have been through our criminal justice system as convicted criminals and absorbed what was positive in that confinement, who could counsel others who might be headed in negative directions. Constructive aspects of our present social and criminal justice system can be emphasized and used in our institutions, and punitive aspects that seek to control rather than to encourage, could be discarded.

Our present laws and institutions have been put in place by thoughtful people who wanted what was best for their society. Every thinking community has participated in a search for order. Often order required that the many submit to the wisdom of the few, or to *a just one*, who they hoped was very wise. Frequently, people have been disappointed in their governments and in their leaders, as none of us has the necessary wisdom to know what is good for all the others.

Our present system may be a diamond in the rough. If we chip at it in the right places, if we know how to cut the stone, we may end up with a gem. We will mourn Old Babylon when she is cast into the sea. Her customs served us very well for many ages. But we will be willing to sacrifice her, if we can have a better model. Now is the time to help Babylon to evolve into the New Jerusalem.

5.9 DO GOD'S HOLY PEOPLE NEED A KING?

When we investigate Biblical history, we find that Abraham was the leader of a clan that gathered around him for their security and their livelihood. When his tribal descendants moved to Egypt, they endured Egyptian authority until the time came when they were willing to substitute that unpleasant servitude for the leadership of Moses. After their arrival in the Promised Land, came the period of the judges. People brought their complaints against one another to be mediated before certain individuals who had a reputation for wisdom. For a time there was a lack of order in the land. Even some of the priests who should have been setting a good example, were notorious for their impiety. Some of the people who felt they would have something to gain by a changed situation, clamored for a king.

The Jews had existed for many years without a king. They had decided in their hearts to follow God, and they believed this God would protect them from harm. Or did they really believe? Their request for a king may have been a reflection of their insecurity and their lack of trust in God's promises. They thought that a king would help to unite them against their enemies.

There is little reason to believe that people need authority figures in order to live a peaceable life. Likewise, there is little reason to believe that we need innumerable rules and regulations to keep us all in line. The important and necessary quality is that we have concern for one another. However, some of us are more inclined to be followers, and others choose to be more assertive. There is a place for role models, and for the imitation of role models, just as there is a place for making decisions as to what is good for humanity. There is room for discussion as to what are approved and positive actions, and the beloved community should welcome competition among its members to show forth what is truly God's justice.

Different communities will have varying needs for leaders and for laws. Abraham did not have the law, and his relationship with God was evidently beyond reproach. Jacob and Esau did not have the law, and they were able to live peaceably in the land together. One thing that Abraham, Esau, and Jacob had, that many of us do not have, is a covenant relationship with God. We do not make strong personal commitments in our hearts, to serve God and to give respect to our fellow human beings. Thus we find ourselves more in need of governing regulations to keep order in our communities.

Natural law, or an understanding of what God's justice should be, seems to be inherent in the body of ethical ideas that exists in the thought layer of earth. In order to keep an equilibrium in our social and cultural environments, perhaps it is necessary for violent erruptions to come from those treated as less than human. It would be more logical to maintain equilibrium by defusing potential disaster situations. If we all made personal commitments to obey the natural laws, or God's justice in our hearts, there would be less need for specific regulations, or for governors to enforce such regulations.

The early Jews cried out for a king, a role model and protector. God warned them that it might detract from proper worship of God, and from freedom and equality among themselves. People would be inclined to shirk their responsibility, and to let the king or the government do all their thinking for them. They would be afraid to oppose the power that they had set in place. People must not act out of fear, but out of love. They must set their sights higher than the mere bending to authority and the keeping of out-of-date rules. Our aim must be for the perfect city, the New Jerusalem, but we live today amid the structures of Old Babylon. We seem to be content to accept the same culture (with its same problems) as that which was wrestled with, by our ancestral fathers and mothers. These old props are no longer the best servers of God's justice. We must search for newer ways with more progressive possibilities, if we are to maximize the flows of life and love in the universe. We must ask ourselves if we need a prime symbol of authority (such as the king who ruled in Babylon). We must ask about the need for laws (similar to those used in Babylon). We must ask about our social structures and our economic structures. How can we set our feet on the road to Jerusalem?

6

THE WAYS

OF

THE OPPRESSED

AND THE OPPRESSORS

6.1 LIBERATION THEOLOGY

In searching for communities that run on love and kindness among persons, rather than on dictatorial authority, we could note different religious sub-groups that have had a measure of success. The followers of St. Francis still shun positions of authority. In the Middle Ages the Beguin women of the Netherlands formed supportive communities, and helped the poor. The Quakers believe in the equal ministry of all members of the group. Some Catholic theologians in the Latin American countries have proposed a method of assisting the common people to make their needs known to those more advantaged citizens who have political control.

This latter method or theology, frequently called *liberation theology*, has to do with transforming the inequitable relations that may exist among different segments of a population. When there are inequities, it may be necessary to free both the oppressed and the oppressor from the respective miseries they undergo as a result of their accepted social milieu. There are many political, economic, and cultural settings around the globe, and where there is an intersection of two or more of these ideologies that refuse to listen or compromise, the group with the greater power tends to dominate, putting the other group in psychological or physical bondage. Liberation or mediation is frequently necessary in such cases, or terrorism may be an immediate result.

If we are not one of the monads or elements in a certain situational setting, we can never quite come to complete understanding of the problems and inequities that exist therein. It is also very difficult for oppressed groups in a culture to relate to oppressor groups and vice versa. Communication is necessary between groups. If we are totally outside the culture, we can never comprehend all the seemingly insignificant happenings that went into the make-up of an individual immersed in that culture. We can never fully understand the outlook of the Pakistani kameen who hauls sewage for a living, whose son and daughter are destined to haul sewage, and whose descendants will also have nothing to look forward to, but this lowly occupation. Neither can we fully comprehend the cultural view of the Hindu priestly caste, who accept their privilege as their due. In still another setting, we who have been produced in the relative freedom of the United States, cannot feel the terrible tug of fear that must eat at the heart of the person returning to a dictatorial regime, as he wonders if he will be met at the airport by the police. There are so many world situations that are in need of ethical and theological analysis, where understanding and mediation would ease the pain of all concerned!

In doing liberation theology, our first task is to start with a real life situation. We can attain maximum understanding and performance in our doing, if we are ourselves immersed in the economic or cultural aberration. Although we may be coming from the outside, we can also learn and help in a cultural situation that is foreign to us, by joining into the community concerned with that situation. Whether we are part of the culture or merely aligned with it, the community is a prerequisite to any action. We are of no help, if we do not know what is the consensus of the people. With them, we can discuss and formulate how we all feel, and weigh the seriousness of our common problems.

If we are being terribly wronged, and are very wounded from an oppressive situation, we may be partially blinded to a solution to that oppression. Our hate may drive us towards unnecessary violence. An outside viewpoint may lead to less hasty action. An example of someone coming from the outside who can help because of the fact that they are an outsider, can be seen in the mediation situation. The doctoral student Paul Lederbach was able to function as an effective third party in Nicaragua, because his purpose was to gather unbiased information from both sides.[1] In surveying both confronting communities, he became useful as a go-between and as a disseminator of opposing opinions. His pool of information, which was able to be communicated to both sides, was a means of freeing both sides from their stereotypical viewpoints.

In a liberation theology arena, after we have asked questions, and proposed answers, we are then faced with the more difficult task of deciding what actions to undertake. In order to find solutions, it is necessary to understand the roots of the problem. When tidying up a garden, slashing of overgrowth brings temporary relief, but often the shrubbery enjoys the pruning, and comes back twice as thick. Violently shooting a few leaders of the opposition party, only brings new and more violent leaders to the fore. One must investigate historical, economic, sociological, and even theological roots that have led to mistreatment of one's fellow human beings. Slavery, greed, and power plays are most often thought of as culprits in situations requiring liberation, yet even seemingly harmless misinterpretations of biblical material can cause social malfunctions that should be corrected.

When one has gotten to the root of the problem, one cannot stop at some place back in history, and either sulk, or propose some violence as a solution. Neither can we throw up our hands and say the economics are insurmountable! The community group must brain storm for all possible solutions. Then we must advance forward from the present moment in positive solidarity. Courageously walking towards the future is not only a statement of trust in humankind, but a cleansing and forgiving action for what has occurred in the past.

Actions planned to be undertaken in the future must be as non-violent as possible. The present state of the oppressed may be an actual life or death situation, and they may have to commit criminal acts to remedy their plight. If the poor are starving, no less an authority than St. Thomas Aquinas, has pronounced that they have a right to steal to preserve their lives.[2] Similarly, general ethics allow for a certain amount of violence, if lives are in danger, and there is no immediate non-violent means of achieving an acceptable result. However, liberation theology seeks to free both the oppressed and the oppressor in a non-violent manner, through maximum communication. The oppressor is set free from his desire to dominate, and his inability to share his material goods. The oppressed is freed from possible material death, and from lack of self esteem. When this occurs both the oppressed and oppressor are enabled to live out together their common human experience as children of God.

The term *liberation theology* had its beginnings in Latin America, and is often associated with violent eruptions of poor people. Comfortable people who enjoy the status quo, have defamed the name of this generally peaceful process, by calling it *Marxist*. Marxism is frequently misinterpreted as *Godless communism* with the accompanying notion of people being led astray by cold and calculating leaders, but it also can be seen as a grassroots community action which is striving to better its immediate neighborhood. Christian thought encourages the poor to band together in loving community, and commemorates with the Jews the Exodus from the land of Egypt to the freedom of the desert. We often speak of a Christian theology of liberation, but in doing this we limit ourselves to a certain segment of humanity, those who claim to follow the person Jesus Christ through membership in certain church bodies. If we speak of a world theology of liberation, we include all those who show empathy and compassion for their fellow human beings, as did the person Jesus Christ, the person Buddha, and others such as Gandhi, Dorothy Day, and Confucious. Our intentions for liberation theology should include the eventual freeing of all the world's people to lives of maximum fulfillment.

6.2 THE PROBLEM OF POWER

There are as many contexts from which to do liberation theology, as there are bondage situations. The overall problem that is in common with these situations is that one group of individuals is attempting to control another group, or to keep them powerless. The in-group wants to be in the seat of power.

There are different types of power. Power can be used for good as well as for evil. Power is tied in with God's gift of free will. We can chose to be a power for good, to transform both ourselves and others; or we can be insecure and self-centered, and tear down and deprive others.

The scene in the Garden of Eden pictures the first sin as a power play. The insecure male blamed what went wrong, on the female, in order to maintain his good image before God. The insecure female blamed it on the snake. They both exercised their free will in an attempt to maintain their power.

Women and men still have power structures that exclude the good of each other. The male power structure is called patriarchy and is participated in by both males and females across the whole world. The female is less likely to exercise matriarchy, or domination of the males in her household, as she is to use an underhanded power structure, which might be termed *feminine manipulation*. Those of us who are women know full well when we are artfully moving males into the directions we wish them to go, by gentle maneuvering actions. This feminine manipulation is not all bad; it can have very good consequences, and be very Christian in its purposes. I merely wanted to point out that it does exist. Patriarchy is not completely evil either. We might speak of a loving responsible father dutifully caring for his family, as a benign patriarch. The evil enters in, when we desire to control, in order to elevate our own agenda at the expense of others.

6.3 WHAT LANGUAGE TO USE

Many world situations are in need of a theology of liberation, or of a process that will free those persecuted or ignored, from domination by an oppressor. Gustavo Gutierrez has proposed such a theology for the Latin American countries.[3] The words that one uses, when speaking of this type of theology, can lead to positive or negative reactions. Perhaps *liberation* is not the right word to use to describe a peaceful and freeing process. When adding the idea of power, to this liberating and overcoming, many might think of an unruly mob. Often when the word *liberation* is employed, an oppressor will shake in his shoes and respond with fear and further oppression. He may take it as a personal confrontation by his imagined enemy, Marxist Communism. For many accustomed to the relative freedom of democracy, words like *Marxist* and *Communist* are symbols that represent total evil. *Devil* has been for many centuries, a useful word for this *anti-God* entity. Name calling, by fearful people, can lead many people into panic.

If one speaks of *salvation*, the process is conceived as more bland. If an oppressor thinks of Jesus as savior, he has the notion that the oppressed will accept their lot, humbly, in the likeness of a meek and self-effacing Jesus, and bear their crosses of starvation and homelessness, gracefully. They will be willing to put off their reward until a future life, awaiting "pie in the sky when they die." In this case the oppressor has no fear that he will be thrown down from his position of dominance. The word *salvation* assures him of his continuance in power. He naturally aligns himself with church structures that promote this *heavenly-reward* mentality. However, this stance on the part of the authoritarian ruler does not make for rapid change in the hardship cases of the persecuted. It does not free the oppressed, house the homeless, or feed the hungry.

What word can we use that neither threatens the oppressor, or condones his oppression? One word that might be optimumly employed is *solidarity*. In the encyclical *On Social Concerns*, Pope John Paul encourages the Christian community to be in *solidarity* with each other and with the earth.[4] The rich are to be in solidarity with the poor, to assist the poor to their fulfillment, and this process will also help to build their own personal self-esteem. *Solidarity* can be interpreted as people working together to supply each other's needs. Its purpose could be seen as an encouragement of the flows of life and love.

Another word that might replace the oppressor-frightening term *liberation*, is a word that draws people together, *reconciliation*. Reconciliation helps opponents to come to agreeable terms with one another. It speaks of forgiveness, even in the bleakest of situations. It allows room for mediation and for win-win arrangements. Oppressors will not be completely destroyed, but will be given every opportunity to live in loving community with those they formerly oppressed. They will be given the opportunity to share their excess material wealth. The term *reconciliation* has been used effectively in El Salvador, where the residents of a bombed out village have returned in an effort to put their lives back together. Both bandits and government forces have signed agreements with the townspeople not to interfere in this project of reconciliation. Because of the tone of reconciliation, the town is not a threat to confronting parties. Those townspeople who have suffered loss, due to terrorism from either hostile political group, have resolved to put their anger and hurt aside in favor of working together for the common good.

The Bible in II Corinthians 5:18-20 makes a pitch for reconciliation. We are to be reconciled to God, and we are given the task of handing on this gift of reconciliation.

6.4 AREAS WHERE RECONCILIATION OR LIBERATION IS NEEDED

Going back to particular contexts in the greater world, we find that liberation, salvation, solidarity, or reconciliation is needed in many areas. The poor or powerless or oppressed are erupting across the world in many situations. Massive unrest is taking place after twenty six years of authoritarian rule in Burma. Young white conscripts refuse to serve in the South African defense force. Bombs continue to explode and harm the innocent in Londonderry and Belfast. Kampuchea waits to see what its fate will be, when the Vietnamese withdraw their forces. Intensifying military conflict in the regions of Eritrea and Tigray, hamper relief efforts in Ethopia.

As a response to life destroying forces, the church in Chile promotes the formation of Basic Christian communities as neighborhood support groups, where people help each other to bear the vicissitudes of the times and of their government. Due to this gentle pressure from the lowly, the military government of authoritarian Catholic Augusto Pinochet is lifting restrictions that have been in place since 1973. When the democratically elected President Salvador Allende was killed, with possible CIA acquiescence, tortures and disappearances became the order of the day, and even farmers' organizations to help grow better crops, became suspect. Through observing the non-violent work of base communities which emphasized the love of neighbor, those who governed were led to listen to the voice of the people, and were enabled to set aside their fear of loosing power.

In Nicaragua the contest between rival groups is also seen as between two factions in the Catholic church. Managua's cardinal, Miguel Obando y Bravo, led a group that favored the Contras. Another Catholic group led by the Jesuits felt that they expressed the feelings of many of the common people, and took the side of the Sandinistas and Foreign Minister Miguel D'Escoto. The base Catholic communities in Nicaragua, are not expressions of the common people as in Chile, but are hierarchically led. For this reason many Nicaraguans leave the Catholic church altogether, and join in with Protestant sects, where they can practice neighborhood solidarity.

The idea that a minority might gain power through small isolated acts, often causes great fears in the oppressor government. In Palestine we find that there is so much fear, that seemingly harmless actions can lead to suspicions that fire needless cruelty. Persons boating off shore in a rubber dinghy in August of 1988, were gunned by an Israeli naval vessel. Observing this, Palestinians in a camp at Rashidiye, returned the gunfire. In retaliation for this response, Israeli gunboats launched rockets into two Palestinian refuge camps further along the coast, and four helicopters dropped rockets into Ain Hilwe and MiehMieh shanty town sites.[5] Parties on both sides evidently had no communication with each other, and had no knowledge of the purposes or fate of the dinghy occupants. If there had been communication and mediation in this instance, many people, both gunners and the recipients of gun fire, would have been liberated from their roles of oppressor and oppressed.

On the positive side Iran and Iraq have made the important decision to listen to one another's representatives. The government in Poland has heard the agonies of the people and has invited what was once opposition, to work together for the common good. The Berlin Wall has tumbled. There is concern in the economic world with the inability of Third World governments to pay their horrendous and unjust debts. With modern communications and television airing of situational distress, those people who fall into the category of oppressors are forced into at least a partial empathy with those classified as oppressed.

The duty of those who serve God is to announce freedom to all who are in different ways in bondage (Isaiah 61:1,2 and Luke 4:18,19). If they are in chains, either they or we must try to discover the basic root cause of their enchainment. If we find the cause, we have the further responsibility of investigating possible ways to help them be rid of this injustice.

To find the root cause of a particular bondage is not always easy. Like roots of growing things, these causes may twist and wind around one another, in the soil in which they exist. Suggestions for the root cause of bondage of women in Latin American countries, might include the machismo attitude of the conquistador, which results for women in unequal wages, lack of education, and sexual exploitation. The blacks in South Africa have been subjected to a master-slave mentality for several centuries, and have been the objects of an unchristian colonial policy foisted upon them by groups claiming a mandate from God. The people of Ireland have an economic problem; jobs are scarce, and consequently, acquiring food and housing places people on a defensive gut level of living. These basic human needs are transformed into fears that it is one religious group or another, that is the enemy. Certain Indian tribes in Canada are at the mercy of logging corporations who want profits, but who also feel they know the best ways of harvesting wood from the forests. The women of Asia, in order to make a living wage, have been distributed around the world as housekeepers to clean up after others, and as sex objects, to gratify the lust of others. Political prisoners are the victims of power politics.

These bondages might all be summed up as due to an illicit use of power, illicit in the sense that God is a God of justice. What is against God's justice and mercy, is an improper use of the freedom with which God has gifted us. In all these examples certain individuals are deprived of their basic human dignity. This is taken from them through various exploitations; some are deprived of economic rights, food, jobs, and housing; some are deprived of self esteem, through lack of education or acceptance of unbalanced cultural standards. The Christian cure or call to freedom is to empower those in bondage with the knowledge of God's love for them, with the consequent acquiring of individual self-esteem. When the oppressed have this knowledge, they are then free to esteem others as children of God, to be reconciled with the oppressor, and to free the oppressor from his fears.

Liberation theology has the characteristic of being able to state through social analysis, the necessity and the method for reconciliation. As there are many different situations that need healing, there are many variations available for the recovery process. Some opponents of liberation theology see its method only as a rabble rousing venture, sure to stimulate armed rebellion among the oppressed. They feel that in an agitated state, the oppressed will rise up and oppress their former oppressors. (Perhaps there is a subconscious belief that this reaction would certainly be justifiable.)

This rising up of the oppressed to become the oppressor, has happened many times. Some supposed liberators do have this type of action in mind, and can hardly wait to get in the seat of power, so that they can vent their long-held frustrations on their enemies, as in the execution of Ceausescu of Roumania. It certainly is not necessary to point out that this is not the truly Christian way, and is unrelated to the justice and mercy of the God of *All*. True liberation theology strives for the peaceful cooperation of all diverse elements.

Another way to deny the effective outcome of liberation theology is seen in the *Reward in Heaven* attitudes. The poor and oppressed are told that if they endure until the end, their souls will enjoy the bliss of paradise. Long suffering Hindus are taught that they will come back in the priestly caste, and their patient wisdom will be appreciated in a future existence. This may ease the pain in the hearts of the oppressed, but it does nothing for the unhappy heart of the oppressor. We must free both the oppressed and the oppressor for a true liberation into the world of God's justice.

6.5 THE HUMAN TENDENCY TO STEREOTYPE

It is very difficult for anyone who is not black to make a liberation theology for an oppressed black group. The non-black has not been brought from childhood to adulthood within the context of the black culture, and has no conception of the power-hold of the slave mentality. Likewise, any statement on women's equality must be formulated by women, but agreed to, and critiqued by men, and then implemented by both. There must be a process of mediation in these operations, whereby the oppressed and the oppressors sit down together to give their unique viewpoints, and thus gain greater understanding of each other.

Let us try to examine the roots of one specific case of oppression, that of whites stereotyping blacks. In this case the difference noted out front, is that of skin color. Each group is inclined to think consciously or unconsciously, that they are different, and therefore may be imperfect. Thus they try to hide from themselves and from the other this lack of confidence. Where they feel a bit unsure, like fighting dogs, they put up a snarling face.

The basic root problem in this connection is the color of skin. Why are some people dark skinned and other people light skinned? There are different opinions on this subject, and many ways that genes can be affected. For instance, it is a fact that an Indian tribe on the east coast of Central America has an albino gene. Every now and then a baby deficient in skin color is born into the tribe. This infant is treated as a special baby, a gift from the heavens, someone to be treated with reverence.

This same characteristic of albinism may have occurred where ever the first human beings congregated in society. Suppose an albino babe were born in the heart lands of Africa. Like the Indians of Central America, the parents would hopefully take this as a good omen. The elders of a tribe would see no threat in a little babe. He may have been separated out from the other children, but it would all be to give him preference and honor, somewhat as we delight in having an albino tiger in a zoo. He or she may have grown up to adulthood in a privileged position. He may have even been chosen as tribal leader. He also may have turned out to be obnoxiously spoiled due to over-catering.

The first albino-black may have been acceptable in the tribal situation, but once in, the gene may have been proliferated, and at some point a group of these "holy children" may have embarassed the tribe in some manner, or posed some threat to the general group. They may have been asked to leave the tribe at spear point. The first act of exclusion may have been dark skinned people turning out their lighter skinned relatives.

Recent writings surmise that as Africa was predominately black, so was Egypt, and that when we speak of the Pharaohs, we are discussing a Black dynasty. We also are inclined to believe that the wandering herders of Abraham's time, were lighter skinned. When famine struck the world in the days of Joseph, these lighter skinned herders turned to the food supplies of the darker Egyptians for help, and they were not refused.

It is rather amazing that the herders managed to keep their identity distinct for the two hundred or more years that they stayed in Egypt. They must have had some outstanding characteristic that set them apart from the local people. The most obvious explanation is that they had a different skin tone. Whatever difference it was, it was a difference that enabled the in-group to make slaves of them, and we find the Israelites building public buildings for their oppressors.

In more recent times we have used the color of skin, for the whites to oppress the blacks, but it may have been the opposite side of the coin in 1400 BCE. Perhaps the whites should be forgiven for their later day evil treatment, because they were only doing what comes naturally. They were operating out of fear of another dominant group. The dark skinned Egyptians, also being human, and also being afraid that the light skinned people would take over, acted out of their need for self-preservation.

There was no modern psychology to tell these opposing peoples that they were asking for trouble. Today when we better understand our ids and our egos, we have little excuse for discriminating because of skin color. As God has given us the freedom to choose, above and beyond our cultural bindings, we can decide to treat all others with empathy, caring love, and kindness. We can accept our inner insecurities and failings, and recognize them as prods to stir us on to further successes in understanding of ourselves and others.

6.6 THE POOR HAVE RIGHTS TO THE GOODS OF THE EARTH

This Black-White or White-Black Oppressed-Oppressor stance is given here as an obvious one from an historical viewpoint, but looking across the world, we can see many places where stereotyping and discrimination take place, because of fear and greed. Often the rich who have more than they need, hang desperately on to their surplus, in their insecurity, and refuse to recognize the God-given right that the poor have to that surplus.

Pope John Paul's *Encyclical on Social Concerns* states that the earth is made for all.[6] Thomas Aquinas' writings have emphasized that the poor has the right to supply himself from the riches of others. When in desperate need, it is no sin to take another's property. Let's consider the possible judgment rendered by St.Thomas Aquinas in the case of theft of a banana from a banana plantation. If a shipwrecked man is cast up on the shores of a banana plantation, who would condemn him for grabbing and eating a banana? If a hungry person living in the neighborhood of the banana plantation, helped himself to a banana, would we think he was acting illegally? If a well-to-do person took and ate a banana, would that be stealing? If this well-to-do person was a friend or associate of the people running the plantation, and at some future date, openly thanked the officials in charge for the fruit, how would we judge him? Would our ethical system find it distasteful if this person ate half the banana, and threw the other half away, wastefully?

How far can we carry this belief in the right of one person to the goods of another? In New York City the poor need apartments. There are many apartments that are empty because the rich or those of the middle class hope to make a profit on them. Do the homeless have a right to those apartments?

Having been educated in a capitalist society, most of us would answer that the apartment owner has worked by the sweat of his brow, for that apartment and for whatever profit might come to him, and that he deserves his reward. It would not be fair for someone who had done no work, to move in, rent free, and profit from the industriousness of the owner who is a stranger to him. We cannot compare this expensive enterprise with a lowly banana. Most of us would agree that it is allright to share a banana with the starving, but going a little too far to donate an apartment.

We would also probably agree that it is scandalous that so many people in the New York City area, especially women and children, have no homes. Our welfare hotels are full, and flow out into the street. Outlying counties pay tremendous rates to put up women and their children in area motels, and seem paralyzed to construct affordable housing. As motels usually have no kitchens, extra money is needed for meals from fast food restaurants. Busing back to the original schools of the children, increases the cost of the welfare package. Can we shrug our shoulders and say that this is no concern of ours, that our lawmakers are taking care of the situation?

The early Hebrews had this same problem of people running up against hard times. In Leviticus 25 they set forth a proposal. We don't know how many people used this Jubilee method, but it seems a little more friendly and people-oriented than disaster insurance. The Jubilee Regulations return the land to the original owner. Fifty years may be quite a long time when you have lost your land, but if the person who has taken over your property knows that eventually it will return to you, he may allow you to share it with him, so that you will, in turn, be generous with him. This claim of the poor to their part of the earth's produce is reflected in Isaiah 3:14. Yahweh calls to judgment the elders of his people; "You are the ones who destroy the vineyard and conceal what you have stolen from the poor. By what right do you crush my people and grind the faces of the poor?"

A contemporary model of the Sabbatical, or seventh year regulations, can be seen in the opportunity given to professors in some universities to study specialties of their choice. If set in place in the total population, it might mean that every seventh year, one seventh of the population would live on public welfare and would do the volunteer work that they believed would best serve the needs of others. Thus there would always be one seventh of the men and women freely contributing towards the good of the greater community.

Profits are a very important part of our present American capitalistic society. We need money to educate our children effectively, and to set aside for our old age. We also seek profits, as with them, we can increase our material possessions. The Jubilee-Sabbatical model doesn't seem to encourage the making of profits. Other sections of the Bible seem to downgrade the accumulation of wealth. The rich young man in Mark 10 was very ethical and very wealthy. His inability to share called into question his entrance into the Kingdom/Queendom. Luke 3:11 requests that the person who has two coats give one to the person who has none. One aspect of liberation theology is to encourage the oppressor to share his surplus with the needy.

6.7 LIBERATION THEOLOGY AND VIOLENCE

It is never permissible to use violence except in a case of absolutely necessary self-defense. All non-violent means must first be exhausted. We must have made some effort to understand the reasoning and rights of our opponent. If we believe that the poor are suffering death in a certain situation, it is our duty to make that situation known to the public at large, and to emphasize the gravity of the situation to those who are causing it.

We have been told of the Nicaraguan woman who knifed in

the back the soldier who was gunning down children. This was a permissable violent action by a member of a group in defense of the group. All-out war can likewise be justified, if there are no non-violent actions available to rescue a damaging situation. Fortunately there are many mediative measures that can be taken before nations must go to war, and modern communications are available to readily emphasize decaying conditions.

We may look at the Holocaust situation and come to the conclusion that the imprisoned Jews should have risen up together in solidarity, instead of accepting the gas chambers. In fact, the non-violent resistance should have begun long before the train ride to the chambers. In hind-sight it is easy to see that the local communities should have been organized to protest non-violently to any removal of the Jews from their homes. The inflammatory rhetoric of a Hitler could have been exposed as hate-mongering by those in authority positions in churches, or by ordinary people reacting with responsi-bility and courage. There is always a need for the prophetic types willing to be jailed for their statements, such as Jeremiah or Daniel Berrigan. There is also a need for all ordinary people to act on moral principles.

When we allow racial hatreds to breed in our hearts, we, the people, both Jews and Gentiles, become guilty of Holocausts, in equal yoke with German soldiers who obeyed orders to pull the switches. This fear and hatred is in all human beings, and can be seen in other mistreatment of individuals, such as the sexual abuse of children. The child who is abused, may grow into the adult sex offender, as fear and hurt has twisted his insides. The nation that undergoes holocaust, with accompanying fear and lack of trust, becomes the nation that persecutes the Palestinians. The Jews as a nation have a subconscious fear:- they feel that now they have a little power, they must keep that power, and protect themselves against whoever might be an unfriendly *other*. Unfortunately, violence only leads to further violence. Hatred in the heart can only be purged with actions springing from forgiveness.

In opposition to violence, *mediation* and *reconciliation* are two methods to be used to encourage all the world into solidarity with one another, into the fulfilled future that God hopes we will achieve. Forgiveness is a necessary ingredient in this formula. One may or may not accept governmental structures as a means to this

SONG FOR THE OPPRESSED
Deuteronomy 28:2-8

All the blessings that follow shall come up with you and overtake you if only you obey the voice of Yahweh your God. You will be blessed in the town and in the country. Blessed will be the fruit of your body, the produce of your soil, the issue of your livestock, the increase of your cattle, the young of your flock. Blessed will be your grain crops and the food you prepare from them. Yahweh will bless everything you do. Yahweh will defeat your enemies when they attack you. They will attack from one direction, but they will run from you in all directions. Yahweh will bless your work and fill your barns with grain. He will bless you in the land that he is giving you.

SONG FOR THE OPPRESSOR
Deuteronomy 28:15-21

All the curses that follow shall come up with you and overtake you if you do not obey the voice of Yahweh your God. You will be accursed in the town and accursed in the country. Accursed will be your grain crops and the food you prepare from them. Accursed will be the fruit of your body, the produce of your soil, the increase of your cattle, the young of your flock. Accursed will be everything you do. If you do evil and reject Yahweh, he will bring on you disaster, confusion, and trouble in everything you do, until you are quickly and completely destroyed. He will send disease after disease on you until there is not one of you left in the land that you are about to occupy.

world-wide peace and order. Often governments can take the lead in achieving just benefits for their people. On the other hand those in authority positions, being all too human, often aggravate situations that the common people could have resolved peacefully. Frequently those leading authoritarian systems see no need to improve the present situation, as they fear loss of power and prestige.

If one accepts poor governmental control placidly in an acquiescing manner, there is no personal or communal fulfillment, and we may be a disappointment to the God who urges us on. To be the best that we can be, we must operate in freedom. Our freedom is not to be used to control others. Each of us must use our personal capacity and gifts in our own unique way. If two determined individuals go after the same prize, or seek the same piece of earth, they must bring the situation to mediation, each discover the other's needs, and in some manner act through that situation to bring a *both-gain* solution for both parties. Money, power, and prestige must all be given second place to empathy and understanding for an opposing person or group. God's justice operates through our loving concern for one another.

Freedom is a gift given to us by God, but excessive personal freedom is able to destroy a family or a community. If we are to be considerate of others, we cannot succumb to selfishness and greediness. A certain amount of deprivation may be necessary for personal fulfillment. As we can be in solidarity with members of our family, and wish for their good, so we must be in solidarity with all the world. Belief in one's right to unlimited freedom can be very oppressive of others; one must always remain cognizant of the needs of others. We must not see the other person as an enemy; the enemy is not the other,- it is the greed and fear that is in ourself.

God wills the fulfillment of the whole world. He wants every monad to rest under the fig tree of contentment. God's plan is that we dwell in the garden with the tree of life, and the tree of the knowledge of good and evil. Only if we are broadminded enough to do liberation theology for the whole world, will we fulfill this dream of God's.

PART II

Practical Applications

Chapters 7 through 12

PART II

In the first half of this book we have set down what we hope is thought provoking material on the human being and his or her relationship to God. We do not expect that you will agree with all the statements made here, and we welcome open discussion on these topics, which are very important for the future of humanity.

On the practical side, in this second section we consider some of the structures that the human has put in place with the hopes of creating order. The thesis of chapter seven is that we have the Spirit of God in us, that all peoples have this Spirit, and that humanity surely should do something with this marvellous gift. Using our God-given talents, we may be able to be living stones for the building of a New Jerusalem. We have heard the command, "Be holy, for I, the Lord your God, am holy!" Let us try to see things from God's perspective. Let us do the deeds we believe a Holy God would do, such as helping to build a fulfilled earth.

How can we transform our social structures in order to be considered as God's holy people? As we believe that for optimum success, governments should reflect the will of those governed, in this next section we give some practical suggestions. There are three specific areas which we hope to improve through their considered use of the relationships of covenant and consensus. Chapters eight and nine look at the Catholic Code of Canon Law and suggest ways this might be implemented to further just relationships in a religious organization. Chapter ten looks at the prison system. If we change its emphasis slightly, this structure could help people to become more than they are, instead of further oppressing them. Chapter eleven turns our vision outward from our own national concerns, and centers on improving relationships among nations, governments, and people. These suggestions would require the concentrated thought of the total designated community before their implementation.

Chapter twelve asks, "Where do we go from here?" The answer is that we are not just participating in wishful thinking. What could be more practical than to believe that by working together we can change the world!

7
THEOLOGY
FOR
AN INTERFAITH MESSIAH

7.1 WHO WILL LIBERATE THE PEOPLE ?

Various people across the world are being oppressed, and we empathize with their situation. Everyone should have the opportunity to
be free, creative, and productive. Above all, people need to find the
way to be fully human, in gentleness, kindness, and compassion. We
feel that the hungry should be fed, the naked clothed, and water
provided for the thirsty. Those of us who aren't particularly poor in
a material fashion, find that there are other situations of a spiritual
vein that need a guiding hand. We glance around us and think that
there is room for improvement in the way people treat each other,
and also in the societal structures that people have put in place to
support their cultures. Some changes should certainly be made. Who
shall we look to for leadership in this endeavor?

　　　We have suggested that we have our origins back in what can
be nebulously referred to as a *First Cause*. We have some sort of
positive relationship with this mysterious force which created us. It
does not seem logical that a good God would create a world, fill it
with freely acting and thinking beings, and then desert it. It is
reasonable to believe that God somehow communicates with the
creation that God created.

　　　The religions of the world proclaim this communication.
There is the belief that God speaks through the Holy Books, through
his chosen ministers, and through the lives and words of ordinary
people. Religious spokespersons tell us that the world is going
somewhere, to the blackness of Armageddon, or to untold evolutionary wonders. They believe that the individual human will be

interiorly rewarded according to how he or she weighs up in the balance of God's justice.

Many believe that in order for all to know and understand these just purposes of God that God planned for a special messenger or revealer of God, known as the *Messiah*. There are various ideas of what this Messiah should be. Religious groups have diverse expectations of such a revealer. Some Muslims project that God himself will come and lead them through the final days. Likewise many Orthodox Jews resent human beings as political leaders in Israel; they feel God should be their only needed guide when they reside in the holy and promised land. The Jehovah Witnesses also are non-political and hope for the leadership of God. A poll of the world religions would show that the peoples of the earth have a collective dream for a peaceful future guided by some form of godly leadership.

Some branches of Judaism have had more practical aspects of the Messiah as God acting in a strong military and political leader. This type of Messiah would come to serve at a particular time when a particular need arose. When the Jews were seeking to throw off the Roman yoke, Simon bar Kochbar led his people in warfare. It appears with hindsight that he was an unsuccessful Messiah, but at the time, he was acclaimed by many as the one chosen to lead the people in God's name against their enemies. He illustrates the messianic figure coming to save the people from the imminent disasters of their era or specifically from the imminent disaster of all-time. Religious people of each era seem to feel that theirs is the final time, and their pessimism coupled with an idea that the world deserves to be punished, may help to bring on such a disaster. In these times some might consider the ultimate punishment to be destruction by nuclear terrorism perpetrated either by governments or by individuals.

The Holy Scriptures have many readings which proclaim both the coming holocaust and the savior of the people. The apocalyptic *Book of Daniel* (9:25) refers metaphorically to a messianic individual. "Know this, then, and understand: from the time this message went out; 'Return and rebuild Jerusalem' to the coming of an anointed Prince, seven weeks and sixty-two weeks, with squares and ramparts restored and rebuilt, but in a time of trouble." Such prophecies are difficult to interpret, and are much discussed. All of us want to be *in the know*. It's our old friend, the ego, flaring up, wanting to be in the secure spot when the fire rains down from heaven. In times of distress we are liable to dismiss our own responsibilites and place our hopes on whomever will promise us safety. In this search for security, those with religious leanings often follow prophets or sages who assert some understanding of God's qualities.

For ages the Jews have speculated on the questions, "How will the Messiah come, and with what body will he or she appear?" This is akin to the theological question, "What is God like?" No one really knows the answer. There are as many responses as there are theologians. Certainly the God who created all things, can either choose to stand outside the material as spiritual Messiah, or mysteriously enter into the creation as person, however God wishes.

7.2 THE MESSIAH AS A PERSON

Some Jews feel that the Messiah will come in human form, as God appeared to Abraham (Genesis 18) or to Jacob (Genesis 32), walking as a man, talking as a man, and even wrestling. For this reason, some of the Jews of Jesus' time felt that it was not scandalous to believe in the person, Jesus, as God somehow come to earth. Other Jewish interpreters of scripture prefer to take these appearances (such as God wrestling with Jacob) figuratively, and are disturbed when others proclaim a human being as containing the essence of God.

Those who see God as working through persons, feel that the only way for God to make known his message to humankind, is through human beings. They claim to see God working through a specific individual to correct human ills. Most of us like to justify our actions, and think that as surely as God made us, God will eventually reward those who do justly. Some feel that one purpose of the Messiah would be to point out the just and give them their reward. Accordingly, for those who have been wrongly imprisoned by others, there is the belief that a Messiah will come to throw wide the prison doors. Those who have been oppressed think that the Messiah will come to head up a kingdom where they can dwell securely omnipotent over their neighbors. A broad interpretation might be to see the Messiah as one who changes unjust structures so that humans might no longer feel the need to control one another, by the use of authority tactics or by the employment of weapons.

The word *Messiah* contains the idea of a messenger. The Christian tradition believes that the person Jesus delivered God's message to humankind about 2000 years ago. He is expected by his followers to come again at an unknown point in future history that they often designate as the *End Times*. This Jesus is an easily understood example of a specific Messiah living at an historical moment. To many of his followers he is also an example of a Messiah that is yet to come.

Jesus is quoted as admitting the possibility of himself as Messiah (John 4:26), and in Luke 4:18-19 announces to the assembled synagogue that he fulfills the Messianic prophecy of Isaiah 61:1-3. This scripture which he quoted enables us to see Jesus' idea of what the Messiah should be like:

> *The spirit of the Lord Yahweh has been given to me,*
> *for Yahweh has anointed me.*
> *He has sent me to bring good news to the poor,*
> *to bind up hearts that are broken;*
> *to proclaim liberty to captives,*
> *freedom to those in prison;*
> *to proclaim a year of favor from Yahweh,*
> *a day of requital for our God,*
> *to comfort all those who mourn*
> *and to give them for ashes a garland;*
> *for mourning robe the oil of gladness,*
> *for despondency, praise.*
> *They are to be called "terebrinths of integrity,"*
> *planted by Yahweh to glorify him.*

This understanding of Jesus as to the possibility of a human such as himself, being the chosen one of the chosen ones, displays that there was a belief among the Jews of that time, that the Messiah might come on the scene as a human being. This human being would be anointed to serve, but would also fulfill other Old Testament prophecy of kingship, leadership, and priestly vocation. Much of the New Testament, such as the Book of Hebrews, is devoted to showing how Jesus fulfilled earlier prophecy, and thus has a claim to Messiahship. Different New Testament authors visualize different degrees of Messiahship. Considering the tendency of Aramaic exaggeration to make a point, we are given ideas of Jesus that range from subservient sonship, to a being that totally possessed God's wisdom.

Let us consider for a moment different ways that present day Christians might find Jesus as the fulfillment of messianic prophecy. Some would insist that Jesus is a godly being, united in his body with God before the foundation of the world. At the other extreme of the spectrum, others would tend to equate him more with the everyday human, perhaps denying all the miraculous occurrences that the first group would associate with him. In between these two extremes we would find people giving this Jesus qualities of both God and man, in varying degrees.

Still another group might not consider Jesus as a specific human being, but more as a spiritual entity. Realizing our inabililties to pin down particular details of an event that happened two thousand years ago, they could look on the story of Jesus as a legend. They might feel that he didn't necessarily have had to come enfleshed in one particular human form. At the time of Jesus we have many people reporting on the Jesus' phenomena, that Jesus said certain things, did certain things, had a certain spirit, and from this secondary information various people were led to believe that the promised Jewish Messiah was incorporated in the reported person of Jesus. The material which was attributed to this Jesus gave to the world inspirational ideas of a caring comunity dwelling in harmony, which exercised full consideration for others under the guidance of a loving Abba, the wise elder who is always with us. God could have communicated his message of loving community by employing the stories told about events and ideas that accompanied this person. This Jesus may have said things that started his friends thinking in positive directions. He may not have existed at all, in the particular manner in which they described him. God's message to love one another may have ultimately been delivered by the early Christian community.

This body of characteristics represented by Jesus or by the people of the period of Jesus might be called the message of the Messiah or the spirit of the Messiah. Although credal formulations about Jesus and his God-man characteristics were not unanimous, many Jews and Greeks hearing of this event, came to believe that this person Jesus somehow fitted the description of the Jewish Messiah. They proclaimed this Messiah to their contemporaries. As

these messianic qualities associated with this first century phenomenon appear to be useful for all time, Christians today feel that this
Jesus was the Messiah for all time, and continue to proclaim him.

The immediate followers of Jesus are pleased to show us the
many aspects of Jesus' messianic character. The unidentified author
of the Gospel of John quotes Jesus as, "Let not your heart be
troubled. You believe in God; believe also in me" (John 14:1). We
are asked to believe in Jesus' Godly concern for people. The New
Testament writer, Paul, not seeing this person Jesus in the flesh, but
coming soon enough after to absorb the spirit of this Messiah, asks
us to believe in the Good News of Jesus Christ (Romans 1:9). Paul
and the gospel writers give body to this message of God's love, and
thus are the bearers of the caring and concerned spirit of their
Messiah. We, too, as those who follow after, attempting to emulate
this Jesus, embody the spirit of our Messiah. If we are going to state
that, as Christians, we believe that Jesus came as the Messiah, then
we also state that as we carry this spirit of the Messiah in our hearts,
and in our actions, we, too, have a part in this messianic destiny. We
and all those who support God's rule in our midst, can be considered
carriers of God's message, followers of God, or Children of God
(Roman's 8:14-17).

Believing wholeheartedly in the Messiahship of Jesus, the
New Testament writers make claims for the divinity or closeness to
God of their candidate for Messiah. Early creeds make the statement that his body rose up to exist in heaven and to sit on God's right
hand. This allegorical affirmation may tell us more about the covenanted heart of Jesus than about the location of heaven. In seeking
to interpret the claims of early church persons as to the dual nature
of Jesus Christ as human and divine, it is not good to fall back
helplessly and declare the whole concept too mysterious for the
human to comprehend. Our minds were created by God, somehow
in God's image, and God must expect us to use them to come closer
to total truth. If we are to speak of a person who proclaims the divine
message of love in his whole being, and if we further state that
heaven exists where God exists, then we could conclude that Jesus
Christ in his glorified resurrected state did not have to go anywhere
to reach heaven and the right hand of God. He contained heaven in
himself. He uniquely kept God's covenant with humankind.

In describing Jesus as rising up and being hidden from sight

(Acts 1:9), perhaps the evangelist is speaking figuratively. He/She may be describing the fact that Jesus' glorified body seems to be no longer visible to the disciples. However, there is also the happy word that as surely as he goes mysteriously, he will return mysteriously through the clouds of our doubts and misbelievings. Those who are in tune with his message will find his spirit in one another. Those who covenant with God in their hearts will aid in establishing God's kingdom on earth.

Jesus himself speaks of heaven and the kingdom of God as a place which is possible in the human community. "The coming of the kingdom of God does not admit of observation and there will be none to say, 'Look here! Look there!' For, you must know, the kingdom of God is within you" (Luke 17:20-21). Those who resolve to act responsibly for God and towards one another, are those who build God's realm, God's kingdom/queendom.

The different New Testament writers seem to have had varying interpretations of the *second coming* or the return of their Messiah. The Beloved Disciple who wrote the Gospel of John seems to expect an immediate spiritual rather than physical return (John 14:20; 15:5 and 17:26). "On that day you will understand that I am in my Father and you in me and I in you." "I am the vine, you are the branches. Whoever remains in me, with me in him, bears fruit in plenty." "I have made your name known unto them and will continue to make it known, so that the love with which you loved me may be in them, and so that I may be in them." This gospel writer tells us that the spirit of Jesus has possibilities of being in each human heart. Thus we can set down here a tentative conclusion that for those who love God and neighbor, God's kingdom is within. In this within kingdom, this inner realm, God dwells, with Jesus at his/her right hand.

Christian Eucharistic beliefs reflect this same type of idea. If we have faith, Jesus will dwell in our hearts. When the glorified essence of Jesus disappeared from human view, did it radiate into the hearts of all those who served God's justice? It is difficult to say scientifically and precisely, what might be the possible capabilities of a glorified being. We cannot make material statements about spiritual qualities. Yet at the *Last Supper* Jesus asked his disciples to bring him again into their midst through the partaking of material bread. Thus many possess the faith that those who truly love and serve others may possess some spark of divinity, a spiritual element derived from a material ritual having to do with Jesus' glorified being. It seems that there are possibilities of the divine in each of us, waiting to be activated.

There are those who might think that this bit of Christ or God directed covenant residing in the individual heart, is too small a thing to be important. Naaman the Leper felt that washing in the Jordan to cure his leprosy was too small a thing to accomplish the great cure of his sickness, but his aides reproved him, "If the prophet had asked you to do something difficult you would have done it...." (2 Kings 5:13). Perhaps a small effort on the part of each of us to act in the Spirit of the Messiah, might effect a great cure, the coming of the Spirit of the Messiah to the whole world.

7.3 THE MESSIAH AS A HOLY COMMUNITY

Some early Christians felt that Jesus had returned as a spiritual comforter to their hearts, and that this spirit would help them to heal the sick and preach the gospel. Other Christians, such as the writer of the Book of Revelation, foresaw a Second Coming when the world would be disrupted and Jesus would come to set things aright. This Book of Revelation is full of threatening implications about this future time, yet on the other hand, speaks of the New Jerusalem, the beautiful community that human kind should anticipate, the city foursquare, lit by the love of the Lamb (Revelation 21). There seems to be some connection between the Second Coming of Jesus as Messiah and people dwelling in harmony on the earth.

As societies and theologies progress across time, the notion of Messiah, has also evolved. Early Israelis felt themselves chosen to be the privileged righteous, preserved by a favoring God. Their notion of a worldly kingdom under the military leadership of a king selected by God, such as David, is an example of this type of thought. But this way of thinking has been enlarged. A more empathetic belief is that the Jews are chosen; but the purpose they are chosen for, is to bring the message of God's love to the whole world. This integrates all races and creeds within the bounds of one loving community under the protection of one God. Today many Jews do not associate themselves so much with an elitist political state under an authoritative leader, as with a united world under the care of a loving God. Having their roots in Judaism, Christians have logically developed a similar line of thought. As all peoples are the evolutionary spin-off of one God-created world, there may be an inherent urge to form a Utopian world community.

Thus, the basic idea of a Messiah which fosters the fulfillment of God's plan can be preserved, without the burden of an older cultural construction. If you are going to expand your belief to that of a Messiah who comes to take care of the whole world under a loving God, this Messiah might be thought of as a spirit which dwells in a community (such as the Spirit of Wisdom in John chapter 1, or in Ecclesiasticus 1 and 24). This Spirit might not be sequestered exclusively in the Jewish community. It might reside in all those who care for the world and who want for all peoples the best possible situation. It might be that we are all to be carriers of God's message of love and justice to one another.

A group of committed and covenanted people such as this, would be basically more humanity oriented than are most of our political leaders. Political leadership is often a search for personal power or for control of others. A messianic community such as we are discussing would undoubtedly use guidance from everyday people, employing processes similar to consensus and consultation of the powerless. Its methods would work slowly, yet effectively, like yeast in a lump of dough. We are led to think of networking and church groups who work quietly and steadily at what is best for oppressed peoples.

Besides worrying about God's messenger or God's Spirit leading them through a future time of holocaust, many look ahead to a reign by God. They attempt to attune their actions to this ideal prospect. The various religions that exist enable the dwellers on earth to hope for a peaceful future. In different regions and cultures, there are many ideas as to how the divine has assisted the human in the past, and there is always hope for what is yet to happen. A common faith idea is that if the person covenants with God, and shows this covenant through obedience to ethical norms, God will take care of that individual. Another corresponding belief is that if people meet in loving consensus under God's guidance, these groups will be able to serve God more effectively, and can hope for a secure future.

As we are human, we and our communities do not become

the ideal. Errors creep in to disturb the harmony of a group. When individuals dwell together in a religious community, they frequently forsake the idea of present consensus in favor of delegating authority to a select individual, or to rigorously following regulations formulated in the past. These regulations may have been set in place at one time by some form of consensus, but are frequently frozen into place, and enacted on the community by an authority figure with no present consensus from the group being governed. Scripture or law handed to us from the past, is sometimes given more respect than is warranted, and may seldom be properly brought up to date. Eugene Kennedy notes that too much law cripples human communities.[1] If we depend on law, we are much more likely to finger point, and much less likely to attempt to understand the human being who is offending.

For optimum community results, all individuals in the community must be listened to, in order to make current regulations, and in order for all in the group to grow into being responsible individuals. We abdicate our God-given gifts when we pass our decision making processes into the hands of someone else. To covenant with God, as Abraham, is to strive to be your best in all situations. Abraham had no previous authority structures or Bible to guide him, and had to rely on his own sense of his relationship with God. Today we are able to refer to Holy Scriptures as guidance in our striving, and to listen to the wisdom of those who have gone before us, but each person must be ready to exercise his covenantal and consentaneous capabilities. The building blocks of a good community are understanding and responsible people. When individuals collectively strive to be filled with God's spirit, then a community can be said to be working from the wisdom of God, or to be acting in the spirit of the Messiah.

In this notion of the Spirit of the Messiah working in the community, there is the idea of God dwelling among God's people. If God's Spirit is present in people across the breadth of the earth, then God's spirit can be said to flood the earth as the waters cover the sea (Habakkuk 2:14 & Isaiah 11:9). Many may prefer to envision God's accompaniment in the person of one charismatic leader who expertly guides those less wise, but God is generous and merciful, and delights to give spiritual blessings to all. We each have been created, each with our special giftedness, and have open accessability to God's spirit. R. M. Brown emphasizes, "In our times, we do not expect such tangible evidence of being accompanied as fire, cloud, manna or angels. It is clear that the evidence of accompaniment in our day is provided by persons. The face of God for us is found in other human faces. Where, after all, did Jesus tell us we would encounter him? In visiting the sick, clothing the naked, feeding the hungry, rather than in building cathedrals or memorizing creeds."[2] If God's spirit is to flood our world, it must be carried by human carriers working together in loving community.

7.4 THE IDEA OF BUDDHA SPIRIT

When speaking of the Christian view of God, we find that Jesus, as the ideal, the Christian Word of God, is a model for all Christians to emulate. Christians freely choose to covenant with God by agreeing to structure their lives on the truths held by this person Jesus. Looking around the world at other religions, we find that Buddhists envision the ideal way to follow as the Eight-fold Path presented to them by their founder, and they covenant within themselves to be the best possible by following this path. Muslims rigorously hold to the teaching of the prophet Mohammed in order to live a life pleasing to God. Jews strive to keep the Ten Commandments and the 613 rules as set down in their Holy Scriptures. The Communists hold up the ideal of the good party member. It seems to be inborn in the interior of all people to think about their origins and their purposes. With average considerate treatment by those who make up their environment, people often equate their ideal to God. They will measure themselves against this ideal and make a personal covenant to do their best. They will compete with their past performance and strive to better themselves. The Christians often describe this covenantal process as walking with Jesus. The covenantal process of the Muslim is in the name, Islam, which means submission to Allah.

Let us try to approach this idea of covenant, consensus, and Messiah from an interfaith viewpoint. First let us propose an understanding by each person of a commitment to the ideal, and, second, a commitment by the One God to each and every community of all such peoples. Thus there might develop a collective voice which would be able to reflect one true wholesome message. We have been implying that Jesus is God's messenger to the whole world, yet half the world feels no need to listen to the claims of either Judaism or Christianity. Their own religions and cultures seem to serve their needs very well. They live gentle, considerate, empathetic lives, and covenant in their hearts to follow the wisdom of great teachers who have lived among them. These teachers may also have proclaimed words similar to those of Jesus. Can these teachers reach consensus on one loving message?

About two thousand and five hundred years ago the people of India wrestled with day to day living, observed the finality of death, and puzzled over what life was all about. Their religion was Hinduism. Hindus pay respect to the unknown *First Cause* through many representations of the different qualities that they feel are evident in that *Unknowable*. They worship the powerful side of God before a statue that has many arms. The gentle, tender womanly side of God is represented by the statue of a woman. The great peace that God can bestow is represented by an elephant. As suffering and evil were also experienced by the Hindus, some of their symbols for God reflect these qualities. God's justice was also felt to exist, and so the Hindus explained this by reincarnation. If you were a good person who suffered an injustice and died, you would be rewarded by returning to earth as as scholar or prince. If you did something wrong and got away with it, you might reincarnate as a pig or a fly.

The poor in this cultural milieu were too stressed to worry about things philosophical, but the upper classes sometimes had sufficient liesure and education to ponder theological questions. A prince of one of the small tribal groups, called the Shakyamuni clan, questioned, developed, and evolved into what has come to be called a Buddha personality. This personality can be described as being comprised of compassion, truth, and wisdom. The purpose of this personality is to spread the dharma, the teachings of truth that will lead all humans to become fulfilled persons. As Prince Shakyamuni had received the privilege of Enlightenment or of being filled with this truth, he was able (and he was compelled by his beliefs) to instruct others on how to achieve this state.

All through his lifetime the prince never lost sight of the fact that he was a human being of the same physical makeup as any other human being. He believed that others were fully capable of achieving this Buddha state. He instructed his followers not to make statues of him, or do him any special honors after he passed to his reward. He had come into the world to serve and share, his purpose being to save all people from the anguish of their daily living.

People recognized the importance of this Buddha message, and the man's followers after his death immediately strove to proclaim the importance of this Shakyamuni prince to whomever would listen. They began by attempting to convince their fellow Hindus to transform their Hindu worship into beliefs in the teachings of Buddha. Hinduism has always been a very open religion, and made room in its temples for this new form of religious truth.

Have you ever wondered how Buddhism grew out of Hinduism? On the surface one can think of Hinduism as a religion that believes in many gods. One can look at Buddhism and say that it teaches a God of absolute nothingness, perhaps no God at all, certainly not a personal God like that of Judaism, Christianity, or Islam; certainly not a series of gods and goddesses as represented by Hindu statuary. Yet surface judgments can be very superficial, and can lead into all sorts of error.

In Catholicism we have many pictures of saints that represent to us different qualities of goodness. The thought of the gentle life of St. Therese of Lisieux inspires those who strive for patience in their battle with the little every day annoyances of living. Saint Francis of Asissi reminds us that poverty can be used to glorify God. We use these statues of those who followed God, to activate us towards good aspirations.

The Muslims use *words* to bring the qualities of God to mind. Instead of statues they set words such as *righteous, compassionate,* and *generous* before the eyes of their people. The Muslim beliefs could only work after writing became a skill that was available to the majority of the faithful. The Hindus follow their pre-writing custom of putting the qualities of God in a form understandable to their followers. The rift between Hindu and early Muslim practice was due to the fact that some Muslims thought that some Hindus were actually worshipping the statue, rather than the all-encompassing God behind the statue.

After the death of Prince Shakyamuni, his followers and the local Hindu religious experts, kept careful control of the Buddhist dharma and structured it into the existing religious forms. It became necessary to have a statue of Shakyamuni as representing the quali-

ties of Buddha. A statue would remind the people that the god-like
qualities of truth, wisdom, and compassion could reside in a human
person, if that person conscientously followed the Buddhist teachings.

At some point certain Buddhists separated themselves from
the Hindus and made their own temples. Frequently there would be
only one representation of Buddha in the temple as the complete
ideal to be imitated. In other temples, one can find the multiplicity of
forms that show that Buddhism was derived from Hinduism.

Let us try to think of the Spirit of Buddha or the good
personality that was finally achieved in Shakyamuni Buddha, as an
evolving of the seed of God that is inherent in every person. Christians might view this seed of God as our free will allowing the Holy
Spirit to work in us. However this concept is pictured, there is some
fortunate combination in our makeup which we do not fully understand that gives room for the growth of goodness in the world.

When we go in a present day Buddhist temple, we may be
confronted with three images of Buddha seated side by side. Their
hands may be in different positions, or they may be holding objects
that portray positive qualities. Each separate statue represents the
Buddha spirit, or the spirit of compassion, truth, and wisdom. This
trio may be the Buddha of the Past, the Buddha of the Present, and
the Buddha of the Future. As the whole world has a past, present,
and (we hope) a future, the meaning behind these statues is that the
spirit of wisdom and love has acted in the past, it acts in the present,
and it will act in the future. Thus this loving spirit is always in control
of all things.

These statues are also here to remind each individual that
she/he has a past, present, and future. If he prays before the statue
of the past, he may need healing for a past event. It may help him to
meditate that when a poor situation was handled badly in the past,
that the spirit of wisdom and truth was still available and acting in the
world, and that the disliked results are acceptable in the universal
Buddhist wisdom. The statue of the Buddha of the present can
inspire the individual to act responsibly and in conformity with
Buddha in the present. The statue of the Buddha of the future is to
give aid to those worried about a future event.

As the Buddha Spirit is all through time, so the Buddha
Spirit is all through the whole earth. There are sometimes four

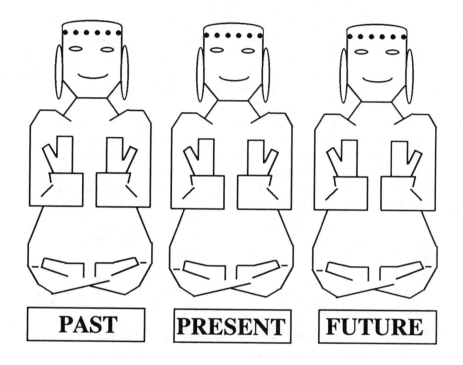

PAST   PRESENT   FUTURE

THE BUDDHA SPIRIT IS ALL PERVASIVE.
IT WAS THERE
WHEN WE PARTICIPATED IN PAST ACTS
THAT NEED
FORGIVENESS AND RECONCILIATION;
IT UNDERSTANDS
THE NEEDS OF OUR PRESENT;
AND IT WILL BE WITH US
IN OUR FUTURE.

Buddhas displayed in a temple, the Buddhas of the North, South, East, and West. One of these Buddhas may be seen holding an umbrella, representing a certain power over adversity. A person can address his appeal to the God or Buddha Spirit behind this image, to be shielded from the rain of circumstance, and perhaps the Buddha Spirit will spread his umbrella over the sufferer. One of these directional Buddhas holds a snake; another, a type of guitar. Moses lifted up a bronze serpent in the wilderness; David played a lyre. Religions often seem to contain similar symbolic material.

Among the variety of Buddha images, there are also a Buddha of Longevity and a Buddha of Healing or Medecine. If one meditates before a statue of longevity and thinks what calm and serious qualities make for a long peaceful life, that individual will be more inclined to work on those qualities and to lead a life that is long and useful. Some representations of Buddha are angry, as there are injustices that must be confronted with righteous anger. There is even a female representation of Buddha. In all this one can see the thread of Buddhism's long-ago origins out of Hinduism, and its emphasis on the Spirit of Compassion and Truth.

7.5 THE TRAVELS OF RELIGIOUS BELIEFS IN SPACE AND TIME

The original Shakyamuni Buddha is credited with having eighteen disciples. This is purely legendary as he may have had more or less. Pictures of these disciples show them to be of many different colors, representing all the races, or nations known on the earth. There are various shades of black, brown, yellow, and white.

We know that Buddhism was brought to China and Japan, and that some of its most diligent followers were from these countries. Many representations of Buddha have a distinctly oriental cast. Some Chinese are very broadminded and have the philosophy that different ethical systems can exist side by side. About the same time as Shakyamuni Buddha, a teacher called Kong Qiu (Latinized as Confucious) was teaching responsible kingship to Chinese royalty. Another Oriental Lao Zi, also fifth century BC, advocated that man should understand himself. An Oriental painter pictured all three of these gentlemen standing together at ease.[3] Confucious is pictured as being the tallest and dark complexioned. This picture may be speaking to the acceptance of all races and all religions, and to the possible compatibility that might exist among all the founders of great ethical systems. Jesus Christ, Mohammed, and Buddha would surely have enjoyed a great conversation, too. When great wisdom and love speak to great wisdom and love, what could they disagree on?

The message of wisdom and love has done its best to penetrate the whole earth. King Asoka reigned over a tribe in middle India from 268-232 BCE. From being Furious Asoka he repented and became an advocate of the Buddhist teachings of wisdom and compassion. He sent missionaries from his country to preach Buddhist philosophy to Ceylon, Syria, Egypt, Kyrene (northern Africa), Macedonia, and Epeiros (northwest Greece).[4] Thus, even before the cultural trade-offs of the time of Alexander the Great, there was much opportunity for knowledge of Buddhist philosophies to be disseminated through out the known world, in which Palestine was centrally located. The Essenes may be a spin off of Judaic Buddhism. The fabled Wise Men from the East may have been Buddhists. The twelve year old Jesus may have discussed Buddhism with the elders in the temple.

There are many teachings of Buddha that ring a bell with Jesus' words. When Jesus asks his followers to believe that the Father is in him (John 14:10), and that those who have looked into his heart, have seen the Father (John 14:9), a Buddhist would understand that Jesus had fully absorbed the Spirit of Love and Compassion. Having this Spirit, Jesus' desire was that all should have this Spirit, that all should know the message of God. His apostles were to carry this message to their fellow Hebrews, and the Hebrews were to carry it to the world.

This work of the apostles was to be an active mission to proclaim peace to all hearts. Often when observing Buddhist monks and Christian monks, we get the impression that they have withdrawn from the world, and are selfishly using their chosen spot of freedom and quiet, in order to experience the thrill of union with The Compassionate Spirit. However, it seems that any approach to our loving God necessitates our recognition of the plight of our fellow human beings. There is no union with God, unless there is compassion for our fellows. There is no rest in the Holy Land, unless we dwell in understanding with the others who inhabit the land.

We are not all called to be monks, and to thus meditate our way into a satisfying companionship with God and the human. The Buddhists recognize this fact, and encourage lay people to covenant or affirm their search for truth through their use of the Eight-Fold Path. Known as a Bodhisattva, this lay person follows a way of service and sacrifice for others. Jesus, as lay person (he was not designated a priest by his Jewish contemporaries), taught and followed this same way of service and sacrifice. The Buddhist who seeks union with the Spirit of Compassion and Truth, is in flow with the same messianic process personified in (enacted by) Jesus.

This poem by a present day Bodhisattva, Lee Kwang Soo, shows how a person of another faith expresses his search for the Spirit of Love and Compassion.[5]

My heart that wants to give everything to you
with no reluctance;that is where I learn alms.
My heart that decorates itself with perspiration;
that is where I learn to observe commandments.
My heart that yearns for you unceasingly;
that is where I learn purification.
My heart that loves only you between heaven and earth;
that is where I learn meditation.
I learn enlightenment when I am humiliated
and forget pleasure and sadness and even myself in you.
Now I see that you are the Buddha who reveals yourself
as my beloved to teach me what is true.

7.6 GOD'S BEING EXISTING IN THE HINDU

Many of us when considering Indian Hinduism from the cultural platform of the United States, have the tendency to conclude that all Hindus have a consistent creed and common beliefs. In fact Hindus have a multitude of sects, comparable to the diversification in Christianity. About the only belief that they hold in common is that it is allright to be different, that there are many paths up the mountain.

We also may offhandedly assume that worship of idols originated in India and that those of us who worship the One God had better steer clear of such heathen practices. However, artistic

Indian statuary shows an early Greek influence, and many Hindus will assure you that they do not worship idols. They will affirm their belief in the One Creator-Sustainer, and the statues represent to them its many aspects. We of the West can usually meditate on divinity without the help of statuary, and are more inclined to describe God's attributes by the use of words.

Hinduism has very ancient roots, and has considered God's being and the human's receptivity to this being, from many angles. One particular idea contained in the Hindu religious traditions which speaks of the *avatar* or incarnation of God, could broaden our theological viewpoints concerning the Spirit of the Messiah. It could inspire us to become better Christ-bearers and urge us forward on the pathway to being guardians and builders of our world.

In order to help the individual to relate to Ultimate Being, God is sometimes represented by a Trinity, Brahma (the Creator), Visnu (the Helper), and Siva (the Destroyer and Renewer). It must be stressed that all Hindus do not think this way. Some name the Great Soul of the Beginning, Atman, as the Creator. At one point in Indian thought, the God Varuna almost became the sole, supreme being, a Hindu national God comparable to the Jewish Yahweh of the Davidic era. Some Indians do see God as multiplicity. One section of the Hindu holy writings lists 33 gods and 3306 devas or demi-gods, but finally reduces them all to one, designated as Prana, which means life-power or breath-of-life. This designation shows rigorous respect for the flow of life in the earth.

Different Hindu sects often adhere to the worship of One God under its various names. I do not say *his* or *her* names, as Buddhist and Hindu thought often consider God as a neuter. As creation of a human takes both a male and female, God, as creator, must contain both these aspects, and is not one or the other.

The Saivites continue this idea of God containing all opposites, in their affirmation of the God Siva, who may be a theological offshoot of the Zoroastrian dualism of the gods of good and evil. Siva is the *one* who destroys, but also the *one* who picks up the pieces. A God representation with a frightening face is usually that of Siva. Similar Christian thought is that we must destroy our selfishness, if we are to be renewed with a generous heart.

The Vaisnavites are concerned with their present condition,

and see their God Visnu as the Preserver. For them God is more
personal, one who is ready to help them in time of need. This
particular god, Visnu, is credited with breaking into history in
various forms, or avatars, which would help the people when they
were in desperate straits, as some Jews visualized the purpose of
their messiah.

The avatar or God-in-man idea became prevalent in Hindu
and Buddhist theology about the second century BCE. Ancient
myths were given new twists to support this theory. The descents or
incarnations of Visnu are usually ten, though some versions list a
total of twenty four. In each of the ten appearances the full essence
of God is believed to have taken on flesh, in order to save the world
from threatened destruction.

The Christian Judaic tradition believes that Noah was saved
from the flood by God telling him to build an ark. In the first
incarnation of the Vaisnavite tradition, Visnu turned itself into a fish
to save Manu (the first man whom we call Adam) from the flood. The
second incarnation was a turtle. Both fish and turtle again give us the
idea of a neuter God.

The third avatar brings us closer to the idea of a warrior male
God. The name is Varaha which is similar to the name Varuna, which
comes from the Greek Uranus. The various god-names of India
easily transfer characteristics and devotees, and eventually Varuna
became associated with the water, such as the Greek god Neptune.
The legend goes that there was a calamity that caused the earth to
begin sinking under water. Visnu turned itself into a wild boar which
lifted the sinking earth on its tremendous tusk. Thus humankind had
a place to dwell.

The situation that brought on the fourth avatar, was a
demon who had been guaranteed that he would be slain by neither
man nor beast, on neither day nor night. This dilemna required a very
special solution, and Visnu incarnated in a man-lion, which was
neither man nor beast, and slew the demon at twi-light, which was
neither day nor night. This is a fanciful story but many theological
implications can be drawn from it. It may be saying that when things
look impossible, God will come into our lives and do the miraculous
to preserve the creation and its inhabitants.

God also is credited with a sense of humor. Another demon
had control of the world and its inhabitants, and Visnu incarnated as

a tiny dwarf. He approached the demon and asked if all the land that he strode over in several strides could be relinquished for humanity. Of course the demon agreed, because how much land could a tiny dwarf cover? Visnu suddenly grew into a giant, and strode across the whole earth! As a consequence, we are all free of the demon and can possess the land. There is a Nordic tale of a plowman that contains this same theme. We can see a theological similarity with the parable of the mustard seed, small starts growing into the Kingdom/Queendom of God (Luke 13:18,19).

The next avatars are all full size men. This list contains no women. Appearances six and seven have to do with Rama. Number eight is Krishna, and nine is Buddha. These three are frequently worshipped as diety in their own right, as being normal human beings totally imbued with the presence or essence of God.

For some the tenth incarnation of Visnu is yet to come. It is believed that a form of God, the Hindu Kalkin or Buddhist Maitreya, will come to save humanity if the world is destroyed by flood, fire, or calamity. Some Hindus would insert Jesus as the tenth avatar, as one who saved the people by showing them the way of true justice.

The Kalkin, or incarnation yet to come, is a late addition to the Vaisnavite myth which prophecies, "At the end of this dark age Visnu will appear in the form of a man mounted on a white horse, with a flaming sword in his hand. He will judge the wicked, reward the good, and restore the age of gold."[6] This description has similarities with the Christian Book of Revelation which describes the battle of the end times, "And now I saw heaven open, and a white horse appear; its rider was called Faithful and True; he is a judge with integrity, a warrior for justice." (Revelation 19:11) The Greeks of Plato's time had spoken of the age of gold as the pre-historic time when all things went well for humankind. Thus Christians, early Greeks, and Hindus display interwoven threads in their mythic tapestries. With common patriarchal backgrounds, Christians and Hindus evidently expect the rider of the white horse to be an individual and a male.

If we look at the definition of avatar as incarnation, embodiment, or epiphany, and see that early Hindu theologians saw no harm in visualizing God in a fish, we might look at our present world and allegorically visualize God in the total community, or in any part of that community. An epiphany is a manifestation of God, and a community is certainly capable of making God's love manifest. It is likewise true that an individual in certain of his actions, can make God's love and concern manifest. To return to the fish as an instrument of God's visibility, watching a fish can make a human being think of the wonder of God's creation, and bring him closer to God. Even the stones will cry out God's praises, if we humans fail to do the honors.

In regard to the Christian faith, the same notions of God incarnate in every human being that does God's will, progress through the Gospel of John. In John 14:10 Jesus queries, "Do you not believe that I am in the Father and the Father is in me?" Finally, John 14:23 proclaims, "If anyone loves me he will keep my word, and my Father will love him and we shall come to him and make our home with him." If God makes his home in us, surely we are *avatars*, ready to display God's love and care to humanity.

If the world today is on the brink of disaster, who will save it? If we are to exercise God's care for the earth and the earth-keepers, there appears to be certain actions we should take, and certain messages we should get across. We find in our present era those who are willing to tackle different aspects of God's care for the world. There is the community of those who wish to clean up acid rain. Are they not avatars in their actions of attempting to save the world from ecological disaster? There are those who oppose nuclear weapons, and suffer mutilation and prison. Are they not avatars as they bear their crosses?

Perhaps we should not look around expectantly for an avatar or a savior, but accept the responsiblity ourselves for rescuing the earth from its dilemmas. Are we not all capable of carrying within the essence of God?

We might conclude from this discussion of an inter-religious messiah, that all faiths await expectantly a spirit of goodness, that will guide the earth towards fulfillment. They may express their expectations with different symbology. Some may visualize a specific person as the starting point for this fulfillment. Some may anticipate a holy community. But all of us as created by a loving God, seem to hope for a future time of justice and truth.

8
THE USE OF LAW
TO BUILD COMMUNITY

8.1 FREEDOM

The law is not our master, but our tool. Likewise, a leader should not be our master, but our servant to encourage us and to guide us to fulfillment. However, our humanity often displays imperfections. We must realize that some expert guidance is necessary as we learn imperfectly. We must expect that leaders drawn from a pool of such imperfect learners will be fallible. We must accept the fact that all of us, even the chosen leaders amongst us, often need wise guidance and well formulated directions.

When we are making duck soup, it helps to have a recipe. Of course it is possible to boil a duck and make soup from the drippings, but this off-the-cuff method may result in a soup that is greasy and indigestible. On the other hand, given a talented cook using a tried recipe, duck soup can taste like ambrosia. In making duck soup and in forming community, it pays off to consult the successful practicioner.

The most important ingredient of the ideal community is freedom. God evidently felt this first need when he created the earth. He made human kind with the ability to choose.

Not too many people have their freedom to do as they please or to do as they feel they are led. People who live under any form of government hesitate to criticize the form of government that is in power. If they are employed by that government or in its army, there is even less chance that they will speak their minds freely. Church men think twice before they tell their superiors that they see room for improvement in either the structure of their church or the leaders of their church.

Fortunately there are always a few people who are willing to

155

think creatively, and let their ideas be known. These ideas usually meet with opposition from those entrenched in seats of power, and from the mass of the people who feel comfortable with where they are. As long as their bread is buttered, people won't complain too heartily. When their bread isn't buttered, people are often too weak to complain.

Thank God for the creative thinkers of this world! They come in all shapes and sizes. We even hear women's voices in their midst. Some niches only a woman can fill. Women in the Catholic Church have a marvelous opportunity to speak out on issues that seemed dead or settled to the leadership of the male hierarchy or to the average acquiescing Sunday-morning church goer. Members of the hierarchy would rarely think like a woman, and would be even more hesitant to bring matters into discussion that might displease those in authority in the church.

Although women have been shunted off to the sidelines, and not given much opportunity to express themselves on how they are being governed, like many of those who are oppressed, they are anxious to find new ways of doing things. Women seeking a fair share of jobs, wages, and recognition, try to make modest changes in socially accepted norms. Women left out of the governance of churches, sit quietly and observe, and notice what the busy people at the top of the power structures, fail to notice. Yet in the final analysis, it may be only women who are able to speak out in freedom about church governance, as men in power will not take them too seriously and may even condescendingly humor their outbursts. Fortunately, in this type of sexist oppression, most women are not left to starve, so they have the physical stamina to continue to protest injustice and imperfections.

Women must undertake their struggle against unjust structures carefully. They must be warned to keep at heart the importance of loving relationships. As soon as they stride on the scene shouting, their male hearers are liable to throw up defenses. For women there is "the temptation to enter the public sphere in a purely competitive spirit seeking enhancement of prestige, wealth, and power, rather than entering the public sphere in a spirit of service, of compassion, of solidarity."[1] If we want a government that guides us in a spirit of service and compassion, we must be compassionate ourselves, and not be grabbing for power and authority.

8.2 THE NEED FOR LAWS AND RULERS

Moses found the group that he guided through the desert to be an unruly and thankless lot. God offered to take them off his hands and make of Moses' line a holy people (Exodus 32:7-10). Moses pleaded with God to give them all another chance, and in hopes of improving the whole situation, *The Tablets of The Law* were given.

The purpose of this *law* was to help the whole group to be considerate of one another. It gave suggestions for maintaining order in the community in an acceptably cultural way. The law did not enshrine certain people in authority. The law was not put in place to glorify specific people as rulers, but as guidelines for the total community. "From this you know that now, if you obey my voice and hold fast to my covenant, you of all the nations shall be my very own, for all the earth is mine. I will count you a kingdom of priests, a consecrated nation" (Exodus 19:5-6). There was a covenantal aspect to the law which encouraged the community member to think about how his or her actions affected personal relationships with God and man. The law was used as a guiding light to illuminate truth, by the judges in Israel, and was not used as a tool to control by their rulers until after the Davidic kingdom was established.

The injunction, "Thou shalt not murder," speaks equally to the king and commoner. There is no way that this can be interpreted as a privilege for the ruling authority to behead his subjects. The law was given as guidelines to keep order in a loving community; it comes from the authority of God only as the human interprets God through the moral consensus of humankind. This consensus must be continually updated in order to meet the challenge of new situations of human invention, which arrive upon the earth. When we discover that our leaders, either self-appointed or elected, are not following given guidelines for optimum loving and truthful community, we are ethically required to bring this to their attention, as the prophet Nathan did with David (II Samuel 12).

The law can be used wisely as guidelines to remind the people of their ethical standards. The law helps to maintain an orderly community. Some structure, not necessarily a king, might be useful to encourage people to renew the covenant in their hearts. Often a king does nothing for order, but in his imperfect humanity and desire to keep power, he may foment hatred between nations, kill people, not recognize true statements from false statements, and treat his subjects with inconsideration. He may observe the poor in his kingdom, become poorer, and the rich become richer, and feel no compunction, as the rich are his supporters and enable him to maintain his own selfish personal image. Some may feel that a king is necessary to enforce the law, but if we are to follow holy scripture, it seems that God reserves for God's self, the right to pay back those who do evil. "Vengeance is mine, and requital, for the time when they make a false step" (Deuteronomy 32:35).

If the law is used in covenantal fashion, in which it is a set of guidelines agreed to by both the community and the individual, then it encourages freedom of thought and holy expression. If the law is handed down authoritatively and imposed from without by others, it squelches the individual's and the community's ability to follow God in freedom.

8.3 CHURCH CANON LAW AS A COMMUNITY BUILDER

Having said all this about laws, we will investigate the effect of one set of laws on a particular community group. This chapter and the next will address themselves to the problem of canon law in the Catholic community. Those of other faiths may feel that they have better rules and regulations which enhance personal freedom and responsibility, but I am using this particular Roman Catholic body of law as it illustrates dramatically how a slight bending of present structures might open up vast areas of understanding. Present authoritarianism with competitiveness to stay on the top of the heap, might bend gracefully to a new method of governance using cooperation and social interaction.

For a long time, Christians did without written law. Jesus had proposed the *law of love* and as a good Jew, supported the Jewish Torah. As different church communities formed, and acquired habits of worship, regulations were put in place to uphold these habits as the community grew in their togetherness by doing things in what they considered to be the proper way. While maintaining belief in loving care of one's neighbor, each group had variations on the worship theme, due to different cultural backgrounds. When church authority became centralized in Rome, those in the seats of power began to feel uncomfortable with these expressions of freedom and creativity. There is often a notion that if someone is not doing things *my* way, then they must be doing it incorrectly. Consequently, there were attempts to mold Christians into conformity. Down through the centuries many minor rules and regulations were proclaimed by those heading up different church areas.

In 1983 a rather important development took place in the Roman Catholic Church. This subset of the people of God were presented with a body of guiding laws which will standardize procedures and assist those certain individuals who are drawn out from the group to facilitate and to organize, to serve their brothers and sisters wisely. It is a very comprehensive code of law, touching on every aspect of life in the Catholic body of believers. The specific canons that are mentioned here will be taken from the English translation of the code, prepared by the Canon Law Society of Great Britain and Ireland and published by W. B. Eerdmans Publishing Company.[2]

The recent code of canon law promulgated by the Catholic Church is written with the equality of all persons in mind, in the majority of its directives. The purpose of this canon law is to foster love, growth, and order in Christian communities. Code regulations should enable the people of God to work for justice, love, and truth "with all things being done decently and in order" (I Corinthians 14:40). The church government should reflect the rights and responsibilities of individuals to serve one another, and thus should make opportunities for both small intimate local communities, as well as larger overseeing bodies.

Although the purpose behind the making of all laws for humankind, is to further cooperative community, there is the danger of law having the opposite effect if it is employed in an authoritarian manner. We have horrifying examples in history of law being used for dubious purposes. There are the well known examples of Hitler's legal measures used against the Jews, and the shameful Catholic Inquisition. Even today in Israel-Palestine we find government officials employing the negative aspects of several different bodies of law in order to deny rights to minorities in their country.

Canon law is a relatively recent development, and another purpose behind its promulgation is to assist in maintaining the tradition of the Catholic Church. Those who promulgate the law must search honestly and deeply for the true Jesus tradition, and make sure that their law, power, or authority, does not wreak havoc on the *good news* of Jesus Christ to the poor, to women, and to all creation.

8.4 NEW CODE WRITTEN BY CONSERVATIVE CLASSICISTS

Until 1917 there was no Code of Canon Law in the Catholic Church. The purpose of the 1917 code was to collect into one place, all the rules and regulations that seemingly promoted order in the church. There had been means of governing, creeds, and laws since the time of primitive church communities, but in an era of mass communication, it seemed wise to gather and standardize this information. With the breath of fresh air that characterized Vatican II, it was decided that these laws collected in 1917 themselves needed revision to make the church more in tune with our contemporary society. Unfortunately this revision like the 1917 collection, was not done in a consentaneous manner, and has a tendency to reflect the minority classicist male viewpoint. It has been criticized "for paying more attention to technical detail than to the practical experience of the church since Vatican II."[3]

Perhaps we are expecting more of this code than it is designed to give. The average American Catholic sees this code and immediately assumes that all these laws are to be obeyed without question. We should rather understand the code more in the terms of Roman Law, where certain guidelines are set down, and exceptions can be made. Having a comprehensive body of law is a rather new development in the Catholic system, although clerical churchpeople have been making rules for the laity to obey for centuries, without the consent or advice of lay persons, as if parishioners lacked mental ability or were deficient in possession of the Spirit of God. One of the purposes of the new code is to get the response, advice, and consent of the governed, even advice from women. Laws require the "Amen" response from the people;[4] in a similar manner the blessing of Eucharist in the Roman Catholic service awaits the people's "Amen", and the Sinai Covenant was ratified by the people (Exodus 24:3). The Catholic laity should be asked if it will agree to obey the law, and what is its opinion of the law, in order for there to be a workable relationship and positive growth. Some of the writers of the code realize the need for this covenantal response.

For sixteen years after Vatican II intensive work went on to produce the New Code. Teams of canon lawyers poured over problem sections when they had a free moment from marriage tribunal duties. Their work was reviewed by cardinals, and further advice was sought from the Roman curia, the bishops of the world, and the faculties of Catholic universities. The majority of these workers were conservative church*men*, and they didn't change much in the law, or give much room to the liberal viewpoint. In corporations where optimization and ultimization are necessary for the pursuit of the almighty dollar, stale department heads are reshuffled in order to give new insights, and to inject fresh oxygen into the blood. In the service of our country and of Almighty God, politicians and churchmen are more lax, and use men (and seldom women) who often seem adverse to new ideas, and more interested in secure retirement benefits, with maintenance of the status quo. Thus the new code "gives less scope to episcopal collegiality than Vatican II may have desired."[5] It "honors less the insights of the council concerning the laity than the dignity of God's people would demand."[6]

Law may be described as an instrument whose purpose is to aid in bringing on the fulfillment of society. It serves as a facilitator and orderer and helps to preserve historical progress.[7] The law must be *appropriate* and *true*.[8] It must be good for today, yet encase what we learned from yesterday. As humans display diversity, the law should be written with this diversity in mind. This same diversity should be represented in the committees who write the laws, but this did not seem to be the case in the writing of the New Code.

The conservatist or classicist sees law as the controller of human activity. The historicist sees community and law as the result of the common experience of human living. The historicist of Vatican II saw a need and urged that a New Code be promulgated. Unfortunately, it was the classicist that was given the job of writing it.

The classicist, an expert in Roman law, still expects to get input from the people, but from hind sight, and built into the new code lengthy time elements, such as thirty years or a hundred years, before allowing legislative change. By the time the changes are allowed, the laity may have given up in disgust and proclaimed their dissent by not being there to be the objects of legislation. The voice of the lay people was heard at Vatican II, and was ignored by the writers of the code in most instances. Normal historical progress was given a setback. The classicist remained tied securely to his abstract principles, and refused to follow the leading of the historicist in his urgings to revise those principles in the light of new authentic human experience.

A clear historicist voice was trumpeted forth from the American Catholic Bicentennial Consultation in Detroit, October 1976. Resolutions were produced urging that women and married men be ordained priests. Open discussion led to consensus on many agenda. Historicists saw this meeting as "a new way of doing the business of the church in America."[9] Classicists saw the meeting as being a group of children attempting to rewrite the constitution. As the Detroit meeting was only consultative, no person with power was required to act on its deliberations.

8.5 REACTION TO THE NEW CANON LAW CODE

The 1971 synod of bishops declared that any church that presumes to preach justice must first practice justice itself.[10] How should the church people and the world in general react to a code of law whose interpretation continues to make women into second class citizens, or less than citizens? When will the bored unloving judges "give her justice?"(Luke 18:5) How will the world react to a code of law that seems to encourage a class system similar to what we have abhorred in India, where who is on the top of the heap, does not depend on heredity as in India, but on celibacy and gender? How will the world react to a code of law that can be interpreted as seeking to enforce antiquated modes of government whose injustices and unholy emphasis on *divine right* have proved to be illicit means for keeping in power?

Perhaps this is the best code we can expect from a church whose governmental roots twist back into Pax Romana. However, we believe we are led by the Spirit of God. We image God as just judge and loving law giver. God is love and made us with the great purpose of our fulfillment in mind. Parts of the New Code do not seem to lead to the fulfillment of humankind. They are written from a position of authority, and do not consult with the human experience of those whom they have placed under their authority. Instead of consultation, we find coercion. The New Code itself condemns coercion. The Spirit is thus seen working in the New Code to protect the people of God. If we interpret the New Canon Law non-coercively in all its codes, it will assist in the fulfillment of the Christian people.

8.6 THE PROBLEM OF AUTHORITATIVE STRUCTURE IN THE CATHOLIC CHURCH

It is difficult to draw out a loving easy-going interpretation of canon law, when we find ourselves in a church structure that is hierarchical and authoritarian. Often it seems that the hierarchy wants the laity to stay in its place, and to acquiesce dutifully before their supposedly more knowledgeable superiority. Ours is to obey, and they want no suggestion. If they are required by law to ask for suggestions, it often seems like they do the opposite of what was suggested, in order to maintain their authoritative position. We of the laity want to feel that we are a part of the church. We want to give something of ourselves into our church government. We know that we are prophets, priests, and rulers, not merely a collective pillow for the hierarchy to rest upon. The Pope and the most ordinary lay catholic are equal partners in the Christian community.

The average Pope may not feel that he has bonds like this with the laity, humble people who may include priests retired because of marriage, or ordinary women, yet he should feel this unity. Father Richard Rohr tells of the Maryknoll sister who went to serve in Peru, who realized that even in her missionary poverty, she was so well off that she could establish no bonds with the poor around her.[11] She understood that they could receive nothing from her with dignity, unless they were able to give something of themselves, or the relationship between her and them would be a cold, authoritarian, rich American - poor peasant, affair. She hit upon the happy idea of asking them if she could borrow a hoe for a couple of hours, using it to garden. Thus, they were able to give her something, and when she returned the hoe, she could give them words of friendship and appreciation. On this give and take basis, she could contribute loving service. Those who find themselves in a privileged position in the church, need to establish ties by asking for help and information from others, if they truly hope to serve others. Perhaps the Pope would like to borrow my hoe.

There is this same give and take relationship set up by Jesus in his meeting with the woman at the well. He does not start off the conversation by telling her he has come to save her. He begins by asking her to do him a favor. He asks for her considerate action in giving him a drink of water. Then in their further conversation, she tells him about the Messiah. In our church experience, is there any of this give and take? We may not even recognize that we bring gifts to the altar. All is done for us by *church*. Do we hear Jesus in our heart asking for a drink of water? Do we shoulder our bucket and plunge it into the well? Does the church grab the bucket from our hands and say, "Let me do that. You don't know the correct way to do it!"

Is there give and take in the organizational structure of the church, between the laity and the hierarchy? In revising the Code of Canon Law, input from the laity was not requested. The laity is given a body of regulations and told authoritatively what religion is all about. Sometimes it seems that the Word of God in the Bible is not even consulted. We might compare the development of church hierarchy and its laws with the constructional history of the tea ball.

The average tea ball is egg shaped, made out of metal, and has a chain on it to hold it to the top of the tea pot. One might surmise that at some point in time, there were tea balls made out of wood, but these may have tainted the tea with woody or poisonous flavors. Originally tea was allowed to float around in the pot, and some people today don't mind floating tea, or tea leaves in their cups, but it doesn't seem to be customary to consume straight tea leaves. Water was hard to come by, as it had to be carried from a distant source of supply. You can imagine that if a woman had to boil eggs for her family to eat, that she would not throw out the egg-boiling water, but that upon removing the eggs, she would throw in some tea leaves, and serve tea to drink, with the meal. In her tea-leaf disposal problem, she may have scooped out the leaves with a handy left-over egg shell. If the shell had a convenient crack in it, she could have strained the tea juice through the crack. In all this supposing, if she were suddenly confronted with another guest for dinner, she may well have set the soggy leaves in their egg shell, back into some fresh water to brew another cup of tea. The first tea ball may well have been two sections of an egg shell, jammed together.

Let's equate the Holy Spirit to the tea, and humanity, to the water. One can mix tea and water, or rather Spirit and humanity, and get a Spirit-filled human being. This can happen naturally, or a prophet can act as a catalyst to bring God to the people. Moses was a type of egg-shell container, that held the tea (Spirit) in the water (humanity). He operated rather spontaneously, but the Levitical priesthood that followed him, was more structural and confining (like a wooden tea ball) and didn't give the Spirit as much freedom to mingle with the people. Skipping over the tea saturated interval of Jesus, we find that our tea balls are being made out of fairly unyielding metal, with small controlling holes in them called *sacraments*. They frequently have a chain on them, to anchor them in one spot, as a bishop is anchored to his diocese. This metal tea ball was probably invented by man, as a more practical and orderly way of doing things. It was an excellent solution for its particular era, but today we have light weight disposable paper tea bags to hold our tea. We have passed the point where we are dependent on rigid authoritative structures. God wants us to consider all things with our informed consciences, and come to consentaneous action in loving communities.

Although we see canon law as part of the rigid structure of our church organization, or as a vehicle created by men to control the spirituality of other men, the Spirit has guided us to this law to assist in keeping order and in facilitating the growth of Christian love in our communities. In its part as rigid metal tea ball, it also holds the tea that insists that *all* catholics have rights and that laws to guide these catholics should be made with their consensus. A new form of church government lies dormant in the Code, waiting for the opportune moment to sprout and to blossom.

8.7 HISTORY OF GOVERNMENT

Ever since creation, humankind has been experimenting with different ways of government, so that there will be relative peace in which to perform our God-given function of tending the earth. Caring for the earth is a community project, usually accompanied with rules and regulations. As the leaders drawn out of the early church community to guide the group, cast their eyes about for a vehicle to promote their purpose, their first glance fell upon the civil government of their time. They admired the *pax romana* of the Roman empire, with its hierarchical steps leading up to Caesar. They incorporated the household codes of Roman law into their teachings. When Christianity became the official religion of the empire, it seemed natural to set down as church law, regulations that were similar to the civil law of the day. Thus our church, our schools, our whole mode of society are based on the authoritarian regime of Rome, rather than on the humble words of the Nazarean, who requested that his disciples not have a ruling structure like that of the heathen powers (Mark 10:42-44).

Many centuries later we have the privilege of seeing that there are many other forms of government than that of rule from the top. We have debunked the *divine right* of kings, and we have come to new understandings about the *infallibility* of the Pope. We have seen mindless democracy in action, and we have watched bloody dictatorships come and go under various guises. We have observed the expressions of opinion in town meetings, and run organizations by means of Robert's Rules. We have seen crowds moved by mass hysteria, and the rise and fall of religious groups such as Jonestown. We have learned about the apparent failure of a communism that gives power to an elite group, as there seems to be a built-in defect that stratifies this type of society into lowly workers and elevated leaders. Even the most well meaning democracy contains this stratifying effect. What is left to try? How do you get leadership that really serves? How do you get rules and regulations that lead to each human "enjoying peace under the fig tree" (Zechariah 3:10)? If we want the promises of the Almighty to become reality, it seems reasonable to put into practice the insights that God has given us. As we "ought to obey God rather than men,"[12] our governance and laws might advantageously reflect the decrees for the Jubilee Year (Leviticus 25) and the forgiveness and humility displayed by Jesus, rather than a show of material power.

Who is eligible to oversee humankind's conformance to Jubilee type regulations? It seems that it is necessary to have some sort of structure to promote the Gospel of Love. Would the flimsiness of a tea bag do? Yet isn't the flimsiness of the individual human being designed to hold the spark of the Spirit of the Most High God?

Jesus spoke to the woman at the well as if he felt her capable of utilizing the living water of God's Spirit (John 4:10). Did Jesus foresee an educational structure? He seemed to feel that if people knew the truth, they would willingly conform. "Go to all peoples and teach them!" (Matthew 28:19). Servants of the truth must discuss this truth with others, so that all people can freely give their "Amen" to this truth. They must also have the freedom to reject and to revise this proferred wisdom. As long as humankind is human, it will need consultative guidelines to help it to tend the earth and to assist it into positive relationships. These guidelines should not be imposed from above, but should spring from the experience of the people, as they dwell as neighbors together and consider each other's needs.

The right to vote on a matter is a first step in this direction, but being able to say *yes* and *no*, and following the lead of the majority doesn't take into consideration the equally well motivated minority. If this minority is set aside, they will develop discontents that can upset the peace of the community and lead to terrorism.

Some believe that you can really see democracy at work in a town meeting, where neighbors get together to thrash out a problem. In a Christian community people should listen considerately to one another's views, and try to reach agreement, not on what is best for oneself, but on what is best for the community. There are pitfalls in this type of governance, as we are very human, and frequently can see only from our own selfish viewpoint. The Quakers, in trying to perfect this system, have developed a method of consensus, which contains the following major points:

(1) There is no voting; agreement must be unanimous.
(2) Agreement is reached by controlled discussion.
(3) An individual who disagrees with the group can agree to stand aside, or to stand in the way of a final decision if she/he feels strongly on the matter.
(4) If discussion becomes heated, anyone can call for a moment of silence.

*(5) The position of facilitator for the meeting is a
rotating appointment, and the facilitator is not
entitled to express an opinion on the matter being
discussed.
(6) If the meeting does not reach consensus, no
action can be taken on the matter.*

Consensus is very difficult to achieve, but it is in creatively
overcoming problems, or approaching partial solutions, that we
grow as human beings and gain fulfillment. We have God's promise
that the Holy Spirit will be with us, and if the community makes an
earnest effort, God will assist it, and bless the earth.

8.8 PROBLEMS OF LEADERSHIP

The problems of our governments to rule objectively and peacefully,
are not due simply to their structure, but also to poor leadership.
Democracy does have potential; majority rule has made this nation
prosperous. Still we can look around and see graft and inefficiency
on every side. For example, some in authority profit from illegal
drugs that destroy the minds of others. Our state laws imprison those
addicts who have acted with drug-mutilated minds, yet we often find
that their destroyers go free to enjoy illicit gains if bribe money has
been passed in the right places. Money is not the only way of bribing.
Individuals act out of a variety of self-interest motives. Often people
view security as a continuance of forms and regulations to which they
have become accustomed. They might see the continuance of poor
leadership, as being more secure for them, than experimenting with
new ways and new leadership.

What can be done about the problem of corrupt or inept
leadership? We in the Catholic Church can't turn our backs on the
problem and say, "This doesn't apply to us. We have all these saintly
priests and sisters to be leadership for us." We are all called to be
leaders, to be saints, to be prophets, priests, and rulers, and to join in
the process of consentaneous government. Very often it is the
inspired or inspirited laity who are obliged to be the life of a parish
that is headed up by a priest grown too old or too comfortable in the
prestige of his job.

We might take a hint from industry. Large corporations have

as their primary goal, the making of money. For this they need active and enthusiastic leadership. Several years ago corporations in this country noticed that the Japanese corporations seemed to have busier workers, better managers, and bigger profits. The secret was the *quality circle*, which some of our industries immediately imitated. Workers would get in small groups with their managers, and discuss where and how improvements could be made. The managers did not lead the groups; each time they met, leadership was rotated among the workers. Implementation of this model was a boon to American business. It could be used profitably in the managing of our religious and political organizations. It would be an excellent way to revise church and political governance.

8.9 CANON LAW AS A SPECIAL TYPE OF LAW

We must not make the mistake of assuming that canon law is a rigid body of doctrine, and that we must toe the line or pay the penalty. There is a wide variety of different types of law in the new code. Some of these laws are rigid; some are guidelines; some codes bow before custom. Some are divine laws, as we believe God has given them to us in scripture and in revelation. Others are natural laws, those that relate to human nature or to the care of the nature around us, yet on which we do not feel we have divine pronouncements. There are liturgical laws that instruct on how to perform ceremonies, which are merely rules of order that may be changed if another method of operation arises that is preferable. There are exhortations and recommendations. There are ecclesial laws that assist in church discipline. There are theological statements, which are open to further elaboration by theologians. The whole code is given to assist those who govern the church into the best possible governance of the church. Written into the codes are descriptions of various gatherings of people. These gatherings are for the purpose of assisting priests, pope, and bishops to know the wisdom and will of the people, so that those in governance with a wise and understanding ear, can make appropriate changes in the rules and regulations for the good of the community. It is the desire of the church that the new code of canon law be a bridge, and not a road block, to better community.

8.10 CANON LAW REGULATIONS SHOULD FURTHER LOVING COMMUNITY

Jesus saw the law as a living thing, changing to meet the needs of people, and himself the fulfillment of the law, his statement of love giving life to the letter of the law. He proclaimed himself to be "the *way,* the *truth,* and the *life*" (John 14:6). Canon law is to further the life of Christ in the community. Christian laws should support and encourage the weak and the oppressed. They should not be made to explicitly protect those in power. Our Christian code of law hopefully is not given by a certain group of *men* to support their power structure, but to insure the development of all individuals in an orderly manner.

If we believe that the church is the people of God, we must be conscientiously concerned about listening to the people of God when formulating our codes. We should implement information-gathering consensus groups as the *quality circles* of church organization, being careful of the possibility of a power mongering facilitator trying to influence consensus. For this reason it is very important that the office of facilitator should be rotated through the whole group.

Certain terms in the code come out of stilted and archaic usage. Using our God-given freedom for the purpose of more open church governance, we can interpret the titles of *Supreme Pontiff, Holy See,* or *Bishop* as *servant* or *facilitator.* Discussion of the College of Cardinals brings up the term *collegiality. Collegiality* and *Subsidiarity* to describe governing groups set up by the code, have stratification connotations. *Collegiality* as used by the code, means the gathering of a brotherhood of priests and equals, to advise a bishop or superior, who does not necessarily have to listen to the advice of these brothers. As the group of sisters is excluded from this priestly brotherhood, there is no true collegiality in this group, and it seems far from the positive performance of the quality circle.

The *Subsidiarity* group is the sub-group of those on the lowest level of the totem pole. The regulations seem to assume that the parish with its common people make up the lowest level in the church. I find this term very discriminating as the dictionary definition of subsidiarity implies aid from a subordinate of inferior status. The parish should really be considered on an equal level with the hierarchical priesthood, especially when you consider that it is the people who know in their hearts what type of wise governance they need. The terms *collegiality* and *subsidiarity* when applied to stratify groups, make one question the purpose of these information gathering groups. Are they bridges or road-blocks? Are these circles being used to put down and weed out the non-conformers, so that the elite may know what discontents lurk in the lower strata and effectively squelch them through various types of mind control?

We are all human and we grab for power as a subconscious or conscious means of self-preservation. Even in writing these words, I am making a bid for a tiny piece of power. It is much easier for the controlling elite to put people down, than to try to understand their needs in love, to be responsible for them in their peculiarities, or to act as mediator when problems arise. Service to help solve the problems of the troubled is much more difficult than slapping on a law, and insisting on *YOUR* authority, and *THEIR* obedience. But such loving, dedicated service is the message of Christ.

Every law and regulation in the new code should be examined from the viewpoint of: (1) Is it loving? Does it put anyone down? (2) Does it come from the heart of the people, or from an authority figure?

8.11 BIBLICAL AND HISTORICAL INSTANCES OF CONSENSUS

Deuteronomy 1:12 describes church organization according to Moses. "'How can I alone bear the responsibility for settling your disputes? Choose some wise, understanding, and experienced people from each tribe, and I will put them in charge of you.' And you agreed that this was a good thing to do. So I took the wise and experienced leaders you chose from your tribes, and I placed them in charge of you. Some were responsible for a thousand people, some for one hundred, some for fifty, and some for ten. I also appointed other officials throughout the tribes. At that time I instructed them, 'Listen to the disputes that come up among your people. Judge every dispute fairly, whether it concerns only your own people or involves foreigners who live among you. Show no partiality in your decisions; judge everyone on the same basis, no matter who he is. Don't be

afraid of anyone, for the decisions you make come from God.'" We
have here an example of the quality circle, without the advantage of
rotating leadership. However, the leaders are urged to exercise no
partiality.

The New Testament relates consensus in the early church
when Paul goes to Peter and confronts him face-to-face (Galatians
2:11-14) on a matter of church custom. Acts 1:15-26 describes an
open meeting with the decision left to the Holy Spirit, rather than to
a human opinion. When we get into the later books of the New
Testament such as Timothy, we find a tilt to authority, and instruc-
tions on _not_ listening to consensus. Gnosticism is creeping on the
scene with strange new ideas, and there is a fear to listen in love, as
there is a threat that the right to rule may be taken from one's hand.
The author of Timothy trusts less to the Wisdom of God, than in his
confidence in the man Timothy's ability to hold the fort. This
authoritarianism is reflected in the description of the marvelous
elder of I Timothy 3 who is without fault. Are there any men without
fault? Are there any women without fault?

The churches in Revelation speak of possible consensus.
The church at Thyatira (Revelation 2:18) tolerates a certain woman,
so at that time they were practicing freedom of expression. However,
they are advised to be tolerant no longer. We do not know if they
silenced the woman, and destroyed their quality circle.

Another purely historical example of the use of consensus
was with Cyprian, Bishop of Carthage. Instead of using the terms
collegiality and *subsidiarity*, Cyprian applied *consilium* and *consensus*, to both fellow priests and laity. Cyprian was not under obligation
to follow the advice of these groups, but he evidently made it his
policy to implement their considered judgments. When persecutions forced him into hiding, and he was therefore unable to consult
with his constituents, he apologized for this deviation from the norm.
Cyprian defined the church as *consentientis populi corpus unum*[13]
meaning one consentaneous body of people. He refused to act
without the consensus of the people, as then the group would no
longer be *church*, but a dominated and stratified assembly of disparate individuals. Under his guidance there was both a clerical and lay
voice in the selection of bishops.[14] Cyprian made a good start in the
right direction, but later church fathers found the monarchical form

of government easier to implement.

Revelation 21 tells us of the New Jerusalem, the perfected community, as opposed to the evil community of Babylon in Revelations 18. Thrown into the sea with evil Babylon are all the things that keep a community or humanity from realizing their full potential as loving brothers and sisters. These negatives might include selfish power, greedy luxury, refusal to see the needs of others, economic oppression of poorer neighbors, improper treatment of God's gift of sex, debasement of women, and not listening to the needs of others. On the contrary, the Holy Community dwells in harmonious consensus. God is in its midst, and its citizens are *all* rulers and thus equals. They walk actively in peace. The name Jerusalem means *to tread in peace*. Babylon who has been disposed of, takes her name from the confusion of tongues. No one can achieve consensus in her city limits, as consensus requires the ability of people to listen and to understand one another. One hopes that the code of canon law is urging humankind to *tread in peace* together. John Alesandro in his article, "The Revision of Canon Law," comments that canon lawyers can't get to basic meanings because of a language conflict which he terms *Babelization*.[15] It is up to us, the loving community, to set this code in the proper city. New Jerusalem may or may not be an historical example of consensus as it is not yet a part of history. Perhaps New Jerusalem is not achievable; it may only be a goal after which humanity should strive. Then again, it may be a process with which we are presently working, the *already* here-and-now section of God's kingdom/queendom, God with us in the present, whenever we do things in a Christian manner.

8.12 PRESENTDAY INSTANCES OF NONCONSENSUS IN THE CHURCH

If there were more consensus activity pervading all areas of the church, certain inconsistencies in church teaching might be more apparent. The South African Bishops took a commendable stand against apartheid in 1977. In their declaration they try to eradicate all possibilities of racial discrimination, such as suppressing "the customs still lingering in some places of having different sections of churches appropriated to different race groups." Women think immediately of the sexual discrimination legislated in our church against women on the altar. The anti-racial declaration goes on to desire "to do all in (its) power to speed up the promotion of black *persons* to responsible and high positions in the church."[16] Women know that the word *person* here does not refer to black *women*. Women are usually put in their place, and it's not a high or responsible place that they are put in!

The treatment of women is a blatant example of how lack of consensus can blind those in authority. We are told that *leaders* are drawn forth from the community to lift up the community. When the community is made up of both men and women, it is strange that only men are drawn forth to lead. Dentists are called forth from the community to serve the community. Teachers are called forth. So are firefighters. All of these can be of either sex, but when it comes to serving others as dispensers of religious tradition, some are excluded from this role, even though they are baptized members of the community and qualified with a theological education.

Setting up requirements for a standardized theological education is another example of church leaders exercising discrimination against applicants for the priesthood. If leaders are to be drawn from the community, they should come from both the educated and the uneducated. One might question here if it is wise to set up stratification in leadership with educational qualifications. Often the Holy Spirit is heard better from the lips of a child, than through the voluminous words of the authoritarian.

Other obvious examples of historical non-use of consensus in the Catholic church, are the disbelief in the knowledge of Copernicus and the tortures of the Inquisition. The church did not listen to the voice of its children, but assumed that an elite subset of celibate males had the total truth. We are deceived by this same belief today when we assume that an up-to-date theological education is necessary for a church leader. When we look at the havoc wrought by the Inquisitors, we might question that assumption. Is it wise to submit the Spirit filled minds of the loving community of people, to the iron rule of the wisdom of authoritative *men*, who feel they have captured the fullness of God in hearts that are just as self-centered as anyone else's? A celibate male trained to conform to the power structures of a church that does not listen to its heart, would need tremendous help from the Holy Spirit in order to know what would be the best actions and beliefs for a humble woman grounded in love for her family.

God loves us, and God gives each of us a model of God's loving care, that springs from out of the way we have been brought up, and which works for us. For example, some of us may work out of a guardian angel model, where a messenger of God has us in its special care, and takes the pressure off God. We feel that God must be terribly busy with important affairs like assisting presidents and holding up the earth, so as not to have any spare time to handle all the work of caring for the little people. Some find angels a concept that is too childlike and would rather picture God as total knowledge and love answering all the prayers for help directly through God's self. Some turn to the saints or to dead departed relatives that they feel are concerned with their needs. Others feel that God is available through a concerned community of the living. If a loving community gathers with a request for one of its members, then, they believe, God hears.

Giving God the right to change God's mind or to say *no* allows these models to work. God makes God's self available to God's beloved humanity. The mistake happens when one group of believers becomes elitist and thinks that another group is wrong. We must be loving and tolerant of other groups. The harm enters when we start referring to the other group as heretics when their model has been just as effective for them as ours has been for us. How can one group condemn another group of fellow humans beings who are equally in contact with the God who made us all? If we all listened to one another in consentaneous groups we would develop love and understanding for one another, that would keep us humble and non-elitist.

8.13 NECESSITY OF CONSENSUS FOR ACTION OF THE HOLY SPIRIT

God's Spirit speaks most clearly through a loving and prayerful community. It may be true that the oracle of Delphi was a *loner*, and yet proclaimed the message of the gods. We do have our Padro Pio's and our Jeannie Dixon's. However, most of us are a little out of touch with truth and with God's reality, and we have had at least one Pope who at times was out of touch with even human reality. Thus it seems odd for the Vatican to insist that all religious are obliged to obey the Holy Father as their highest superior in virtue of the vow of obedience.[17] Peter, who may or may not have been our first Pope, insisted that we ought to obey God rather than men (Acts 5:29). It wasn't just Peter, either; it was the other apostles in consensus with him! Jesus also tells us that where two or three are gathered in his name, inviting his Spirit, that he will be in the midst as advising love (Matthew 18:20). Nowhere does he assert that his friends and apostles are to obey fallible Peter as their highest superior. Obedience should be related to understanding the will of God as discovered in a consultative group of equals.

On the one hand we must respect the Spirit of God working in people, as we feel that God is in prayerful consensus. On the other hand, we must be wary of giving too much respect to individual wisdom, in calling any man *father*. Jesus gives this advice in Matthew 23:9. Do not relinquish your God-given freedom of reasoning before the authority of any human, who may well be working out his subconscious frustrations on your pliable id. Perhaps the code is implying that it's not the Pope that the vowed religious should be obedient to, but the consensus of the loving community, of which the Pope is a visible sign. This authority that the superior is to claim over the vowed religious, comes from God through the church or community, when the church or community have consentaneous beliefs and actions, and deliver them to the superior who is to act as spokesperson. Even the title of *Superior* is unchristian. Jesus said that in his community there should not be one person lording it over another as was customary with pagan government (Matthew 20:25-26). It would be much better to use the title of *spokesperson* rather than *superior*, and to have the position rotated frequently so that delusions of grandeur don't set in. A human being in authority often comes to believe that he/she merits that authority, and people set under that authority, often have a tendency to adulate the person who is merely representing the abilities vested in that office.

It is necessary for God's word in the community to be spoken to the community and to the individuals in that community. This word and the power to speak it, do not originate in the spokesperson, but this temporary facilitator in his capacity as server of others, should be able to relay the message to those who need it. If God truly lives and speaks in a community, it seems logical to consider the many opinions possible in the community, and not to relinquish all authority to a truncated section of it. A loving community should give listening room to all of its members. It also should make allowance for changes that take place over time, as often the Spirit speaks differently in a different age, or even only several years later, or the next day, depending on what sort of thinkers are included in your community group. Different people should be able to express individual feelings on topics under consideration. With many viewpoints there would be a fuller picture containing more opportunity for truer input from the Holy Spirit.

The Baha'is have thought about this community process, and have come up with a form of governing called Consultation.[18] In Consultation "there are two important factors which Baha'is must always remember. First, that every individual has the right to self-expression: he is free to declare his conscience and give his personal opinions. Second, that once he has expressed his views, he must not dogmatically cling to them with utter disregard for other people's opinions. He should always be prepared to look into ideas advanced by others and consult with them on every matter in a spirit of sincere fellowship. When the principle of consultation is carried out in an Assembly, the decision arrived at is usually very different and far better than anything the individual members first had in mind when they started their discussions."

The Baha'is emphasize the need for love and understanding among members, and the necessity to pray for help from *The Realm of Glory*. Discussions are to be confined to spiritual matters that have to do with "the training of souls, the instruction of children, the relief of the poor, the help of the feeble throughout all classes in the world", and other matters that concern the proper caring for God's gift of the earth.[19]

Unfortunately the Baha'is don't go far enough in their consideration of minority viewpoints. When they come to a time consuming disagreement, they yield to the voice of the majority. "If (a unanimous decision) does not happen, the vote of the majority becomes the decision of the Assembly."[20] It is easy to see that a church schism might result with the minority group leaving to form a new community. If you close off discussion with even one group member, you limit the full disclosure of the Holy Spirit. The Catholic Church closes off discussion with more than fifty percent of its members. It does not consult with women, children, and a majority of its men. I am convinced that what the Holy Spirit wants to say through this unconsulted group, is of vast importance to the human race.

8.14 NEW CODE OF CANON LAW CONTAINS A VISION FOR THE FUTURE

When arguing for consensus, and against monarchical authority of the Pope or of a religious *superior*, we must keep in mind that the Code of Canon Law is not a dead weight. It has a positive thrust. It is a document in which change is expected. It is a document whose purpose is to enhance love in the community. Like your average person, it is far from perfect, but hopefully headed in the right direction. A person is considered to have a good fundamental option or purpose in life, when that person opts for Jesus or decides to act responsibly in love. You might say that the hope or option of the code is that the monarchical authority of the past will be replaced by a genuine collaboration,[21] collaboration which does not entail token collegiality or gently degrading subsidiarity. The code looks into the future and envisions a unity in a diversity that is represented by both male and female, lay and cleric, in every aspect of church structure.

We apologize for limiting this critique to the Catholic construction. Other churches may have an equally well designed format to guide their organization, or one that encourages even better community, yet we are not acquainted with these other groups. It is necessary for us to speak out of the culture in which we are immersed. We are actually very pleased with the broadness of the rules and regulations that direct the Catholic Church, and also with the broadness available in their interpretation. We see possibilities in these guidelines to enhance the flows of life and love and to change the course of the world.

9

ARCHITECTURAL DIMENSIONS OF THE ROMAN CATHOLIC COMMUNITY

9.1 DISCUSSION ON LANGUAGE

Human beings have problems with language. Our codes of law are written in human words, and open to many varying interpretations. Language brings problems, but like the gift of life itself, it is filled with overwhelming possibilities.

What potential for love is unleashed with the gift of language! We can communicate with one another! I can tell you how I feel, and you can relate to my feelings, and reinforce me. Before language, we communicated with grunts. We could not possibly describe theological thoughts, or even human emotions. A male dog, confronting a female dog, cannot say in a delicate or courtly manner, how attractive he finds her. She has no words to turn aside his unwanted advances. There may be a biting match. We with our language, can each describe our feelings. We can get to understand one another. We can decide that being friends is more important than succumbing to selfish urges. We can sublimate our angers, and grow in our love and understanding for each other as persons. In discussing our concern for each other, we can learn about all the people in the world, who are our brothers and sisters, children of God, and thus build loving community in the world, and eliminate the need for nuclear weaponry. All this -- through language!

The variations in and additions to our language make evident stages and cycles of the human being and his growth in human understanding. A baby's first words, and the earliest words of the human race, reflect the parents and their caring concern. We hear *da-da*, *ma-ma*, and *no*. Early tribes sought to explain their origins, and invoked gods and goddesses to protect themselves. Nations and rulers attempted to keep order and power in the world, and all this is reflected in language. Science has led us into a whole new area of words to describe the inner workings of micro particles, and the macro wonders of outer space. All these words are living words. They change as people and customs change. They change as people learn more, and reform their ideas. As our human understanding grows, our language grows from legalisms to empathetic love.

As God is love, and created us, our notion of love changes as we grow and can perceive more clearly. Early tribes believed they were the favored recipient of the love of their particular God, and that this God would punish their enemies. Now that we can understand that the whole earth, even the whole universe, is God's creation, we can communicate to one another the wonder of this love, and try to assist God in caring for this wonderful earth with which we have been entrusted.

Language is the key that has unlocked this comprehension of love! Unfortunately, there are some problems with language. We speak different tongues, so we often find it difficult to understand one another. Even when we speak the same language, we have problems with listening, and often follow the leading of our own mind, rather than attempting to see the meaning in the words of the other. With language we can also bind the other, and harm the other. What emergent love can be stifled with the incorrect use of the gift of language!

Using this wonderful gift in a positive manner, what possible new interpretations can we derive from certain behavior codes, in order to further loving community? The New Code of the Catholics was written with the purpose of emphasizing the notion of Church as people of God in accord with the teachings of Vatican II. It also sought to promote "that rights and prerogatives of Church people be delineated within this context."[1] This canon law is a statement put forth that waits for the *Amen* of the people. In reviewing canon law one can agree with a proposal; one can say nothing, and thus the proposal is accepted as reasonable law; or one can disagree with a proposal, and it will be carefully reconsidered. If the voice of the people decides against a proposal, they will over-ride the law. Promulgating a code of law, is one way of finding out how the people feel about things. Listening leaders will change laws to suit the feelings of the people. In this chapter is proposed an action that the Catholic community could take in order for its law to be used as the guiding force to shape its structure more closely to the form of holy community.

9.2 CONSULTATION IN THE HAGGADAH

For the Jewish community the Haggadah relates that before the creation of the world, the Torah, as God's wisdom, was consulted by God. The Torah advised God that if no one is there to express homage, Lordship doesn't amount to much. We are told that "the answer pleased God exceedingly. Thus did God teach all earthly kings, by divine example, to undertake naught without first consulting advisors."[2]

The creative abilities of God were used to set in place peoples and governments who would assist in caring for the earth and earthly communities. In following God's example, have those who have been placed in leadership roles listened to advisors within their communities? It is interesting that God is credited with listening to the Torah as the advisors, and it seems God was not listening to a merely consultative voice or to a majority, but that God was taking the consensus of thought as presented in the Torah and acting on that advice. Do we use the Scriptures as if they were merely a consultative voice that we could disregard, or do we try to get the total message of the scriptures and to live it in our lives and to put the message into our bodies of law? Do our leaders use the power of the Holy Spirit speaking through the people in general, and through God's word as coming from the people, as a merely consultative voice that they can disregard? God's wisdom may be implying that those who guide us, should do so through a manner of consensus, or we might not be there, to be guided. Those in leadership positions should listen and act on the voice of the people. The people should listen to each other, and act in loving consideration of each other's needs.

9.3 CONSENSUS IN CONSULTATIVE BODIES: PARISH COUNCILS

Is it possible to take a present legal system, such as the Catholic Code of Canon Law, and interpret it freely to mold it into greater conformity with the Law of Love? Can this New Code of Canon Law which we have been discussing, incorporate the voices of the people, and thus merit the *Amen,* or acceptance response, of the people? The hope of the hierarchy who fathered the code of canon law, is that the consultative bodies described therein, will bring us all together. They believe that the laws are not set up to promote altercation, but to promote unity. If one has ever attended a parish council meeting, one can see that the design of the meeting can tilt in either of the above directions. Meetings begun with a prayer can end with a walk-out. People can become very frustrated when they are on one end of a very divisive issue, with only a consultative voice; and the pastor is on the other side, with total say, and he's not even listening. If there were no vote, no final arbiter or decider, but use of the process of consensus where every person gets the chance to tell all that he/she knows on the subject, and why he/she feels the way he/she does; where the pastor is just one of the gang, whose opinion counts no more than the opinion of anyone else; where guidance is earnestly sought in prayer in troubled moments; then the Holy Spirit would guide the group into peaceful action and unanimity.

When considering the parish council or group of people selected to meet with the parish priest, Canon 536 #1 of the Canon Law Code, states that the pastor presides over such a parish council. As a part of the People of God whose *Amen* is anxiously awaited, we choose to recognize this presiding as a suggestion, and not as a binding final law. It seems that other presiders should be tried, such as rotating presiders, and that a particular presider for a divisive issue should preferably be a person who is unprejudiced on that issue. Canon 536 #2 gives the parish council a consultative vote only. This word *consultative* should be interpreted even more positively than the Baha'i manner of consultation, and should dispense with following the vote of the majority, so as to encourage true consensus. This consensus should be binding on the parish, unless a future meeting brings an opposing consensus, as is possible as new information on a topic becomes available. If a pastor of a parish has a council that agrees together on a matter, and if he is a true pastor in loving unity with his parish, he will naturally follow the plans on which his council agrees.

It is easy to form a poor parish council and to be discouraged with the results. Careful planning is necessary on the parts of both pastor and parishioners, in order to form a cooperative consultative group that feels it is really being heard. The importance of the council should be insured through an annual parish assembly where the whole parish is given the opportunity to give input and to choose parish council members. It is important to keep the roots of the parish fresh and vigorous. There is no point in polishing "the top of the ecclesial pyramid while its baseline withers away."[3] The spontaneity and strength available in the parish council is seen in the action of the first such council described in Acts 2, where a group of people in the power of consensus, put concerned love into history.

Canon 537 describes the finance council of the parish. The pastor is not mentioned as presiding here, as in Canon 536 for the parish council. It is recognized that the pastor may not be the financial wizard of the group. 537 is a more realistic canon than 536. 536 should recognize that the pastor, as drawn from the group to serve as chief liturgist, is not necessarily equipped to be the presiding officer over meetings to discuss a variety of topics. There seem to be fewer frustrations with finance councils, as they are usually run on a more consentaneous basis.

9.4 CONSENSUS IN CHURCH STRUCTURES ASSOCIATED WITH THE BISHOP

As we rise up from the parish level in the hierarchical structure, we find that a group of parishes are under the care of a bishop in an area of church governance called the diocese. The pastoral council, the priests council, and the diocesan synod are three groups of people described in the Code of Canon Law, that can be of great aid to this presiding bishop. The pastoral council, made up of selected heads of parishes or otherwise assigned priests in the diocese, is to be convened by the bishop at least once a year (Canon 514 #2) to assist the bishop with pastoral affairs. Progressive bishops who are willing to listen can invite the pastoral council to meet even more frequently than the four times a year that its by-laws provide.[4]

The priests council (whose members are appointed by the

bishop and by the priests themselves), assists the bishop with organizational matters and the governance of the diocese. This council has a vote on certain issues, but its voice is usually consultative, again with the meaning that the bishop can ignore the proffered advice. Giving this freedom of action to the bishop, leaves a positive and progressive bishop, free room for a trial of the process of consensus, especially if when he presides (as he should according to Canon 500), he does it in an unobtrusive manner. A lot more is learned in a meeting when everyone sits in a circle, including the presider, and everyone is given a chance to speak. In like manner a seminar type class is usually more productive of learning than a lecture by a teacher confronting the students.

The bishop (Canon 462) can also convene a diocesan synod on the advice of the priests council, if a problem that needs airing, comes up in the diocese. The make-up of this diocesan synod can be very heterogeneous. Much valuable input as to the mind of the laity, can be disseminated from such a gathering. Many women feel strongly that they should be allowed to become deacons and priests in name as well as in their actions of service. If this subject could be aired at well-represented diocesan synods, having both pros and cons invited to participate, we might see consensus in action. Canon 465 assures women that if they get invited as a delegate to the synod and the subject is women priests, they will be heard. "All questions proposed are to be subject to the free discussion of the members in the sessions of the synod." Two other issues that need intelligent and open consideration are capital punishment and the place in society of those oriented homosexually. If the church is to achieve a living law, it is necessary to collect living people together, to discuss issues, under the guidance of the Spirit.

Having pastoral councils and diocesan synods are steps in the right direction, but will they really work to implement guidance by the Holy Spirit? Under a classicist type bishop, they could be no more effective than a cocktail party. Under our present system, conservative bishops are being appointed by conservative superiors. If we are to grow and change in the direction of human fulfillment, it is necessary to have progressive leadership listening to the grassroots. It takes an open-minded bishop to convene a synod, and much cooperation among all members of the church to carry through with requested reforms.

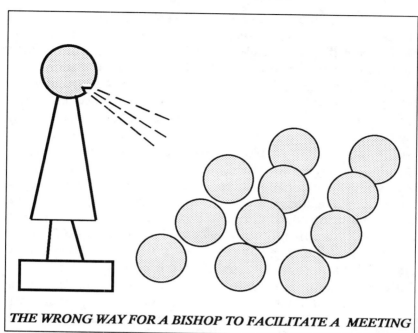

THE WRONG WAY FOR A BISHOP TO FACILITATE A MEETING

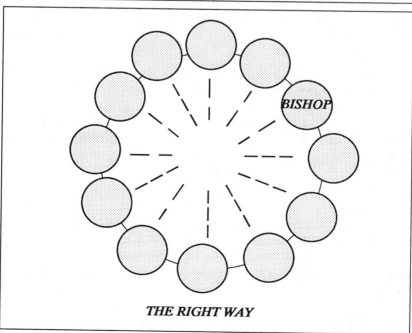

THE RIGHT WAY

Bishops themselves can meet in supportive groups to discuss issues. If an episcopal conference or meeting of bishops is being held, a counciling group called a particular council may be called to supply information and advice. Particular councils (Canons 439-446) and episcopal conferences (Canons 447-459) have great possibilities for being effective in their governance procedures. The councils must respect the laws of the church, but on their own, they have certain legislative powers. Their purpose is to ensure that the pastoral needs of the people of God in their territories, are provided for (Canon 445). "(The council) can, therefore, determine whatever seems opportune for an increase of faith, for the ordering of common pastoral action, for the direction of morality, and for the preservation, introduction and defense of a common ecclesiastical discipline." Note that these councils can introduce a specific ecclesiastical discipline, such as acceptance of women as servers on the altar, and that they can determine what is needful for making the faith more relevant to teen agers and other questioning individuals in their care. After determining the relevancy of an issue, they can order a common pastoral action that enforces and displays the equality of slave and free, Jew and Gentile, male and female, priests and laity. Unfortunately, the flow of living water from particular councils can be turned off at the tap by the faucet labeled *consultative only* (Canon 466). Again, it is to be hoped that if there is a consensus of opinion, that a bishop or pope who has the best interests of his people in mind, will interpret *consultative* to mean *consentaneous*.

When looking for positive examples of consentaneous church government, we find that there are items in the code that should be noted and encouraged. There are possibilities of rotating leadership with the episcopal conferences (meetings of bishops), as each conference elects its own president (Canon 452). This process of rotating leadership selection seems to be necessary for the truly consentaneous meeting. Each of the church governing bodies described in the code, should have this same leader selection process.

According to Canon 455, Section 4, the conference can't act in the name of all the bishops unless each and every bishop has given his consent, which is also a very consentaneous statement! The aims of an episcopal conference (Canon 447) are very noble:- "to promote, in accordance with the law, that greater good which the

Church offers to all people." If bishops and priests are encouraged to activate these aims, and there is a minimum of infighting for power slots, these bodies could become models of wise governance.

In meditating on positive changes in code interpretation, it becomes obvious how carefully organized the church is. If you have well organized and thoughtfully built structures, it is very difficult for an unqualified person who happens to gain leadership or wants to assert power, to totally damage them. The structures can be lightly binding (like a tea bag, with its tea) allowing ideas and spirit to flow freely. Then, poor leadership, either clerical or lay, becomes less important, and wise guidance from other members of the group, has opportunity to encourage growth.

For consultative and consentaneous church governance, it is necessary to begin with small groups of people, and then to send one person to represent each of these groups to a secondary group (such as a parish council). The second step would be to have one member from each secondary group be selected by the group to go to a third larger area group (such as a vicariate, a vicariate being a section of a diocese). This vicariate group should select one of its members to convene with the next group from an area still larger, such as the diocese. Those lay people selected to represent different diocese, could join in a state or country meeting of Catholics, both lay people and those ordained.

There are several things wrong with the selection process presently used in the Catholic Church. The first problem is that the selection in the local parishes is not done by base communities of about thirty individuals. The average parishioner doesn't care who is put on the parish council, and is willing to let the priest assume full responsibility for running the parish. Truly covenanted people should be willing to assume their share of responsibility for government.

Another problem is that bishops are not selected by their constituents or from among the people they serve, which keeps a conservative stranglehold on church governance. Furthermore, lay consultants from the base communities are not seated in collegiality when the bishops meet in episcopal conference. Those in positions of power in the church assume that if you leave representation up to a rather random voting system, that those chosen from the base gatherings will not be educated enough to write pastorals on peace and the economy. However, if the church were organized with more freedom, the Holy Spirit might find qualified people, drawn from these base communities, who might even have degrees in economics, or have actually suffered economic oppression, and whose ideas might be more relevant than someone with a background in ancient languages and liturgy. With fewer vocations to the priesthood, we may have to consider this more random method of selecting leaders from among the people, in thirty years, or sooner.

9.5 CELIBACY AS CONTRIBUTING TO A CLOSED SOCIETY

A further problem in the above groupings, is the homogeneity of councils at "higher" levels. It is fairly easy to get a basic consensus (that may not necessarily represent the feelings of the total community) when all members of the group are cut from the same cloth. Much more is learned at a truly consentaneous meeting of people from widely varying backgrounds. If we are all God's people, by right of God's creating us, and if we all have something of God's Spirit in us, it seems that a more heterogeneous grouping for the final consentaneous decisions, would be in order.

The Holy Spirit working in the code recognizes this need, and gives us the means to broaden the variety of the individuals at these meetings. These individuals are all celibate males with theological educations. To have more heterogeneous participation at these councils, we should consider the question of celibacy. We should first see what the Bible and tradition have to say about the problem. Then we should investigate the Spirit of the code in relation to celibacy.

The church made celibacy a law, in order to better control church property.[5] St. Thomas Aquinas, who died in 1274 had a lot to do with present church misconceptions on celibacy. Thomas based his sexual information on guesses of Aristotle, and on Augustine's interpretation of the role of women. Thomas agreed with Augustine that sexual contact as in the married state pulls down the mind from its lofty heights and thus destroys a good relationship with God. This is an obvious misconception. Neither Thomas or Augustine evidently had the experience of two loving Christians offering their love in thanksgiving to the Communal Creator of Community. No one told them in a consensus-type meeting about a loving God who created this sex urge in both male and female and said, "This is good!"

In 1563 the Council of Trent (no women allowed) affirmed the weak positions of Augustine and Thomas (and thus Aristotle) with its tenth canon: "If anyone says that the married state surpasses that of virginity or celibacy, and that it is not better and happier to remain in virginity or celibacy than to be united in matrimony, anathema sit."[6] This statement may be true for each individual who participated at that council, but we need to get consensus from councils with more diverse representation. It is easy to see that the opinion of these men originated from the misconception that they had based their life on, and viewed from a more understanding generation, the whole situation is very sad. If you are a celibate priest and you have become celibate in order that you might be given the reward of the priesthood, you are not about to let your conscious mind admit that there may be some defect with celibacy.

In order not to be squeezed under the Trent anathema, I should like to say that there is something good in celibacy. Metz considers the three vows of poverty, chastity, and obedience, and has the following positive observations.[7] Poverty is a visible sign to the poor of solidarity with them. Celibacy is a sign to the lonely, of the religious person's acceptance of loneliness. Obedience is a sign to those such as slaves and women and the oppressed, of solidarity with them. These reflections of Metz obviously go beyond the concerns of religious orders, and can be participated in by all those who are so inclined. They should be optional signs, in a similar manner as fasting in Lent is an optional sign of solidarity with the hungry. Displaying these signs should not be something into which one is coerced. The Trent directive with its anathema can be interpreted as saying that those who have freely chosen to be celibate, had better believe that celibacy is the best state of life for them. However, with full representation at Trent they might easily have concluded that each one should be able to choose his or her own preference, and that no person or organization should criticize another's preferred state of life.

With this background on the basics of celibacy, let us look at the Code of Canon Law to see where it might give an opening to new thinking on this matter. If one gives heed to God's inspired word, it is easy to believe with the psalmist (Psalm 119:105) that the law "is a lamp to my feet, and a light to my path." If one pours over and pursues this law, one will find oneself wandering in the foot prints of other human beings who have meditated and who have been inspired by Spirit to try new ways of service to love. There is wonder and beauty to law, captured in language by those who have dreamed dreams for the human's fulfillment in a community under God. The greatest lawgiver was Christ, who entered into the stream of humanity with his *law of love*, who himself was the living example of what was possible for human fulfillment, and who was the final Word on centuries of humanity putting together frail little human words in an instrument that they believed would lift them closer to their God.

Jesus came as the fulfillment of the law, but we are still busy putting down words to interpret Jesus. We are still awaiting the time when the Word will be in each human heart. The words we use in the code must enable us to create new forms of loving service, they must help us to modify and perfect existing forms, and they must give us the strength to restructure forms that no longer serve any positive purpose. The words of the code should help us to abolish obligatory celibacy and to encourage optional celibacy as a sign of solidarity with the lonely.

The code is standing ready to help us with this problem. Canon 219 tells us that all Christ's faithful have the right to immunity from any kind of coercion in choosing a state in life. The question is not celibacy;- it is coercion to celibacy. Canon 219 is firmly against any human being being forced into celibacy.

In looking for the code's reason for celibacy, we must go to Canon 277 in which 277 Section 1 contradicts 277 Section 2, and then in Section 3 gives the local bishop the right to ease the situation. Section 1 states that "celibacy is a special gift of God by which sacred ministers can more easily remain close to Christ with an undivided heart, and can dedicate themselves more freely to the service of God and their neighbor." God gives this gift of restraint in varying quantities to different individuals, and a particular priest may find this gift rather limited when the neighbor he is called to serve is a glamorous woman. Section 2 finds it more important for the priest to maintain his prideful virtue of celibacy, than to expose himself to scandalous talk in the process of helping a subset of needy Christians. Celibacy is an obligation forced upon the priest from outside himself, which causes him problems in personal relationships, so that, according to Section 2, he has to avoid a certain category of Christian. Section 3 of Canon 277 gives a solution to the dilemma. The bishop can dispense with celibacy if he finds he isn't getting enough priests with undivided hearts, with which to serve the total Christian community.

We find that custom is the best interpreter of the law (according to Canon 27). It is true that celibacy is a centennial custom, having been around for over one hundred years, but it is also true that there was a time when celibacy was not the custom. We admit Episcopalian priests who are married into our community, as their customs differ from ours. If two customs exist side by side, they are both legal options. It seems as if the Code of Canon Law is putting it up to the bishop to present the choice of whether or not to be celibate, to his clerics.

The final argument has to do with divine law. Celibacy is not divine law. It is not natural law. Total celibacy of the human race is against divine law. If total celibacy is practiced, that is the end of the human race. God's command as given to Noah, is the opposite, "Go forth and multiply!" Recognizing the problems of humanity (Matthew 19:12), divine law permits occasional celibacy. If a priest chooses to be a sign to humanity of solidarity with the lonely, or to mirror how things will be when we rise from the dead, than celibacy is a good sign, but it is only a sign. However, if the loneliness to be endured in celibacy is to be supported by some manner of common life (as described in Canon 280), then it seems that women are being denigrated. Men are not undertaking celibacy in order to be lonely; they are undertaking celibacy in order to have male companionship. The problem being brought to the fore is the inferiority of female companionship. Half the human community are creatures who are temptations and irritations to the priest who is called forth from them to serve them!

St. Thomas, St. Augustin, and Aristotle had many positive ideas, but as they were human, they were bound to make a few mistakes. They should have discussed celibacy in a consensus circle made up of fifty per cent women. Other ideas of St. Thomas reflect a wider range of consultants. Looking at Thomas Aquinas' definition of law as reason bringing order into the community in the service of the common good, I find the law open to optional celibacy. *Coerced* celibacy is not for the common good, or for the individual good.

Optional celibacy is reasonable. Also reasonable is allowing married men to be priests, as we do not have enough priests to properly serve the Catholic community.

9.6 SEXISM AS CONTRIBUTING TO A CLOSED SOCIETY

If men don't take the time to find out what women are thinking, how can they represent that thought in community meetings? How can they serve the female subcommunity? They can best serve women if they lovingly invite women to join their group as equal members. The Code recognizes this equality in many of its canons, and in particular in Book I Part I Title I where it gives the obligations and rights of all Christ's faithful. Canon 208 proclaims that there is "a genuine equality of dignity and action among all of Christ's faithful." Canon 212 assures us that the "faithful are at liberty to make known their needs." Canon 214 says that the faithful "have the right to follow their own form of spiritual life, provided it is in accord with Church teaching." Canon 219 emphasizes that "All Christ's faithful have the right to immunity from any kind of coercion in choosing a state in life." This last code interpreted freely, means that women can choose to be priests if they feel that that is the state of life to which they are called. The New Code of Canon Law is very open to all sorts of possibilities of loving community.

The various church governing councils would function with greater understanding if half of their members were women. The Holy Spirit shows her care best, where people of many varying opinions gather and show love and concern for one another. If one observed the actions of women in groups and men in groups, they would see that their separate patterns of behavior compliment one another. The woman is usually interested in maintaining pleasant personal relationships while the man's method is to have the group decide on rules and regulations that will make the group run smoothly. It would be interesting to see if the Pastoral Council of the bishop would function more effectively if half its members were women intent on making the group into a happy and contented family. Most of the Code of Canon Law is written with this possibility of women priests in mind.

In considering the prerequisites for ordination, we see that

Canons 1033 to 1054 are all applicable to women. Canon 1037 has a problem with celibacy, but not with women. Canon 1041 Section 3 also specifies celibacy, but 1041 Section 4 seems specifically addressed to women in the notation that excludes those who procure abortions, from the priesthood. At first glance it appears that only women fit into the category of being able to have an abortion. However, this canon can be interpreted to mean any other person who assists the woman to have an abortion. Canon 378 with its qualifications for bishops doesn't exclude women, as long as women are eligible to make it to the priesthood. Unfortunately it does set up stratifying educational standards. All wise humans do not have the opportunity for graduate education.

Some canons, such as Canon 235, speak of young *men* who intend to become priests. It doesn't exclude young women; it just doesn't mention them. If we understand the term *men* generically, we find the Code very open to the idea of women in the priesthood, and thus open to fresh inspiration and love in the leadership of the community. There is a problem with Canon 1024 which states that "only a baptized *man* can validly receive sacred ordination." If we choose to think of this canon generically as speaking of a baptized *human*, then we can read into it that only baptism is necessary for ordination.

Unfortunately, those of the hierarchy who have the task of interpreting the law, understand this word *man* rather firmly, as the opposite of *woman*. They do not admit to the possibility of changes in language and social customs gradually taking place in the last two thousand years. The position of the Vatican is that no women were ever apostles. In believing this, they ignore the fact that the Bible states when Jesus rose from the dead, he commissioned his friend Mary to go and apostolize the brethren who had deserted him. The Vatican feels that as Jesus was a man, no woman can properly represent him as priest. If we are going to exclude one set of human beings from priesthood because of a dissemblance, we perhaps should also exclude all who do not physically resemble Jesus, such as non-Jews, those of a different blood type, those with different color eyes, etc. But God did not call us to be excluders. Truly loving Christians know that God is fond of diversity, and that love can accept and unite diverse elements, for the greater fulfillment of all.

If the sacrament of ordination is to be denied to women, then the Vatican should be consistent, and also deny them the sacrament of baptism. The church teaches that in baptism, women and men equally share the identity of Christ. We put on Christ (Romans 13:14). With baptism, women have the same relationship with Christ as men do. It seems that ordination should work in the same manner as baptism, Christ himself supplying our lack, so that both men and women could be responsible servers of the community. Communities do not need authoritative fathers, as much as they need responsible servers. Jesus warned his followers against docile submission to authority with good reason. Exercising power, keeps those in authority very busy, and they don't find the time to listen to others, or to see the equality of others. Those in power should make it their business to accept input from those they consider to be the weaker and humbler members of the community, so that they will be able to dwell in loving consensus with all.

9.7 CODE INTERPRETERS MUST CONSIDER CUSTOM

Celibacy contributes to much misunderstanding among members of the community. No one should practice celibacy from coercion, but only from a true desire to signify the Queendom/Kingdom of God as being present. When our hearts become God's territory, there will not be a need for strict interpretations of rules and regulations. When we all affirm one another in love, then we will make full use of one another's capabilities. Patriarchy in society has devalued the intelligence and capabilities of women for countless generations. "From the beginning, it was not so" (Mark 10:6). God created all peoples to be capable of loving community and to have possibilities of living together in a peaceful world. True consentaneous community is possible only when there is humbleness of self and openness to the other person. The New Code gives adequate room to immediately further the loving objectives of equality in community.

Let's get on with building this loving community! What is holding us back? Persons in authority in the structure of the Catholic Church want to keep things running in the same manner as they have run for centuries. They feel more secure on *terra firma*. They do not hear the Christ telling them to get out of the safe boat and walk to him on the water. They do not understand that growth requires change, and that if humanity is to *move* onward towards fulfillment, there must be movement. The rules and regulations that these authority structures have drawn up, have been guided by the Holy Spirit and are ready to blossom and to bear fruit. If women are not allowed to influence immediate change by their voice and action, surely their prayers will be heard, and God's justice and righteousness will flow through the earth as water flows into an open cavity.

The Code of Canon Law itself tells us that custom is the best interpreter of law (Canon 27).[8] There is a distinct possibility that women had an equal share in church guidance in former times. This custom should be reactivated. Tradition takes precedence over present day interpretations. When one is in doubt about a previous law or tradition, "the revocation of a previous law is not presumed; rather, later laws are to be related to earlier ones and, as far as possible, harmonized with them" (Canon 21). I should like to challenge the interpreters of canon law, to harmonize their present day regulations on celibacy and female participation with the customs of the early church. Seeing the New Canon Law is so open to it, I would also like to see its visions of true consentaneous community tested in order to harmonize with and to fulfill the practices of the original Pentecost community.

Seeing that the true brotherhood/sisterhood of those with Christian hearts is such a serious matter for the existence of the Queendom/Kingdom of God among us, the canon law issues that are raised here are very important and should be researched thoroughly. To assume that a woman, or a married man, is unable to participate fully in leading the worship community, is not a Christian attitude. If Bible scholars prove satisfactorily that women and married men were accepted as apostles, and thus as community leaders, by Jesus, then those responsible for the implementation of canon law should do their best to encourage this type of leadership. True community is built by the cooperation of equals.

To install one particular leader as a person closer to God than all the others in the community, is not realistic. It encourages the person so selected to think of himself as superior to the rest of the members of the group. He loses objectivity, and comes to believe that his beliefs are the correct beliefs. Thus we have the pope proclaiming himself infallible in certain matters. In reality, popes come closest to the wisdom of God when they listen to the voice of the Spirit speaking through the people. Some priests or leaders are warped by power phenomena and come to believe that they can do no wrong. It is best to rotate group leadership frequently, or even to use a disinterested person to receive the information engendered in the group. This disinterested person, or machine, then can tabulate the output of the group, without unnecessary comment. Catholics do not need to abdicate their right to decision making, to any man immersed in an idiosyncratic cultural milieu. "Do not put your trust in men in power, or in any mortal man - he cannot save" (Psalm 146:3).

9.8 THE RISK INVOLVED IN EXPERIMENTATION

The Catholic Church as a responsible religious organization firmly seeking the betterment of all the people of the world, has the duty to experiment freely with the forms of government that it has suggested in its Code of Canon Law. If it shows the form of a successful community to the rest of the world, especially to secular organizations, then these organizations may be tempted to follow suit. If there is no lead community to demonstrate how a peaceful community can be run effectively, for the good of all its members, then there will be no pattern to follow. The Catholic Church, as infused with the Spirit of God, should run an organization that displays the mind and heart of God.

As bishops are given a certain amount of freedom in calling meetings of their constitutents, they could easily gather consultative groups together to discover the feelings of fellow members of their church, on the important subject of women and married priests. Also discussed could be the related subject of servants to the community, as opposed to authoritative leaders. A solution to the problem of a lack of celibate priests needs to be addressed. Do we really need one particular person to always lead the congregation if all God's people are prophets, priests, and kings? Is there a place for male elitism in the truly holy community? There is a risk involved when an institution examines its structures, but no one will deny the wisdom of checking over an old building for possible termite damage.   If checking over the structures and implementing positive ideas, leads to a better world, the examination is worth the trouble.

10

COVENANT

AND

CONSENSUS

IN THE PRISON SYSTEM

10.1 THE DESIRE FOR ORDER

When we look back at our discussion on how God might work in the universe, we see that there is order maintained, but sometimes this order is difficult to envision. The same might be true when we shift our gaze to the process of crime and punishment. If we look at prison systems across the world, our first reaction might be to shudder in horror at man's inhumanity to man. Organizations such as Amnesty International are continually apprising us of individuals tortured for their beliefs, or imprisoned without trial, who are subjected to the whims of their captors. We are in deep sympathy for those thus imprisoned, but we anguish even more for the spiritual well-being of those who are led into doing the torturing. How can they live with themselves when they have been so cruel to another human being? How can leaders of states imprison opponents of their oppression, when they, and the whole nation, might profit from working to-gether? How do those who guard our Berlin walls feel inside when they gun down another human being whose only aim was to escape to a free way of life?

On the other hand, we can see joy when an officer who formerly prevented citizens crossing the line of the Berlin wall, is able to hand a rose to a West German citizen. We can see vast progress when the Communist government of Poland is able to work constructively with the ship workers' union which it formerly op-

posed. Often peace and order grow out of what seem like insurmountable situations. God works in strange ways in the affairs of
humans. She/He can use a Cyrus of Persia or a Gorbachev of Russia
to give freedom to people whom they have never met.

We can see God at work in the universe even though
nebulae explode and meteorites crash upon us. We admire God's
handiwork as the massive planet Jupiter circles around our local star,
the sun, each celestial giant toeing its own line precisely. We can also
look at the prison structure and see its overseers as a group of men
anxious to find a solution to societal problems, who work very hard
at this project according to a predicated set of rules. Going back to
Jupiter and the sun, let us set up an analogy with the workers within
the prison system. We can picture this group of working individuals
as the sun, and visualize another group (comparable to Jupiter) that
goes according to another set of rules, and maintains a balance with
the emanations and properties of the sun, or first group. Perhaps
both Jupiter and the sun are necessary for us to see God at work.
Perhaps both an officer group and a balancing inmate group are
necessary in order for us to see God fully at work in the prisons.

If both those in charge of the corrections system, and those
incarcerated in the system have for a common purpose the psychological and spiritual restructuring of all individuals connected with
the system, then they would be in solidarity with each other. Viewing
the universe from our small piece of earth, we can see God at work
in the vastness. Detaching ourselves from the immediacy of the
prison system, and viewing it impersonally, we can also see God's
order in process. As people covenant within to do the best for each
other, as they work in groups to encourage non-violence and understanding, as they join in solidarity with opposing forces to achieve a
positive purpose, God's hand is evident.

Humankind desires a peaceful world. He does not want the
heavens crashing in on him. He does not relish earthquakes and
typhoons. He wants his government to avoid conflicts with other
nations and to keep peace within its own territory. We seem to
believe that to have order, there must be some authority around to
enforce that order. We expect God to keep order in the natural
sphere. We believe that God is in firm control of the gravity pressures in the heavens, and will help us to exist through the earthquakes that are necessary due to pressures within the earth. We

rather expect God or unknown forces to take care of major physical happenings, but we often do not credit God with the ability to take care of our everyday problems. Being not too sure of ourselves to handle these real life situations, we feel there must be someone more capable than we are, who will have the wisdom to guide us. Therefore we select authorities to direct us among the lesser pressures that are rampant on earth.

It is a separate question as to whether the just community really needs these governing authorities. If we all accepted our share of responsibility for what goes on, and lived with consideration and concern for our fellow human, perhaps we would not find religious guides or governmental leaders necessary. Truly covenanted individuals should not have to go to a religious specialist for his supposedly superior judgment on moral matters. This type of ethical consultation has a different aspect than a consultation with an auto mechanic who is going to repair your car, or with having a Greek language expert teach you Greek. Basic moral issues should be meditated on, and discussed in consensus circles. They have to do with growing the seed of God that is within each of us as created by God, and that also is within the community. We will always have to go to experts for help in tasks that have to do with our material affairs, as that type of knowledge has variations with time and culture, but dealings with people by people maintain a certain similarity across the flow of generations. We each have our needs, and we should each personally be able to work for better relationships, without creating father figures to tell us what to do. It is our insecurities and our shedding of responsibilities, that make us turn to authorities, and obey them on ethical issues, instead of listening to our inner reasonings. Often we find that the religious guides that we select may have psychological problems themselves. They may make love to the church secretary. They may comfort the bereaved widow sexually. Would be leaders often are themselves in need of the full consultation and support of their community.

So many of us look for authorities to back us up, rather than meditating on what might be God's will or just actions. We need both consultation and meditation to aid in the formation of our optimum inner strengths. Ultimately, we alone are responsible for our thoughts and actions. We cannot ever truly say, "The devil made me do it."

Abraham is an example of a person who thought things

through himself. He could not fall back on the authority of the Bible, and he refused to unquestioningly accept the idols of his father's household. Having many established religions, we are inclined to blindly follow their proclaimed leaders. Having the gift of God's word in the Bible, we accept others interpretations on what God is saying. That wonderful book written under the inspiration of God, condemns our trust in authorities. We do not heed Psalm 146:3. "Put not your trust in princes, or in any mortal man." We disobey the injunction in Matthew 23:9, "Call no one on earth your father, since you have only one Father, and he is in heaven."

However, due to our imperfections, the problem of authority is still very much with us. We seek a just society, and we want order in our lives. Thus we choose authorities to make judgments for us, and we allow them to build armies to control us when we object or disobey. We, the people, make it possible for others to be in authority. Once in a position of authority, with an armed force to back them up, it is difficult to dislodge those in high places with low morals and lack of concern for others. We can see this problem in some of the governments and prison systems around the world. When we look in this country at the prison systems, we can see that the situation is more positive. Those in authority are frequently individuals of high caliber, who are very concerned with rehabilitation of those trapped by poverty, drugs, and a fascination for weapons.

To increase order, rehabilitation, and self esteem in our prison systems, we must have a balance between the consensus of those in authority and the consensus of those incarcerated. We can see this balance as similar to the gravitational balance between the sun and Jupiter. They act in their own area, but they have a certain relationship to each other, and they have a common goal, which is to maintain order in the universe. To be in solidarity may be to go by different routes, but to work on a common purpose. The prison authorities and those incarcerated can be in solidarity with the common purpose of fulfillment of all that humanity connected with the prison system. The authorities have a distinct organization out of which they can work. It is necessary for those incarcerated to have a loose organization so that they also can voice their covenanted beliefs. An interlocking consensus circle of these two balancing groups would increase constructive order in the prison system.

10.2 FREEDOM OF ACTION

We have said that the most important ingredient of the ideal community is freedom. Would it be possible to have government by covenant and consensus inside barbed wire? If we are to consider order in a community as the result of freedom of action to guide itself, then prison may not be the place to experiment.

When there is a need for confined space and confining rules, as is certainly necessary with a two year old toddler, there must be other ingredients supplied by the caretakers, to encourage cooperation rather than negative reaction. With a child one can use gentle removal from danger, and humorous reasoning. With an adult convicted of a crime, it seems that other strategies are necessary.

Even before the crime is committed, we often find that the individual is not free. He is a prisoner of his society. He does not have satisfactory housing. He is not able to hold a job. His educational level is frequently below par. His life is one frustration after another. Through guns, drugs, and *acting out* he seeks to acquire the material goods and supposed achievement that he feels others have.

Upon conviction, he goes from the frying pan into the fire, for his crime puts him in further chains created by our laws. He is treated as still less of a human being, and given very little opportunity to explain his actions, even if he could. Being sentenced according to the law, he enters into the prison system with its own brand of societal legalities. Prison rules and regulations can be smothering and riot inducing. How can we inject a sense of personal freedom behind the walls of a prison?

10.3 PRISON REFORM:- INCENTIVES FOR PRISON PERSONNEL

The prison administration is not without knowledge of the problems of the incoming prisoner. Unfortunately, due to the influx of drug related cases, it is economically unable to supply enough qualified personnel to implement psychological know-how, and to rehabilitate. There is very little opportunity for the average 18 to 25 year old entering the system to hear the good news for the prisoner:- that you can choose in your heart to think kind thoughts, to contribute to the flow of life and love in the universe, and thus influence the world and all creation positively, in spite of a confining situation.

If funding allowed each sentenced inmate to be greeted at the prison reception center, by covenanted prison personnel, an inmate's stay in the correctional confines would be more profitable. In order for this to happen, there is a need for dedicated personnel. An understanding group of inmates at New York State's Otisville Correctional Institution came up with a plan for attracting correctional officers who could assist them in making their prison stay profitable, thus easing their return to society.

They called their recipe for fulfilled officers, *The Campaign for Correctional Professionalism*. Its aim was to set up higher standards for corrections officers, who would be able to minister to and to rehabilitate convicted felons, and thus to ease tensions. These professionals would also serve as role models for felons, reducing the recidivisim rate, and thus lowering the prison population.

It was suggested that there be a one year training for correction officers which would include:

1. *Psychological evaluations*
2. *Training in non-violence techniques*
3. *Training in counseling*
4. *Training in behavior modification techniques*
5. *Training in leadership dynamics*

The requirements for this one year training would be:

1. *BA or BS in behavioral sciences*
2. *must be between 25 years old and under 50*
3. *knowledge of management techniques*

The salary (1989 levels) would encourage participation:

1. *$20,000 during training*
2. *$25,000 during 1 yr. probation and re-evaluation*
3. *$30,000 once accepted*
4. *salary increases annually based on performance with periodic review up to ten years, with tenure*
5. *supervisor's test mandatory after 10 years*

This program for correction officers also could be given to qualified inmates near their release date, who would wish to hold a job in the corrections system after completing their sentence. What better way to get empathetic employees?

There is a higher officer to inmate ratio in Chinese prisons than there is in U.S. prisons as there is great desire to resocialize the felon and make him into a profitable member of society. There is less recidivism as a result of this program. However, this positive recidivism rate is only operative for those convicted of lesser crimes. In the Chinese system the death penalty is applied more frequently, and in such cases, of course, no rehabilitation is possible, which also would explain the low recidivism rate. Inmates in the Chinese system may prefer to stay and work in the prisons and rehabilitate other incoming inmates, rather than to return to their own neighborhood where they feel they have been a cause of shame.

A good educational background is not all that is needed for an inspired and covenanted officer in the corrections field. Many persons with excellent educations remain the prisoners of their own selfish egos. Often knowledge and education can be used to cruelly enforce one's own authority on a less powerful group. The dedicated officer must also have the good of each and every inmate in mind. He (or she) must see clearly his part in society as supporter and role model. He must be able to build self esteem in others through his solidarity with positive progress in society throughout the world. He must be in consensus with his fellow officers and sensitive to their needs. Constructive personal qualities in official personnel are immediately noticed by those inmates of whom they are put in charge.

10.4 PROGRAMS AND SUPPORT GROUPS FOR THE INMATE

It is not so difficult to build self esteem in people. Each person really wants to believe what is best about himself. It is necessary to give each inmate the opportunity to learn about himself, and to learn abilities that will help him to get along in society. For this we need positive prison programs that assist inmates to become covenanted and responsible individuals.

In becoming a covenanted individual each inmate that enters the corrections system should be given an opportunity to choose his program, and decide how he could best spend his time in prison. If his sentence could be seen as an opportunity to improve himself and to make amends to those he has wronged, then it would be better than viewing it as a punishment to be dragged through day after monotonous day. If we are seeking the fulfillment of all humanity, the prison system is a good place to start. There are so many wrongs to be righted. There are so many voids of ignorance to be filled with knowledge. If a covenantal process could be initiated for every entering inmate, then personal growth and fulfillment could take place behind the ugly cement walls and barbed wire.

The first problem that must be addressed when an inmate enters prison is the justness of his sentence. He may not even be guilty. He may have acted in self defense. He may be paying back someone for something that was inflicted on him. He may be guilty of his crime, and eager to make amends. He may be guilty of much more than he has been charged with. In all this, the inmate should be given the chance to speak with a confidential counselor on how he feels. If he believes that his sentence is unjust, if he was framed, he must be given help in having a rehearing. His viewpoint must be heard, in order for there to be justice. If he admits his crime and wants to compensate his victim, some program must be put in place, so that victim-offender reconciliation can occur. If one accepts ones sentence as just, one is more likely to serve that sentence responsibly.

After one has an adequate supply of covenanted correctional officers, the next need is for inspirational programs to offer to inmates, both covenanted or uncovenanted. To serve a sentence responsibly, and to get maximum benefit from the time behind the barbed wire, there must be helpful programs available. The largest section of the prison clientele is made up of substance abusers. Our prisons are being filled up with men and women who have gotten mixed up with drugs, alcohol, and guns. What is often needed in prison are the resources of a drug rehabilitation center. Drug free individuals need a supporting community, and a personal commitment to do their best. Forming such a positive community of dedicated inmates within the prison walls, would make the job of the correction officers easier.

A second group that needs support to maintain inner harmony are the sex offenders. They are generally very reticent about their crime, as other offenders shun them for it, but they need group therapy similar to that of the drug and alcohol abusers. Only recently has their need been noted in the prison system, and psychological group counseling been implemented.

Besides the special needs of those addicted, there is the everyday need of being self supporting. We should put prisoners to work and also get them educated. Many inmates are in prison because they were improperly educated and couldn't find fulfilling jobs. If the legalisms were worked out with unions, we could turn correctional institutions into factories and schools. In the Swedish prison system, labor unions train men in prison for various tasks, and then have those qualified join their unions upon release. Union members in this country object to the competition given to them by prison inmates, who can manufacture goods for less. Prisons are often hampered in giving creative jobs to inmates, as goods made by state prison inmates can only be used within state institutions.

The pay for inmate work in most prisons in this country is ridiculously low, hardly enough to buy hair shampoo or a can of tuna at the prison store. While these items may not be necessary as the prison supplies basic needs, it is a further blow to ones self esteem not to be able to afford to pay for gimmicks, and not having the right to choose and make decisions. Prisoners should have the chance to be trained in factory jobs, and produce goods for outside consumption. They should be paid a reasonable wage, and they should have the opportunity to learn how to manage their own money. This money management should include the willingness to pay recompense to a victim, as well as to give support to their families. Under such an arrangement the state would save welfare money owed to the wife and children of the felon, who are punished for his mistake by the degrading methods of welfare, although they are innocent of his crime. The state also might save welfare money that would go to the family of the victim. A covenanted inmate would be able to use pay from his prison job to compensate a victim, or to support the victim's family, thus increasing his own self esteem.

It is more difficult to say that an inmate should be given a stipend if he chooses to acquire a college education while serving his prison sentence. It seems like rewarding him for bad behavior. We might have young persons committing crimes so that they could get a paid-for college degree. Those interested in education should plan their programs for a combination of work and study. Those working towards a degree in psychology and counseling should be pressed into service as prison support personnel. They could be advisors for incoming felons, and the facilitators for drug, alcohol, and sex offender programs. Those going after a health related program, or desiring to help fill the shortage of nurses, would be assigned in the prison Aids or hospital units. In New York State there is already in place a theological degree program, whose participants assist the prison chaplains. Also to be implemented as viable programs to provide marketable life skills for those incarcerated, could be computer operations, business administration, barbering, cosmetology, and para legal work. Such work-study programs to educate and increase self-esteem should also be in place in the community for the sake of potential offenders.

The state has expressed its interest in the general education of all students up to the age of eighteen. It seems that in the case of failure to educate, that the state should encourage those individuals in prison who were unable to get their highschool diploma. Often an undiagnosed learning disability is at the seat of their personal problems. The under-educated offender should be given special educational help and adequate pay for the housekeeping jobs in the prison complex, so that they, too, would be able to support their families, and learn financial management.

Some in-prison activity can take place without established programs. As with most situations, people are given a choice. Even in its present form the prison system in the United States offers the inmate alternatives. The first option that many of those who enter the prison system exercise, is to do time in self-enforced solitude. Many believe that if they stay to themselves, they will stay out of trouble. A second option offenders have is to go with a gang. They can congregate with those of similar race or religious belief, and show by their attitude that they don't want to have anything to do with inmates of different leanings. Attitudes like this have possibilities of fomenting racial and religious hatreds. The third option is to learn a new way of forming community, by associating freely with those who differ racially, culturally, or religiously. They can respect the other's opinions and their personal pride in being who they are. Each inmate, male or female, can do all this through his own choice by determined covenantal action.

Even though this type of activity can take place on a personal level, in some prisons there are groups that will assist the inmate in this broadminded pursuit. Some chaplains encourage positive community relations by organizing interfaith groups where inmates can exchange ideas and learn about each other's beliefs in a non-threatening atmosphere. If people in crowded prisons can exercise this third option in order to better racial and religious attitudes, it seems that we in the outside world who are under less tension, should certainly be able to change our negative and stereotyping ways.

10.5 MEDIATION AND THE PRISON SYSTEM

Besides undergoing education, job training, and cultural broadening, inmates should be trained in non-violence techniques. They should have experiential training in community building, and in the facilitation of support programs.

Mediation is a tool that would be useful to the dedicated individuals in the prison system, both officers and inmates. There are six ways where mediation can be considered that relate to the prisoner: (1) mediation between inmate and inmate, (2) mediation between inmate and guarding officer, (3) between prison employees, (4) between inmates and people outside the prison, (5) mediation as an activity that would be useful for an ex-inmate to use on the street, either officially or unofficially, and (6) victim-offender reconciliation.

Inmate versus inmate mediation would make for a less inflammable and therefore a more secure facility, and would also have economic advantages. Those inmates caught in physical conflict with each other are usually given time in solitary confinement. Special officers for solitary confinement make the budget mount up! Doubling of officers due to tense situations raises the budget! When two men are put in the *box* (solitary confinement), they are usually separated as far from each other as possible, and when their solitary punishment is served, one or both will be shipped out to different prisons. If they meet each other again in their various prison transfers, they will still have the same grudge, and feel called upon to refight the same fight to save their honor. If they could be given the opportunity to have a mediation session, they might come to a better understanding of the whole situation. If some of their *box* time were cancelled as a result of a positive mediation agreement, money would be saved, and other inmates, viewing this example, might find it more profitable to seek mediation instead of confrontation.

Who would do this mediation? Perhaps a mix of inmates and officers could be used as a mediating team, or perhaps two inmates, as mediators, with no officer in the room, would be more successful in getting the disputants to make a verbal agreement. There are possible drawbacks to inmate mediations. Inmate mediators might be open to bribes (such as packs of cigarettes) as is the prison custom. Also, any mediators would have to watch their image. Would they be looked upon as snitches? Would they hold to their promise of confidentiality? In the high schools where mediations are set up, it is known that if a student mediator breaches his confidentiality, he will be removed from his post. As he values his assignment as mediator, he holds his tongue. The same stipulation could be made for the prison mediator.

It should not be necessary to screen out the violent inmates for suitability as mediators. In the school systems where mediation is employed, it has been shown that the *at risk* students make the better mediators, as they have a greater understanding of the problems under discussion.

Some prisons have a special program area where positive proceedings in inmate versus officer mediation is under experimentation. There is also the tier system in some prisons where an inmate can get a rehearing on an unfavorable report from an officer. The tier system is based on due process. Small infractions (tier 1 tickets) go immediately to a sergeant, and an inmate can then give his side of the story. Tier 2 tickets are reviewed by a lieutenant or higher, and for the most serious, tier 3, the superintendent assigns a special hearing.

If it seems like a particular officer is harassing a specific inmate, he can claim a grievance, and have it investigated. In both the instances of ticketing and grievance, mediation is not used, and the parties leave the situation without learning what goes on in the mind of the other person. It might be a very time consuming procedure to mediate every ticket that was handed out, but it seems that in the case of possible harassment by a particular officer on a particular inmate, a mediation would clear the air better than a submission of grievance. Perhaps in a covenant-consensus prison

unit both grievances and tickets could be mediated, and such procedures would help to increase self-esteem in both officers and inmates.

Relationships between inmate and officer don't have to be
a case of *WE* versus *THEM*. It is not necessary to be overbearing,
because one is wearing a uniform. If you have established a reputation for being a reasonable officer, open to mediation and willing to
listen, it is possible to deliver a ticket without violence, and to
maintain self respect.

Mediation among members of the correctional staff would
have to be voluntary on the part of the personnel. They have a
serious job to do, and may not see eye-to-eye with each other on how
to best do it. They, too, need their consensus groups and their times
for meditating on covenantal attitudes. They must see the humanity
in the persons whom they are charged to guard. The state mandates
in-service training for its officers. Instead of having them perfect
their target practice (within hearing distance of the inmate population) let them perfect attitudes of non-violence and understanding.
A good army does not run solely on marksmanship, but depends
heavily on the psychological health of its members.

Inmates and people who are associated with them, positively
or negatively, on the outside may profit from mediation. When inmates leave the prison situation, they encounter many problems.
Both women and men leaving prison often want to regain custody of
their children. It might be helpful to have a mediation between an
inmate and his outside family. Social services can help in mediations
of this type.

Another problem is the explosive situation that an inmate
may have left behind in his old neighborhood. Often there is someone out on the street who has a score to settle, or with whom the
inmate wants to settle a score. If these antagonists could be voluntar-
ily brought together, and have their situations mediated by local
volunteer mediators who were willing to go into the prison, some
further violence might be avoided.

Mediation can be taught in the prison as a job skill for an
inmate going back into society, or it can be taught as a skill which
would help him enhance his personal life. It could make for better
community relations, both in the facility and in society, and aid in

understanding among family members. This is a skill which would promote greater self esteem in the prison inmate, so that he can function satisfactorily when released.

When considering victim-offender reconciliation as an alternative to sentencing, or to be done concurrently with sentencing, a mediation program could be done experimentally. It is to be hoped that such a program would lessen a criminal's sentence, and would not mean that he paid twice, once to pay back the money, and again, be given the usual time to serve. At present there is not much done to compensate a victim of a minor theft. With victim-offender mediation the victim would have the possibility of some restitution, and thus might be more willing to forgive.

Although there are many problems connected with installing mediation in the prison system, mediation would help the prison to be a more peaceful place, allowing inmates to defuse, and if the box, or solitary confinement, became less used, a lot of the money to pay for special duty officers, would be saved. Finally, let's not forget that the mediator, through his experience of dealing with people, becomes a more responsive and a more responsible human being. As the prison population skyrockets and surplus inmates are forced to sleep in packed gymnasiums, it becomes more and more necessary to have peaceful settlement processes. The criminal justice system could enhance the self esteem of both officers and inmates, and be more cost effective, if it incorporated a viable mediation program.

10.6 SPECIAL PROBLEMS IN MAINTAINING ORDER

Prisons are unique places. Most of us are used to having a secure spot of privacy where we can sleep and think. Can you imagine being in a three bed cell, and trying to sleep peacefully when your two cell mates obviously don't like you! One of them dislikes what you say so much that he won't even communicate with you. Perhaps they smoke pot, and think that you are liable to snitch on them. You may have decided to restructure your life and to stay off drugs. Your positive attitude may be an unspoken threat to their way of life. With prison overcrowding, a different cell is a long time off into the future. How do you maintain your sanity, and hang on to your covenantal commitment?

Strange as it may seem, drugs are available inside prison

walls. Convicts are very inventive people, and if they are so inclined, they can find ways to carry on a profitable drug trade. There are always secondary individuals who will want to get in on the profit, and there are always people who will use drugs to blot out the insecurities of their present. What can one solitary inmate do to help his fellows over their insecurities? What can one person do to convince drug profiteers that they are destroying their own souls for money, as well as the lives of others? Those who are on drugs have such a waste of potential; the drug profiteers are contributing to this waste.

Those selling drugs often feel that they are doing something kind for the addict. They are selling him something that will give him the desired "good" feeling. They do not even want to think that they are also selling him the *letdown*, and not just the temporary letdown, but the letdown for his whole life, this life that still has the possibilities of being a shining inspiration for other lives.

Prison authorities often turn their eyes away from the drug dealing situation. If an angry man takes a few puffs of marijuana, he may forget what his rage was all about, and he may be easier for the guards to handle. For the same reason, calming medication may be given to inmates, to make them placid and less sensitive to their everyday living problems. Some of those who manage prisons find that keeping within the present year's budget is easier, if they encourage the prescribing of sedatives and ignore inmate drug dealings, than if they hired qualified employees to inspire inmates to lead creative lives.

10.7 THE RETURN TO THE COMMUNITY

With dedicated inmates working diligently at positive programs under the direction of understanding prison personnel, reformation and rehabilitation would be a foregone conclusion in many cases. The second part of the job would be to make the changes stick, when the inmate returns to society.

Intersecting circular groups should be formed that would be able to guide the inmate through the morass of his prison exit to a secure job situation in his community. This dual inside-outside program would aid in emphasizing to the inmate his responsibilities to his community, his family, and himself. TV could be used to help publicize such a program, and to secure the understanding and support of the outside community by making the public knowledgeable about the problems of inmates. Whenever possible, if the offender has a bad relationship with a victim, both parties must be given constructive support. It is very important that the victim should be apprised of the felon's desire to change and to be a responsible citizen.

With its lack of emphasis on covenant, our present system often encourages a man to serve his crime time by lounging in front of the TV set, and continuing his drug addiction. He has no reason to become a responsible citizen. With emphasis on prisons as factories and places of learning, an inmate's whole outlook on life may be subject to change. But just inspirational prison programs will not work. Although there are many drug fighting programs in prison, the sense of community and dedication necessary for success in society disappear just when the person needs them most. When he returns to the street where his former drug-dealing associations are, he may leave his support community and his good resolutions behind in the prison. Programs in the prison to educate and rehabilitate must be geared to the needs of the inmate returning to society. In most instances the *ex-con* has for support only an overburdened parole officer. Inmates going out to the street are frequently forbidden to associate with other ex-cons, who might give them support, as they might also lead them astray.

The Swedish prisons have thought about the ex-con's lack of community support. Parole personnel in the Swedish corrections system are assisted by volunteers. These volunteers are available by phone to the ex-con when he feels the need for a friend. They get a free meal once a week when they take the ex-con out to dinner to see how he is doing. They get their transportation paid to the place of meeting. They get a sense of personal satisfaction knowing that they are helping to keep a man on the right track. They report any problems to the parole officer, who also sees the ex-con at regular intervals, and more often if there seems to be a problem.

Perhaps not too many people in New York City or other big cities in the United States would want to offer their services as volunteer parole assistants. However, if a covenanted group of ex-cons were to apply as volunteers to stand by and support new members who came out of the correctional institutions, they would fill a great need, help acclimate the latest ex-cons to society, intro-duce them to the proper substance abuse and sex offender support groups, and get a restaurant meal once a week. As there are many ex-prisoners, there should be many who would be willing to help and empathize with those in similar positions.

10.8 INTERSECTING CIRCLES AS PRISON GOVERNMENT

We mentioned that Jupiter and the sun had a certain orderly relationship. It is likewise possible to have an orderly and construc-tive relationship between prison personnel and inmates. We have been speaking here of changes in the hearts of both the inmate population and of the officers who guard them. We have suggested support groups made up of inmates, and we have also discussed covenanted officers and community groups willing to be involved in helping in the personal fulfillment of those no longer incarcerated. How would such groups work?

Side by side with the state department of corrections with its prison supervisory system and its ranks of officers, exist the unspo-ken rules and codes of ethics of the inmate population. In some prisons the officers on duty allow a certain amount of rule by the strongest, as long as the ruling team doesn't violate prison regula-tions. This can make prison doubly terrible for those inmates who are not *in* with the favored gang.

Other more structured government by inmates is available, which also teaches positive attitudes and helps in the return to society. Some prisons have *Network* units, where inmates are al-lowed to live together in a special area in the prison, take positive programs together, and give each other mutual support with prob-lems. Within the unit the inmates draft their community rules, and even coordinate the supervisory personnel into their plans. This government by consensus could be enlarged to include the whole prison, and could exist along with the regular prison administration.

There are other prison programs that teach self-governing techniques. Substance abuse programs such as *Compadre Helper*, *Exodus* type programs that assist in the release process, and groups that train in alternatives to violence help participating inmates to make more effective community life inside the walls.

Many prisons have a positive and understanding *grievance* process where inmates are allowed to air their problems and get a hearing. If an inmate feels that the official prison government or a particular officer has been unjust, he can go before a board composed of prison personnel and some representation by fellow inmates. Thus we see that the beginnings of free interchange between inmates and officers are falling into place.

Positive inmate organizations need strengthening, without giving power to one particular inmate. Discussion groups need to be formed to discuss common problems, and in these groups rotating individuals should be selected to meet with members of other inmate groups and officer groups. There also is a need for groups of ex-cons and others in the community who could give feedback to the groups within the prison.

We could begin by likening the prison governing organizations to two triangles, one large and one small. The larger triangle is the power and authority of the state, with the prison supervisor at the top of the triangle, the guarding officers the next layer down, and the inmates on the bottom. The small triangle is contained in the bottom layer of the big one, and its interpretation is that there are some inmates that have some kind of authority or power hold, over other inmates.

To improve these triangles would be to turn them into circles. In some prisons the supervisor meets with a board of prison personnel, and they discuss prison problems, and brainstorm solutions. These personnel are the spokespersons for other personnel, and thus we have some prison governments operating with a type of consensus system. If inmates were also allowed to be a part of this circular government, more empathy for each other's problems would be the end result. If representative members were rotated from all concerned groups, there would be more understanding governance possible.

Until more expertise is achieved in shared leadership by all members of the group, we must use those with special abilities to help us to this goal of using the abilities of all. In small cooperative beginnings, the facility and inmate organizations could work together to balance the decision making about who's right and who's wrong, between the officers and inmates. An inmate with leadership

TRANSFORM
TRIANGULAR PRISON POWER STRUCTURES
TO CIRCULAR CONSENSUS STRUCTURES!

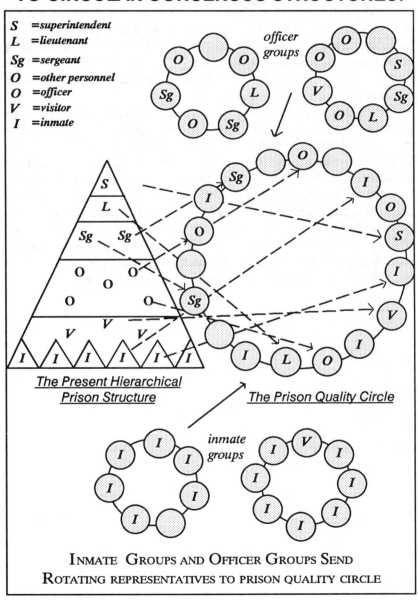

S =superintendent
L =lieutenant
Sg =sergeant
O =other personnel
O =officer
V =visitor
I =inmate

officer groups

The Present Hierarchical
Prison Structure

The Prison Quality Circle

inmate groups

INMATE GROUPS AND OFFICER GROUPS SEND
ROTATING REPRESENTATIVES TO PRISON QUALITY CIRCLE

qualities and the head of the facility could attempt to mediate *both-gain* results for officer-offender explosive situations. Looking ahead to the release of the offender, there should be a circular group made up of personnel in the prison, inmate assistants in the prison, those expecting release in the near future, parole officials, ex-offenders that can support from the outside, and other citizens who do not have a criminal record. The more of this work that is done in consensus circles where everyone has a chance to be heard, the more understanding there will be in the whole community, and the more encouragement and growth to fulfillment.

All this would be very positive, and could make the prison a place where freedom could be exercised to establish justice, if inmates and officers on duty become freely covenanted individuals. Both officers and those they are guarding should make an effort to understand each other's responsibilities and problems and give respect to each other. There should be a certain acceptance of the place that punishment does play in our society, and a desire to turn this emphasis on just punishment into constructive rehabilitation. Many prison supervisors and those concerned with criminal justice are coming to the conclusion that encouraging such freedom within the prison system can lead to a more successful society.

11

THE USE
OF GOVERNMENT
TO BUILD COMMUNITY

11.1 OTHER ADVISORY BOARDS

As we have a right to expect that in a God-created world, all human beings should have inward intimations of God and the possiblity of being covenanted with God, we should expect to find in ordinary governments a certain sense of God-directed order. When we consider the British government, we see behind their parliamentary form, the ancient notion that government must be ratified by the ruling monarch, as the representative of God. In reality, there is no power to change laws given to the British monarch, but for some reason, the British people like the idea of supporting the royal family as a symbol or figurehead. It makes them psychologically comfortable.

The present Israeli government copied much from the British form, but omitted the support stipend for royalty, as an unnecessary expense for a vestige from the past. Those in the new State of Israel who yearn to have God personally leading their nation, rather than a group of politicians, might see a place for God's directive hand in their government, if state procedures somehow received God's royal ratification. If before implementing any rules and regulations,the Israeli government officials listened to God's word or saw God's will, as coming through a consensus of the *holy community*, they would be giving God's spirit the opportunity to once again lead God's people. There would be a similarity to the British process of requiring ratification by the king or queen, if laws or government actions required ratification by God's holy spirit working through the holy community.

Another aspect of the British government that should be taken under consideration is the cabinet. The British cabinet or body of advisors came into being under the reign of a British king who spoke German. He needed some assistance in getting his views heard in Parliament. Once this advisory group formed, they became more and more powerful, and when a later monarch became mentally ill, they had to exercise their power for the good of the people. From this group, one individual became the most important or necessary leader, and the position of *prime* minister became the true power spot of the nation.

The British cabinet is not just an advisory board of knowledgeable people; it also has law making capabilities, and great influence with Parliament. On the other hand, the United States cabinet implements law, but cannot make laws, and membership, while appointed by the President, is subject to the approval of Congress. Various other countries have variations on the cabinet theme. Cities can have councils as well as mayors. We see that cabinets, councils, and advisory boards can be consultative, legislative, or kept in check by another branch of government, such as the judicial.

11.2 SIDE-BY-SIDE WATCHDOG GOVERNMENTAL BODIES

How could present day Israel-Palestine organize to allow the voice of God to speak through a covenanted people? How could the people keep a rein on what sometimes seems like a government that is getting out of hand and going its own way, particularly in its defense department? Picture that side by side with the present governing bodies in Israel, there is set up a system of parish councils, pastoral councils, and diocesan synods patterned after the model of the Catholic Code, with which to compliment the secular divisions of government. These groups would be consulted, and their consensus would be taken as the final truth for that moment of time, and for that particular problem. They would differ from the Catholic system in that there would be no authoritative spokesperson at the top of the ladder, but a consentaneous pronouncement of how a covenanted people felt on whatever issue was under consideration.

Is God's truth as spoken through the people, open to change? A pronouncement on a controversial issue, made by one group can certainly be changed as more truth is revealed on the subject at hand. Feeding infants a nutritious formula can seem like a good idea for some mothers, but after further investigation, and a living out of the situation, the same people may decide that breast feeding, and making sure the mother received vitamins, would have been a better solution. In like manner, consentaneous decisions can be recinded or revised as more information becomes available. There is no need to feel threatened by worries of infallibility. The world turns, and new knowledge is revealed.

These *quality circle* groups meeting to discuss God's will in governmental matters, could be used on the local, national, and international level. It seems like it would be fairly easy to set in place rotating members of the community, so that each monad in the community would have his or her slot in which to serve, and all opinions would eventually be heard.

To begin with, each household would be expected to send one member to a general community election meeting. Different members of the household who had reached covenantal age would each have their turn to participate in this yearly assembly. This local community election would then chose thirty from among their own members to participate in a monthly parish level meeting, for the term of one year. In what might be a multi-faith community at this parish level meeting, God's guidance would be petitioned silently. The presiding facilitator for this parish type group, could be chosen by lottery, and would be rotated for each meeting. At both the parish or the community election level, there would be a finance council, which would be knowledgeable of the finances of the local government, and would implement all financial matters that were discussed by, or needed for the running of the consensus meetings.

When advancing to the next larger governmental unit, such as a congressional district or parliamentary area, a second duty of each of the local community elections would be to select two members from their group to advise the parliamentary representative from their area, as to what they believed was the will of God for their area. This level could be patterned in the format of the pastoral council. According to its size, it might be broken up into committees of varying interests. At the meetings of each of these committees, a different member would be chosen by the group as temporary presiding facilitator. His further duty would be to communicate decisions and advice from his committee to the national governmental parliamentary member. This parliamentary member would not treat these groups as purely advisory, but would be required to implement their suggestions to the best of his ability.

When the national government made decisions or proposed laws, they would have to be approved by a third body which could correspond to the diocesan synod. A third duty of the community election group would be to propose candidates for this diocesan synod type of watchdog governmental group. This would be a consensus group which would give direct advice to the house of parliament or legislative body. This group would contain both minorities and majorities, so that both sides of every issue would be thoroughly heard, and possible satisfactory solutions for all groups would be aired before advice was given to parliament or any action taken.

In the United States we believe in separation of church and state, and we see that often these two groups act as effective checks on each other. When viewing the issue of abortion, we note that legal decisions are hotly contested by religious groups. In our democratic system of government, there is opportunity for modification of laws through minority group operation, but often there is no room for open exchange of ideas as in consensus groups. There is all too often the notion of one side being all right, and the other side being all wrong. In a balanced consensus type of government, the processes of mediation, conciliation, and arbitration would be available at all governmental levels, insuring that all possible information on the subject was heard by opposing groups.

We find that in the United States, the personal ethics of governmental employees often becomes an important issue. Regrettably, the buying of a law maker's opinion through gifts and political funding, is a commonly accepted practice. As church and state exist side by side in this country and influence each other, so do the personal lives of the law makers exist with their public responsibilities. All of us have behaved incorrectly, and have the problem of uniting our good impulses with our less noble actions. We are all human. If a lawmaker's first responsibility is to his associated consensus group, the situation will be such that he will be less likely to be influenced by money.

As we proceed up the ladder, we find that more and more

THE PEOPLE
SELECT

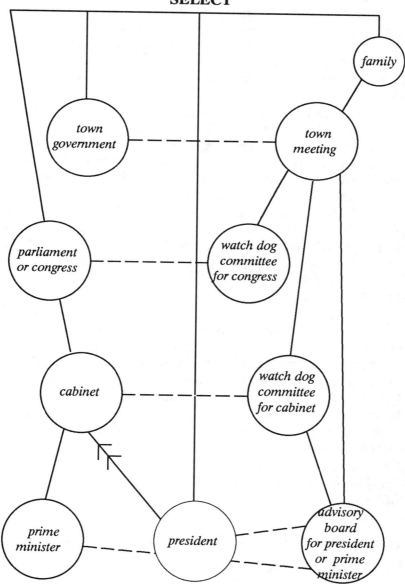

AT ALL LEVELS THE GOVERNMENT MUST LISTEN TO THE CONSENTANEOUS VOICE OF THE PEOPLE

adulation is given to those feeble human beings who get elected to top political positions. "Power tends to corrupt, and absolute power corrupts absolutely."[1] The king often felt that he was God's representative, and could do no wrong. A Pope can easily begin to believe in his infallibility. As humans we seem to have a natural bent to hero worship. Why can't we worship good qualities, as represented by God, and accept humans in leadership positions, as covenanted yet fallible humans?

A second problem with leadership is that many of us are followers. We are glad to slip out from under our responsibility, and let someone else do the work. In charismatic church groups we often notice that leadership drifts to those who can read well and speak clearly. Those who have the same opinions cheer them on; those who disagree, drift out of the group.

The government of the state may still feel the need for presidents and prime ministers, but the secondary consensus government, which would keep a check on the state government, should have no need for authoritative leadership. In the example we have been following of the Catholic Church's consentaneous groupings, the College of Cardinals would be unnecessary, as leadership would flow from below. However, as cardinals and bishops in the Catholic system make statements on ethical issues, there could be a group of writers who would write position papers on problems that have arisen in the area being governed. The office of pope or president as final spokesperson would not be necessary in the secondary watchdog consensus groups, as the voice of God would be heard as coming through the people. In the community groups of watchdog goverment corresponding to the parish, pastoral, and synod levels of the Catholic Code, the rotating job of presiding facilitator would replace the stationary chairperson of the Code. Structures would not be held tightly in place by authoritarian figures, but would be lightly binding (like a tea bag).

11.3 THE CYCLIC NATURE OF POSSESSION

Ezekiel heard the voice of the Lord speaking to him in circa 600 BC. "Mortal being," the voice said, "tell the Israelites that their land is unholy, and so I am punishing it in my anger. The leaders are like lions roaring over the animals they have killed. They kill the people, take all the money and property they can get, and by their murders leave many widows. The government officials are like wolves tearing apart the animals they have killed. They commit murder in order to get rich. The wealthy cheat and rob. They mistreat the poor and needy and take advantage of settlers in the land. So I will turn my anger loose on them, and like a fire I will destroy them for what they have done. Their conduct will recoil on their own heads." Ezekiel proclaimed what the Sovereign Lord had spoken (Ezekiel 22:22-25; 27; 29; 31).

The problem addressed by Ezekiel is that people having to do with governance were making the land unholy by their perverse actions. Ezekiel tells us the problem as it was seen in his day, and it seems to be the perennial problem. God has punished such conduct before, and will punish our inconsideration of the other, again. This prosperity which leads to self-centeredness, seems to be a natural process. Certain people get greedy and oppress others. These others rise up and execute God's judgment. The newly favored group, in their turn, develop complacency and forget the needs of the out-of-favor. The cycle repeats.

Ezekiel heard God speaking again. "Mortal being, say to the House of Israel, 'I take pleasure, not in the death of a wicked man, but in the turning back of a wicked man who changes his ways to win life. Come back, come back from your evil ways. Why are you so anxious to die, House of Israel? If I say to a wicked man: You are to die, and he renounces his sins and does what is lawful and right, if he returns pledges, restores what he has stolen, keeps the laws that give life and stops committing sin- he shall live, and will not die. All his previous sins will no longer be remembered- he has done what is lawful and right; he shall live" (Ezekiel 33:10a, 11, 14-16).

Ezekiel gives us the problem, and he gives us the solution. His inspirited words have been there for many generations to hear, but those of his time did not seem to listen. We today like to believe that his strong words do not apply to us.

When the people of a nation undergo military or economic upheaval, they seem to be unable to think clearly. They try desperately to hang onto the material things that are crashing around them, and find it very hard to return pledges, restore what has been procured unjustly, and to keep the laws that give life. They listen to God's words as spoken by the prophet, but no one puts them into practice (Ezekiel 33:32b). Collectively, as a people, they tend to live from hand-to-mouth, and take little time to think or restructure their mode of national behavior.

When the biblical prophets denounce injustice, they are not only warning the past or present *Israelites*, but as God is God of the whole earth, all nations can listen, and all are invited to reform their ways. What is said here about Israel can also be applied to conditions occurring in South Africa, and also to actions of the United States. Many religious organizations have need for internal revamping in order to come back to basic truths. The gentle prophet Mohammed would be scandalized upon hearing of two supposedly Muslim nations engaged in fratracidal warfare. The Catholic Church could restore rights to its minorities (such as women), that have had their equality unjustly taken from them. Individual people can use these warnings of Ezekiel and treat their neighbor with respect.

As this favored position of privilege in the secure land seems to be a cyclic occurrence, and depends on generous treatment of those who share the land or earth with you, those of us who have exploited the earth's resources should be careful to exercise our incumbent responsibilities. What would Ezekiel think of the actions today of rich nations who have ruined poorer nations through massive debt obligations, which lower both countries' standards of living and block economic progress? The required justice according to Ezekiel might be a Jubilee Year action of forgiveness as described in Leviticus 25:28. The wealthier people of the world, collectively, could forgive the pledges to pay of the third world debtor nations, by willingly accepting personal interest losses. According to cyclic theory, this Jubilee Year type of action could prolong the wealthier nations' time of relative security.

11.4 THE ROOTS OF THE PROBLEM

As the Holy Land is a trouble spot in the world today, it might be good to use it as an example for this problem of mistreatment of the other, which seems to lead to disaster. By using such a specific case, we may be able to identify a common root for all such problems.

In reading the word of Ezekiel, we find that in his time the Holy Land had become unholy. Conditions today might lead us to come to the same conclusion. The challenge for contemporaneous

Israel is not only to self-examine its policies, but to put ethical and non-military reforms into practice.

Surely there could be nothing wrong with Zionism, the desire of the Jewish people to return to the land of Abraham and of David, their ancestors. The covenant God made with Abraham states, "I will give to you and to your descendants after you the land you are living in, the whole land of Canaan, to own in perpetuity, and I will be your God" (Genesis 17:8). The promise to David is that "your house and your sovereignty will always stand secure before me and your throne be established forever" (2 Samuel 7:16). Taken literally, the promises have to do with Abraham's descendants, the land of Canaan, and the sovereignty of the nation. Taken metaphorically, we can understand that the seed of the just, will live securely in the land, and peace will reign.

There are two sides to every covenant, and Abraham and David had certain responsibilities. Likewise, the descendants of Abraham had to be *the people* of this God, and accept his leading through the deserts of this world. Only if we consciously agree to follow God, can we be considered his people. It is a dramatic moment when a nation proclaims itself to be the *people of God*. It is a very difficult task to follow through this covenantal pledge with appropriate God-serving actions and to omit the non-God-serving actions of elitism and domineering authority.

God fulfilled his promise to Abraham, as the descendants accepted God's leadership out of Egypt. God fulfilled his promise again, when a latter-day group of Jews returned from Babylon to build a second temple. It seemed only natural that in this day and age, God would lead the Jewish people home again, and both contemporaneous Christians and Jews felt that they were helping God in assisting the present process of return. Unfortunately, many only looked at the positive part of the promise. They forgot that a covenant has two sides, and that the other side of this covenant was that the people had to conduct their lives so that in practice they acted as God's people. It was not enough to be physically a Jew and circumcised; it was necessary to be spiritually a Jew, obeying God's rules for just conduct, and having a circumcised heart.

Theodore Herzl was one of those who was very instrumental in this return to Zion. His knowledge of government was limited to the nation-states that surrounded him, and so his only way of visualizing Zion was as a state with a legal constitution and political leaders. He proceeded to implement this vision with all his vigor.

Other Jews held back. Rabbi Isaac Mayer Wise felt that "the object of Judaism is not political, nor national, but spiritual, and addresses itself to the continuous growth of peace, justice, and love in the human race, to a Messianic time when all men will recognize that they form one great brotherhood for the establishment of God's kingdom on earth."[2] Many felt that those chosen by God, were not chosen for privilege, but were elected to bring the knowledge of God's compassion to those outside the community. Their foremost duty was to make God's being revered in the world that God created.

While many fundamentalist Christians and political Zionist Jews cheered at the results of the Six Day War, others wondered if it was God's will that the property rights and water rights of others should be disrespected. Some saw the crime of unjustifiable murder in Jewish attacks on Palestinian refugee camps. With the Zionists and their Fundamentalist backers clapping so loudly, at the physical appropriation of property in the land of Israel, those who believed God to be a God of compassion sank into meditative silence. Many felt that God was righting the suffering of Holocaust victims, by bringing his people to a place where they could dwell securely, but they did not see God's leadership in an aggressive military regime. If they spoke out too loudly, they were accused of being anti-Semitic.

Due to the enthusiasm of many Americans, both Jews and Christians, the United States government continued to support the Zionist government in whatever it did. Its main concern was to punish the terrorism of Palestinian groups, whose actions may actually have been understandable, if not justifiable. Ethical philosophers tell us that if someone attacks you for the purpose of stealing your home and eliminating your person, you can defend yourself and your property rights. This may have been what the Palestinian terrorists had in mind, even though their aggressive methods were destined to escalate violence.

In spite of biblical injunctions to respect the rights of the stranger in the land, the Zionists deprived Palestinians of equal citizenship and herded them into camps. They felt that God had promised this land to those of Jewish genealogy. This homecoming of the Jews to the Holy Land was seen by Fundamentalist Christians to signal the *Millennium* and the personal return of Jesus. However, others thought of the Millennium as a time when men would melt their swords into ploughshares. They did not find God's actions in the military might of a political government. These disparate opinions originated from two variant interpretations of God's word, and as people have diverse and unique personalities, it is to be expected that different viewpoints should arise.

The view that one people are the justly favored ones of God, can fail to emphasize that God's love extends equally to all. Given a conviction of our being uniquely beloved by God, we can easily interpret everything to support that elitist view, even to the point of oppressing others. The basic message of the Bible is that we should treat every person as a beloved child of God. When we don't, there is an underlying sense of guilt, whether we admit it or not. Still, we desperately want to believe we are the most beloved of God. The myth we often create, therefore, is to exaggerate the evil in the other (relative to ourselves), to justify our mistreatment of the other in the name of God.

One consequence of that predisposition to fingerpoint, is the inability to think objectively. Every attempt at communication likewise becomes subject to that predisposition. In part, the root of the problem may lie with our incapability to effectively communicate our differing ideas to each other. From the days of the Tower of Babel until now, such mishandling of language has led us into trouble. One of our main faults is that we do not listen to each other. We hear a few words and our busy minds follow through with the way we see the situation. We hear what we want to hear.

The same is true for how we listen to God. We seek security for ourselves, so we only listen for the words that promise us a safe community. We believe that we want to live in the New Jerusalem, but we do not wait to hear what our responsibilities will be, in order to dwell there. Some over emphasize the promise given by God for a safe community. Others avow that we must practice God's justice to stay in God's land. Both sides can quote scripture to justify their beliefs.

11.5 GOD HAS KEPT GOD'S SIDE OF THE PROMISE

Now that the Palestinians have gotten world attention, now that the Zionists see the extent of their problem, perhaps all those in Israel-

Palestine will listen to the list of responsibilities for those who hope to dwell in Zion. God has certainly upheld God's end of the bargain. At least four times God has led Abraham or his genealogical descendants to the Land of Promise. God invited Abraham to leave his country, his family and his father's house and to go to a land God would show him (Genesis 12:1) and Abraham went. Abraham remembered his responsibilities to the Lord. He served God as best as he knew how.

God asked a commitment of Moses to lead the Israelites to Canaan. This return is commemorated by Psalm 105:42-45. "Yes, faithful to the sacred promise given to his servant Abraham, he led his happy people forward, to joyful shouts from his chosen, and gave them the pagans' territories. Where others had toiled, they took possession, on condition that they kept his statutes and remained obedient to his laws." The particular individuals that were with Moses never made it as they disobeyed God's injunctions. Moses himself never set foot on the Promised Land. Joshua finally led the second generation in, but with bloodshed and not much respect for the property rights of others. Eventually David united the descendants of this group, and it seemed like God had decided that the Jews were well behaved enough to merit a peaceful kingdom. With the ensuing prosperity of some, came oppression of the poor and military upheaval, and the dark side of God's promise was fulfilled when the Jews were carried off to Babylon.

With repentance a remnant returned from Babylon, for a third try at dwelling in a secure land, under God. This group, too, was anxious to exclude the foreigner or the settler in the land, who they felt did not worship God in what was conceived by them to be the proper ritualistic manner. As they excluded others, and practiced elitism, it became their turn to leave. This time it was the Romans who carried out the promise's darker side, destroying the symbolic city of blessing, and God's material temple.

However, the Jews did not need either the material city or temple in order to have God's Spirit with them wherever they were cast up. Many Jews were willing to believe that the temple where God dwelt, was the loving Jewish community, and that the special land was any place on earth where this community flourished. Jerusalem came to have a spiritual meaning signifying God's care for the whole earth. The displaced Jew, Ezekiel, described the temple in this spiritual Jerusalem as having a river of life which flowed out to the sea making all things wholesome (Ezekiel 47:1-12).

Yet a fourth opportunity arose, out of the sadness of the Holocaust, for God to lead his people to the fabled homeland. Who would deny the hand of God in this action! They went back "to Zion shouting for joy" and were fairly confident that joy and gladness would go with them, and that sorrow and lament would be ended (Isaiah 35:10). But the political leaders on both sides seem to have forgotten the important list of responsibilities to be fulfilled in order for the group to have permanent peaceful residence. In the past it seems that God has had other world leaders act to take his people from their secure homes when the people did not comply with God's will. If such cycles are not to repeat themselves, a *new heart* is needed. Jeremiah (31:31-34) says of God, "I will make a new convenant...Deep within them I will plant my law, writing it on their hearts." God will certainly keep his promises of a peaceful land if all of his people (for example, both Arabs and Jews) accept the way of true brotherhood in their hearts. Otherwise, non-compliance may again bring a natural cyclic downfall and removal from the land.

11.6 GOD KEEPS GOD'S PROMISE TO ALL RELIGIOUS GROUPS

Uncountable times, God has led trusting communities to secure homes. The Mormons have their Zion in Utah. A successful community that emphasizes responsibility to God and man, is that of the Amish in Pennsylvania. On the other hand, we have the story with the sad ending, of Jonestown in British Guiana.

What constitutes a *New Jerusalem*? According to Christian scripture (Revelation 21:12-16), the New Jerusalem is four square. It has gates on all sides, three in each direction of the compass. These gates are never shut. One can interpret this to indicate that the New Jerusalem is built on equality, totally open to all directions, and thus to the whole earth. The loving community of the New Jerusalem is open to all who come.

In considering the small compact communities that God has led to their particular peaceful land, they may lack this total openness to the other, and this four-square characteristic. They may not grant the stranger or foreigner equal rights, responsibilities, and acceptance. They may deny women equal wage and equal justice, and they may not make the surrounding world or the sins and oppressions of other people, their concern. Their commitment is inward. It may be gentle and considerate of the foreigner in their confines, but they may not have the world-wide vision necessary for understanding the needs of all who may come to them. They may find it difficult to handle the bigotry, the famine, and the militarism in other world communities, and in shutting all this out, they may engender jealousy.

Perhaps what God envisions for the New Jerusalem is a community that uses the wisdom and compassion of God to truly serve all others on the earth. It is difficult to talk about what God envisions, as we do not have, and cannot ever truly have, a God's eye viewpoint, and as we can not comprehend the vastness of the mind of God. If we talk about the New Jerusalem, it is necessary to speculate on what God might be like, and what such a God might encourage in the ideal community. We must enter into any discussion of God's mind and will by first admitting our basic ignorance of what God is like. The more dedicated individuals we can compare notes with, the greater the wisdom we have a chance of procuring. On the topics of God and the responsibilities of a New Jerusalem type community, it would be good to compare intuitions through the consensus circle arrangement.

11.7 WATER, A SAMPLE PROBLEM

If we consider the aim of the Israelis to be such a New Jerusalem type community, with a desire to make a success of dwelling in the Holy Land, what actions should they take? One internal situation that could be worked on by the Israeli government and by watchdog consensus groups is obviously the problem of Israelis living in peace with Palestinians. A more international problem concerns the water rights in the Near East area. This could be linked to the world-wide problem of deserts, land erosion, agricultural productivity, and mass starvation. These environmental issues have to do with our previous theological presentation of the flow of life and the flow of love. The mistreatment of Palestinians is also a very important aspect of the relationship between God and the human, yet the proper sharing of the earth's environment has to do with the final survival of the whole world and the possible ending of all God-human relationships. A terrible waste of money is going into armaments, that should go into continuing the productivity of the earth. Instead of promoting nuclear weapons in South Africa, which doesn't seem to be furthering the peace process, let Israel and its neighbors work on an abundant water supply for agricultural productivity.

Water is one of our most valuable resources. We cannot exist without it. Fresh water is necessary to grow crops to feed this worldful of people; any kind of water can be used to make electricity to supply energy to turn our machines. Non-polluting hydro-power potential is being neglected as investors entice us to turn to the more glamorous nuclear energy which can damage our environment with excessive radiation.

When we look at the quantity of water throughout the earth, and see the vastness of the oceans, and the rising of the tides, and look ahead to possible submersion of Florida if the Artic warms from the *greenhouse effect*, we surely see a need for the nations of the earth to get together in consensus and make important decisions for the future of all the earth. Why can't humankind put irrigational water onto the Sahara desert? It seems that Bangladesh gets too much water, at certain periods of the year. Why can't people make vast holding lakes of monsoon water, and pipeline this valuable commodity around the coast of India to Saudi Arabia?

Instead of using funds and international alliances to distribute arms that physically and economically destroy the poor, let humankind use their know-how to bring water and natural fertility to worn-out soil. In the Near East less than eight percent of the land is cultivated and able to produce crops. The rest is desert, mountain, or swamp. Instead of polluting the world and its waters with nuclear waste, or nuclear testing, or even nuclear winter, so that no one can drink, let us devote available money and human resources to make it possible for all Africa and the Near East to have enough water to farm their spots of earth. Then the world will come closer to each one resting under his own fig tree.

The leaders of Israel have seen this need for water to irrigate the desert, and also to supply plentiful water to flush toilets and to shower in high rise apartments. They have gone about getting this water in a self-centered fashion. There is little concern for the future of the whole area, or for the present needs of their immediate neighbors.

The National Water Carrier conducts water from the Sea of Galilee to near Tel Aviv, which diverts some of the water that would flow into the Jordan, the main river in Israel. Thus Israel wants to be sure that the Sea of Galilee is plentifully supplied. Galilee receives water from the the Baniyas, the Dan, and the Hesbani Rivers of Syria. For this reason it is very important to Israel that Syria does not dam up or divert the waters of these rivers.

The waters of Galilee flow into the Jordan River, and these same waters also flow to the Negev, via the Yarkon Negev pipeline and canal. To increase water to the Sea of Galilee, Israel has its eyes on a diversion of the waters of the Litani River in Southern Lebanon. There is also the Orontes River which rises in Lebanon and flows east into Syria. Of course Syria has its own water needs, and depends heavily on the Orontes for drinking water, electric power, and irrigation. There is obviously not enough water for the needs in the area. International law states that water within one catchment area should not be diverted outside that area until needs within the catchment area are satisfied.

Listening to International Law, Israel has turned towards the Mediterranean with hopes of desalinizing the sea. It has plans for the Med-Dead canal which would run sea water into the Dead Sea and supply electric power. This would raise the water level in the Dead Sea area, as it is far below sea level, and the country of Jordan on the other side of this sea, is not pleased at the prospect. Its industry and farm land would be flooded out. There would be the further problem of salinization of the Jordanian fresh water streams in the area.[3]

Even Egypt has not solved its problems with its grandiose Aswam Dam, and the plentiful waters of the Nile. There has been an increase in productivity in the new farmland at the head waters, but an upset in both agriculture and fishing down river. It is very difficult to plan for all eventualities when redistributing the valuable commodity of water. It is very necessary to get a consensus of agricultural and water experts, and to include input from all the farming areas which will be affected.

The Bible promises that the desert will blossom like the rose, but how is this possible with the slim supply of water? Isaiah tells us, "People of Zion, you will live in Jerusalem ..... On every lofty

A GIANT SIPHON

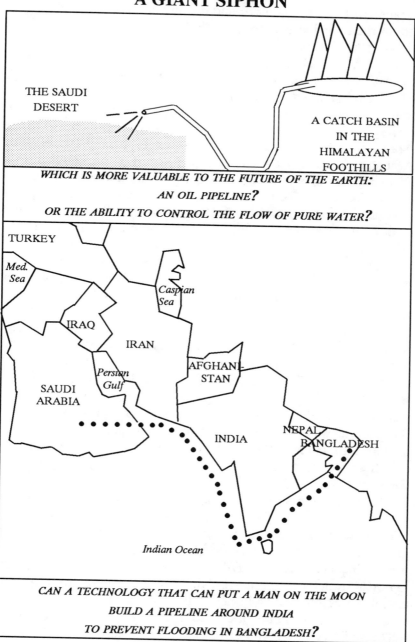

THE SAUDI DESERT

A CATCH BASIN IN THE HIMALAYAN FOOTHILLS

WHICH IS MORE VALUABLE TO THE FUTURE OF THE EARTH:

AN OIL PIPELINE?

OR THE ABILITY TO CONTROL THE FLOW OF PURE WATER?

TURKEY

Med. Sea

Caspian Sea

IRAQ

IRAN

Persian Gulf

AFGHANI-STAN

SAUDI ARABIA

INDIA

NEPAL

BANGLADESH

Indian Ocean

CAN A TECHNOLOGY THAT CAN PUT A MAN ON THE MOON

BUILD A PIPELINE AROUND INDIA

TO PREVENT FLOODING IN BANGLADESH?

mountain, on every high hill there will be streams and watercourses."
(Isaiah 30:19, 25) "The poor and needy ask for water, and there is
none, their tongue is parched with thirst. I, Yahweh, will answer
them, I, the God of Israel, will not abandon them. I will make rivers
well up on barren heights, and fountains in the midst of valleys; turn
the wilderness into a lake, and dry ground into waterspring." (Isaiah
41:17, 18) "I am putting water in the wilderness (rivers in the wild)
to give my chosen people drink." (Isaiah 43:20b) Ezekiel adds that
he has a vision of a stream flowing eastward from the temple to the
Arabah, and from thence to the sea. Geographically, the Wadi of
Arabah empties into the Gulf of Aqaba, a part of the Red Sea. This
Wadi appears to be on the same geological fault line as the Jordan
and the Dead Sea. Ezekiel continues that there will be "fishing nets
from En-gedi to En-eglaim."[4] He cautions that "the marshes and
lagoons, however, will not become wholesome, but will remain salt"
(Ezekiel 47:1-12). Joel 4:18 promises, "All the river beds of Judah
will run with water. A fountain will spring from the house of Yahweh
to water the wadi of Acacias."[5] Revelation 22:1 tells us that the river
of life will be "flowing crystal-clear down the middle of the city
street."

These visions of a park-like city and country may be merely
speaking figuratively of the flow of love that should be present in the
holy community, but they also may refer to the physical needs of the
community. The Israeli leaders have seen these promises in the
Bible, have interpreted them for the physical earth, and have been
busy trying to set up these water courses. But how are they to have
this plentiful water without destroying their neighbors, and disobey-
ing international law? Surely, if they got together with neighboring
countries in consensus communities, they could come up with creative solutions.

Oil is a very valuable commodity, and no expense is spared to
build oil pipelines. In Alaska we have built an 800 mile environmen-
tally-questionable pipe line, in our need and greed for the energy oil
gives to us. In 1982 a pipeline to transport gas from Africa to Europe
was put in place. There is a 2780 mile gas pipeline from the gas fields
in northern Siberia. Humankind does have the ability to transport
commodities that he feels he needs. Israel has devoted some of its resources to making a network of water conduits within its territory,
but there isn't enough water to fill them. If the deserts are to bloom,

there must be more water.

If we look at the map of the Near East, we see that there are larger bodies of water than the Sea of Galilee, and greater deserts than those of the Negev. If we were going to restructure the whole world for the benefit of the people of the whole world, where would we lay our water conduits? Where is there an excess of water? Urban dwellers must realize that their need for fresh water is secondary to that of the farmer. Even the United States would do well to examine its water shortages and surpluses. If we are to have food on our plates, we may have to have impure water for showering.

The Caspian Sea, north of Iran, contains less salt than the ocean, yet has a bitter taste. It is about 800 miles from Jerusalem. A pipe line laid from it across or through its surrounding mountains would be no longer than the Alaska oil pipeline, but would require the consent and cooperation of the two enemies Iraq and Iran. It would have to service the needy in its catchment area who had assisted in its construction. There might be so many needy groups along its path that only a trickle would reach Jerusalem. When considering the total Near East area, another approach might be for Saudi Arabia to fund a Caspian water line to flourish its deserts, using its oil money, and to have the pipeline path go across Iran and the Persian Gulf.

We find that the Black Sea is closer to Jerusalem and also less salty than the Mediterranean. Laying a pipe line across Turkey and along the Mediterranean would also be feasible, as there would be less water required by farmers along the way. There would be need for careful environmental studies and desalination with the consequent salt marshes and lagoons as foretold by Ezekiel. Surely Syria, Lebanon, and Jordan could share in this flow. Putting their combined resources into water lines, rather than armaments, might generate enough know-how among Arabs, Palestinians, Israelis, Lebanese, and Jordanians so that they could service the water needs of the whole earth. Then it would become a simple matter for Africans to grow forests of fig trees and date palms on the Sahara.

Smaller projects should also be considered, such as the Gaza Storm Water conservation Project[6] and one-village dams as in the Huon Peninsula in Papua New Guinea.[7] Small floating power plants, strategically placed along water carrier routes would increase the quality of life for those living near areas of downhill flow. The people in the concerned areas could form groups who would work side by side with already existing governmental bodies who would be willing to listen to the voice of the people. The soldiers must lay aside their arms, and use their energies to help in the construction of roads and irrigation ditches and in the planting of trees. Even before the ditches are dug, and the water is flowing, it would be wise to convert tanks into tractors, and the non-productive land mine factories, to the manufacture of farm tools.

It has become more and more evident as time passes that weapons destroy the earth. If the people of Israel and of the world wish to build an earth for future generations, they must put aside their militant attitudes, and cooperate to preserve and propagate the resources with which God has blessed us. To feed the earth's people, you need food. To grow food, you need water. To share the earth's water, requires cooperation of the earth's people. With proper care and planned sharing the whole world can regulate its water resources, so as to grow the food we need.

12

THE WAY

OF

GREAT

EXPECTATIONS

12.1 BACK TO THE DRAWING BOARD

We have tried to make a rough artist's sketch of the universe and of the present cultural milieu in which we are emeshed. We also have attempted to paint a glowing picture of where we might be going. It is surely difficult for us as fallible creatures to survey the whole scene from a God's eye viewpoint, but each of us as creative partners with God must strive to enlarge his or her view as much as possible. Our vision must be broad enough to include *ALL* humanity; our hearts must be wide enough to feel God's concern for *ALL* life, for *ALL* creation.

The understandings of humanity change as the world grows and changes. As communication of events can be instantaneous and worldwide, our centers of concern have been able to expand. Primitive man, living close to nature which could at times be very threatening, sensed the sacredness and fragility of the life that he carried in his body and in his sperm. His private parts were his most sacred parts, and solemn vows were ratified by placing the hand under that organ, rather than over the heart.[1] The vower was dedicating the life that flowed through him and his offspring to the success of a project.

Recognizing the importance of this flow of life, the human attributed to the gods he worshipped some of the same sexual and creative properties. It was necessary to have dedicated men and women attached to a temple complex, who would be ready to

237

perform sex with the gods or goddesses who were in residence if they chose to appear. We have Jupiter descending to Io. We have the male adherents of Astarte.

Today we seem to have outgrown the myths of both the sacredness of sex and the holiness of life. Many consider the sex organs as *fun and games*. If a potential life results from this physical amusement, it is liable to be quickly snuffed out. Circumcision which was a dedication of one's life-flow to God through one's descendants *ad infinitum,* has become for many a health measure with no symbolic overtones. In today's world it can be associated with the Jewish race, but in the early days of earth's human habitation, circumcision occurred wherever man was found, perhaps being related with the spread of humankind over the globe. Some American Indian tribes practiced circumcision. Australian Aboriginees and Africans also performed this rite. For their day and age it emphasized their obligation to their deity to support the creation in the space and the time allotted to them.

As our horizons have broadened, some of our past history has faded in its importance. The circumcised male of today does not think too often of the manifold symbology behind the minor operation on his reproductive organ. Likewise many in today's world do not sense the spiritual holiness that is associated with all physical life. In particular, ethnic, religious, and national groups cannot seem to see the God-createdness of other people and groups. This, too, is a carry over from our primitive history when gods were localized, and people were not broadminded enough to believe in one God who created all beings. They put their trust in the god of their particular area or group, and tried to believe that their god was more powerful than the god or goddess of their neighbors. Consequently, gods became noted for their power (and for destroying the opposition), rather than for love (and for caring for the community and for all creation). It really is a miracle that any part of God's message of love and cooperation has penetrated into our power-wielding and competitive cultures.

We must admit that we are the haphazard product of assorted previous generations, and as we have freedom to choose, it is not too strange that we seize on some aspects of our ancestral beliefs, and tend to forget other themes. Many of us become busy with the soul-occupying business of everyday living, and can't take time to weigh out our beliefs or those of our predecessors. We accept the fact that there are many religions in the world, and we do not ask why. We don't prod below the surface to discover what all these religions have in common. We do not diligently search to find what God is really like, or whether there really is a God at all. Often the whole idea of what we can't see, frightens us, and we would rather put disturbing thoughts of the supernatural far from our minds. There is the further semi-subconscious worry that if God is all loving, he or she might expect us to share our comforts with the less fortunate. It is so much easier to believe that the less fortunate have somehow displeased God, and therefore deserve their wretched lot. Many of us find it hard to welcome these unfortunate ones as brothers and sisters, equals with us, in the One God's creation. We do not want to believe that we owe anyone anything for our present economic advantages.

Individuals are not the only guilty parties. Even communities will band together and stereotype themselves as somehow better than another community. How we work together in groups also derives from out of our early beginnings. Religion and government are a social and historical phenomena. In very early cultures, humankind was dependent upon nature. It is not surprising that when the rice harvest was very important to life, a goddess should be associated with this important event. Later, when persons trespassed on other persons' rice growing and animal herding territories, it became necessary to have a more mobile god who would go out to war with you. Only as humankind has spread out in its environment, have we been able to come to the conclusion that one noble force has created and controls the whole earth and the heavens.

Likewise our governments have evolved. In agricultural societies the elders of the village met to resolve community problems. As territories enlarged, control was assisted by soldiers. These soldiers obeyed an army leader who established a central government. We entered an era of petty rulers and kings whose main object seemed to be to control one another's territory. Only as weapons became more formidable, have people begun to ask themselves what is the purpose behind aggressive governments. Often if people would accept personal responsibility for their problems, they would be better off with out supervisory government and the hampering of its accompanying red tape. When highly placed officials make profits on trade in drugs and arms that degrade and destroy the poor, the flow of God's life and love is not furthered.

The part played by governments could be that of consentaneous groups put in place to care for their constituents. Their major responsibility would be to guide the people in their territory to show optimum consideration for each other and for those in other territories. Their police would exist to aid those citizens who needed help. Their armies would be those eager to serve outside of their own territory in order to supply the needs of other nations. In this manner governments would help to insure that all nations and peoples understood the positive aims and possibilities of human existence.

Jesus, as God's messenger, came preaching the *good news* of concern and understanding for all. Other religions throughout history have emphasized the same message. If all of us incorporate this message in our hearts and take part in group actions to understand and help others and the environment, then the earth as it turns on covenant and consensus, can look forward to a future.

12.2 GOD TRUSTS US

God has entrusted us with our world. God has entrusted us with springtime birds, with chipmunks, lizards, and deer. God has lavished us with sun and rain and even the marvelous sight of rainbows. God trusts us to treat these gifts with reverence. All this seems to imply that God must hold a substantial hope for the design of creation as workable. The human being that God has put together is evidently a viable model and is able to make constructive decisions, both individually and collectively. If a wise leader is needed to correct a poor position, he or she will arise in the community. If a wise community is needed to correct the errors of poor leadership, people will band together to ease a situation or to promote the common good.

God helps us to govern ourselves, both individually and collectively. Looking back at God's guidance through history, we recall God inspiring Moses to propose regulations that still serve us well today. God trusted Moses, even though Moses had committed a murder, and Moses confirmed God's faith in him by leading the people out of Egypt. Having done in his youth what he felt was against God's will, Moses could empathize with the failings of others.

He doubted his own inner resources, and proclaimed his unworthiness to guide others. God let Moses know that he depended on him, and Moses responded to God's trust. It would be good if our present day communities could trust the expertise of other ex-felons in the same manner as God trusted Moses.

When Moses died, the community took over the administering of the law. At times the community rulers became too harsh and legalistic, but prophets and other members of the community maintained a balance between God's justice and human justice. Specifically, Jesus emphasized the dictum of Leviticus 19:18, "You must love your neighbor as yourself." He found the whole law to hang on love of neighbor and love of God (Matthew 22:37-40).

Primitive man found God and the sacred everywhere in nature. Our ancestors progressed from worshipping God under sacred trees, to assigning a special house where they could worship God. Some communities began to feel that God was *only* in the temple, and *only* at the beck and call of the religious specialist. But God trusts us, the individual and the community, and we have learned that God does not dwell only in temples made with hands (Isaiah 66:1-2 and Acts 7:48). God is not locked within an idol or other symbol; such human restrictions on God have a tendency to emphasize surface differences and to divide. The One God is not confined to any one spot. God's reign is over the whole heavens and earth. God is pleased to dwell within each and all of us.

After a period of trying to confine their God of the land in a temple under priestly control, the Jews were hustled off to Babylon. There they found that God trusted the ordinary people to carry God's laws in their hearts and to remember God in community meeting places called synagogues. It became evident that God could not be tied down to the confines of the Jewish temple.

The exiles in Babylon also discovered that God was not tied down to service of one particular individual or race. God even trusted those outside the Jewish community, such as Cyrus the Conqueror, to send a remnant of the Jews back to their *Holy Land*. The Jewish people still connected their God with that particular spot of land. They had not yet broadened their minds to see the One God as God for the whole earth, and the whole earth as the *Holy Promised Land* for all who served God and neighbor.

God trusts us with our societal structures. When the early

Israelis looked around them and saw other nations with one person in control, they demanded a king, and God gave them a king. This governed people slowly discovered that their well-being depended very much on whether this king feared God or displeased God, whether the king encouraged or hampered the flows of life and love. Early Christians, too, seemed to feel the need for centralized authority to standardize and to increase order. They agreed to listen respectfully to the voice of another human being, the Pope, in spite of his obvious human failings. Sensing his possible imperfections, they organized what has finally become known as the College of Cardinals, to give a consentaneous balance to the Pope's pronouncements. This balancing act is not always used. Those of us who have observed the sometimes notorious history of popes, kings, dictators, and presidents, are not too anxious to hand over control of our minds and our hearts to one like ourselves.

Today many still seem to feel the need of one person to look to for leadership, but still others see that each must try to be responsible for his or her own inner covenantal core beliefs. Pledging allegiance to primarily serve a pope, a king, or allowing some novel other to have control over us, distracts from the commitment we should consciously make to God. It should be our fundamental option to be in solidarity with the whole earth. Covenanting with a specific leader may set us in opposition to another leader, and lead to situations where there is competition for power, rather than for cooperation in service. Individually, we are to care for ourselves and for those less able to function who are in our areas of concern. Collectively, we must decide the guidelines necessary for optimum operation in our specific areas. God is trusting us to do this, and God knows that we will come to fulfillment only by exercising our creativity and our responsibility.

Some of us shirk our responsibility by asking God for leaders, kings, popes, or even astrologers to lean on, that will inform us as to auspicious actions. However, God has given us God's word and wisdom down through the centuries, and has inspired each one of us with sensitivities. God has designed each of us to have the seed of God within, the urge to further God's flow of life and love; and God trusts each one of us to come through. We must not off-handedly pass over this tremendous gift for someone else to manage for us. Many kings and popes cannot relate to the inner needs of those they supervise. Our separate dreams and projects for the care of the earth and one another, can be shared, shaped, modified, and improved in an understanding consentaneous community, better than under an authoritarian despot.

God trusts us to share. One of the human's prime problems is greediness. It is good to work for a livelihood for yourself and those you love, and much satisfaction can be derived from acquiring the necessities of life. God trusts us not to be greedy with our surplus. God gives us the wisdom and the vision to see the needs of others. He gives us hearts that can empathize. He gives us the spiritual strength to act in opposition to our greed, for the good of an individual (who may be ourself) or for the good of the community.

We are reminded by banners and bumper stickers of the truism that "Love isn't love till you give it away!" The same holds true for life. God has given each of us a marvelous multi-faceted gift of life. What do we do with it? Do we hoard it? Do we grab all that we can, some of which may have been intended for others? Do we let the wonder of it all, flow through us to those who are in the present and to those who may be in the future? Life isn't life till you give it away.

We must not be greedy, and collect all the world's material goodies and exciting experiences for ourselves. We could become like a stagnant pool. The flow of life needs an outlet to the *now* to be healthy in the present; and we must keep in mind the healthiness of the world that is becoming. God is trusting us.

Down through the years God's trust has inspired wise persons to guide us gently and to display to all God's message of love. God has given reasonable guidelines to us, which help human beings to relate to one another and to God. In using this wisdom, and in obeying these regulations, humankind has put in place certain societal structures. Some of these structures implement the processes of God better than others. The Catholic Church has developed a code of canon law that could be used to encourage consensus on ethical matters of grave importance. A structure described by such a code could also be used by a government to discern the will of those being governed. The Founding Fathers of the United States, with time, effort, and God's help, came up with an excellent constitution for a democracy with rule by the majority. Relying on God's continuing support, we can surely formulate an even more consentaneous government, which would be able to recognize the needs of minorities, and which could eliminate inequalities, graft, and the evil of power structures.

12.3 SERVING OTHER GODS

It would not take too much of a push in the right direction for governments to behave in a covenantal and consentaneous fashion. Even a king in former times could guide his people to be reverent and just. I Kings 9:4-7 promises, "For your part, if you walk before me with innocence of heart and in honesty, like David your father, if you do all I order you and keep my laws and ordinances, I will make your royal throne secure over Israel forever, as I promised David your father when I said: You shall never lack for a man on the throne of Israel. But if you turn away from me, you or your offspring, and do not keep the commandments and laws I have set before you, and go and serve other gods and worship them, then I will cut Israel off from the land I have given them, and I will cast out from my presence this Temple that I have consecrated for my name, and Israel shall become a proverb and a byword among all the nations."

The above passage has meaning for both Jews and Christians. Some Jewish people are inclined to take it literally and expect a descendant of David to sit on the throne of Israel as the Royal Ruler. Some interpret it as self-rule by the Jewish people. Many Christians take this in a religious sense with Jesus, the Jewish *Son of David*, ruling justly through his followers in the church they feel he established. A more overall interpretation might be the rule of God's justice throughout the earth.

Both Jews and Christians slide over the negative side of this prophecy. Who would want to admit to themselves that they were serving other gods! But how often will any political group that is formed to guide and govern, move easily into the worship of power and authority. From following true justice and loving consideration for others, they seek to maintain high position, and demand compliance to rules and regulations that they have constructed for their convenience. If there are weapons and armies involved, they depend on them to enforce their will instead of searching to discover God's will, or meditating on the commandment, "Thou shalt not kill."

When the stakes are so high, you would think that all those

in positions of authority would search their souls to see what other gods they might be worshipping. When God's prime concern seems to be gentle and just treatment of God's creation, how can one ever believe that anyone should ever carry a gun? Guns are used to wound or kill people. Why would anyone ever want to do that?

Our basic insecurities, or a need to use weapons to protect ourselves, comes out of a lack of understanding of ourselves and others. This can be seen in both the person and in societal structures. We fear the unknown. We find communication difficult with foreigners. Governments try to convince their citizens that a differing type of government is an evil empire, not admitting that there is an honest attempt by such foreign governments to serve their people. In such blind stereotyping, one government will fail to notice that it may have more hungry and homeless and dissastified citizens, than are in the government it is criticizing.

As a country what gods do Americans worship? We worship the private automobile, trusting it to get us to work every day. It takes a sizable bite out of every American's take-home pay. Our economic system is based on this extravagance, and as economics are distributed and interconnected over the world, the poor woman in Brazil may be on a starvation diet, so that I might pollute the air with my automobile.

Some of those individuals who carry weapons, may feel that their weapon is a friend, a companion for their journey. They give to it a worship and a trust that should be given to God. Likewise countries who store up nuclear weapons and rely on huge armies, are making a statement about trust. God has given us this wonderful world that supports our every breath, and all we can do with it is build weapons that will destroy everyone's breath. God trusts us! Why do we find it so difficult to trust God?

12.4 A COVENANTED PEOPLE AS THE ROYAL RULER OF ISRAEL

A group of people who have pledged in their hearts to do God's justice, to be in solidarity with the oppressed, and to care properly for God's creation can do much to improve the future of the earth and its inhabitants. This covenanted consentaneous group guiding the earth, could be considered as the *hand of God* or *Royal Ruler*.

An example of this *hand of God* working down through the centuries can be seen in many loving synagogue communities. Their acting together in faith has been the means of bringing their descendants back to the land of their beginnings. Working through human hearts, God's guiding Spirit has led the Jews across time and obstacles to a promised territory. When a people cry out in anguish from being oppressed, it seems that God hears, and those who try to serve God, hear. Those concerned with God's justice work to further that justice. First, there is the anguish of the people, and then there is the recognition of their needs and statements about the problem. Then the community that seeks after God's justice, proposes possible courses of action. Only after much concerned effort, dedicated discussion, and earnest prayer, does the community come near to a solution of the problem. Continuous concerted action and admission of fallibility on the part of the community is needed to establish God's justice in their particular area of earth.

The formation of a loving, serving, problem-solving community which can take on the job of *Royal Ruler*, is a process that requires many ingredients. The first need is for covenanted people. The particular elements of the group must be willing to give of themselves to form a unity. Even chemical elements need the electric attraction of other elements to become something more than their original state. Common bonds and a God-directed purpose contribute to an ecstacy of passion at conception. The members of the group congeal and nurture one another in a womb-like warmth and protection. But no group is immune to outside forces. The problems of the world make their influence felt. The group trusts in God, intends to do God's will, yet it must realize it is not onimpotent. Serving as caretakers of God's creation, requires many careful decisions on how to best advance. As we are human, there will be anguished nights of planning. Although praying to walk in God's ways, it is difficult to know when our actions are optimum.

To manage the earth through the consensus of many God-fearing base communities, may seem to some a rather reckless proposal. There is no obvious reason why we should trust the common man (acting in groups) over the single authority (often chosen by his peers). We have been obedient for so long to power structures with capitalistic agendas, that we are used to coping with their defects and dishonesties. This change to trusting one another as the expression of consentaneous groups, may give us an initial feeling of insecurity. Yet there is always a time of trial and a feeling of unrest before a new idea or an improved social structure is set in place. Birthing is never easy, but we and our communities are called to this caretakership out of necessity. We are to bear the Messianic message of concern and solidarity across the earth and to be the conduit of God's life and love to future generations.

This time of indecision and fear for the community is spoken of in Jeremiah 30:5-7. There will be a time of panic before the time of consolation.

> *Yahweh says this:*
> *I have heard a cry of panic,*
> *of terror not of peace.*
> *Now ask, consider:*
> *can men bear children?*
> *Then why do I see each man*
> *with his hands on his loins*
> *like a woman in labor?*
> *Why has every face changed,*
> *turned pale?*
> *This is indeed a great day,*
> *no other like it:*
> *a time of distress for Jacob;*
> *but he will be freed from it.*

This period of inquiet before freedom is interwoven with Jewish beliefs, and is reflected in their hope for the coming of the Messiah. At dismal periods in their history, such as the Roman destruction of Jerusalem, they were sure the Messiah must be near at hand.

Another period of agony was when the pogroms swept across Europe. The Jews found Messianic leaders in men such as Jacob Frank who attempted to ecumenize his people, thus reducing their elitist notions that invariably brought on persecutions. In his way of living, Frank showed that a Jew could obey the Torah, follow the path of Islam, and also perform all the religious observances of the Catholic Church. His approach opened the possibilities for other universalists who advocated absorbing the spirit of all religions, and dismissing the forms as dress-for-show.

The most recent upheaval for the Jews was the Holocaust. On the world community's horror at the suffering of those victims, came the seeming blessing of return to the Holy Land. Some saw the action of God's Messiah in Theodor Herzl or in Moshe Dyan. Some felt God's spirit led them back. Some conservative Jewish groups felt that God should lead them back somehow in person, and be their ruler; that a humanly led Jewish state was wrong. Martin Buber foresaw that treatment of the Palestinians which excluded God's concern for people, by the political powers, would endanger the ability of Israel to remain in the land. The trust of the community in the guidance of their God had brought them back to the Promised Land; their lack of trust and their inability to form loving community with the people of the land has bred another sorrowful historical moment. What Messiah is to guide them through this?

If we are to believe the prophets, the Spirit of the Messiah, when it comes, is to somehow come to the whole earth. Isaiah 11:9 and Habakkuk 2:14 foretell that "the country shall be filled with the knowledge of the glory of Yahweh as the waters swell the sea," yet Isaiah emphasizes that "the root of Jesse shall stand as a signal to the peoples. It will be sought out by the nations and its home will be glorious." This Messianic root shall be available to all to form the whole world into glorious community, and the present age with its threat of nuclear war, is terribly in need of this helping and healing community. If a great period of disaster is to precede the Messianic event, surely the Messiah will be with us soon.

There is a longing in the hearts of the Jews for the Messiah to come and to bring peace to the people. Not only the Jews, but those who trust in a positive creative spirit, hope for a messianic time of fulfillment. For the Messiah to come to you and to me, and to all the earth, we must open our hearts to the wisdom that is in the Messiah. When we hear God's message of love and act on it, only then can we become the dream God has for us. When we join in loving community and act lovingly towards the other inhabitants of the earth, then the Messiah will be able to dwell in our hearts and work through our hands. It will be possible at that time to affirm that the covenanted consentaneous community is like a Royal Ruler who reigns in the earth.

12.5 HOW TO FORM LOVING COMMUNITY

The threat of nuclear war bodes total destruction of God's plan for loving community upon the earth. In this, our day, we need to understand the message of God and the reason for our existence, more than at any previous time. Grave situations breed noble actions. If we open our eyes and acknowledge the gravity of our societal predicaments, perhaps we will be able to collectively birth God's spirit in our world. The saving and reconciling spirit of the Messiah will be born in our positive actions to form a loving, functioning world-wide community.

In order to form such a consentaneous and covenanted community, we first have to visualize a possible model of God. Your model may be different from the one set down here, but in general, humanity sees a reasonable, moral God that has some relationship with people caring for other people. We cannot put God in a box and describe him/her completely, or state God's will for all time and all peoples. However, we can propose certain directions to go in, and certain actions that seem more godly than others. Then we must act on those theoretical propositions. If the Messiah, or God's message, is to be accepted in the hearts of all human kind, people must reflect all that they see as positive in God and God's creation.

Humanity has tried very hard through the course of history to improve itself, frequently asking for God's guidance. It has set down laws whose purpose usually was the forming of individuals into better community. It has put in place educational systems to teach those laws and other collected community knowledge. It took upon itself punishment of the wrong doer, or the individual who found it difficult to conform to society's legal and educational aspirations. It devised political, economic, and military means of dealing with groups outside of the community. The Spirit of God is often reflected in these main societal structures. Unfortunately, sometimes the original good purpose of a structure becomes warped.

In our country we have a legal system that frequently supports the property rights of the rich over the needs of the poor. From an educational system that began in the churches, we have developed an unrealistic public program that avoids prayer, advocates memorization over experiential learning, and has inadequate goals, principles, and role models. Many of the poorly educated end up in prison. While there, they don't become immersed in creative projects for self-fulfillment, but are merely *doing time* with little emphasis on rehabilitation. However, these inadequate social institutions need merely a slight push in a positive direction, in order to improve them and head them towards the model of the New Jerusalem. Forward moving implementations could be encouraged by a different emphasis on the part of those in the structure of government. Military states, such as Chile, should gradually relinquish more say to the people. Democracies should put in place means to hear and service deprived minorities and the mentally discouraged.

In our democracy we frequently hear the words, "Why should I vote? Those politicians do what they want, anyway." This assumes that our convictions are not heard, and that the other, the politician, has no principles. If our hearts were truly committed or covenanted, we would not only vote, but also do more to make sure our politicians heard our complaints, and we would even attempt to influence the politicians to be committed people themselves.

If each person made a covenant with God at some point in his life, then he would be thinking seriously about what was best for him and what was best for the community. This knowledge would move him to better actions and help him to anticipate better reactions from others. You might ask how an atheist can make a covenant with God, seeing any good government has to make room for the unbelievers. An atheist can make a contract with himself, but should express his aspirations to some encouraging member of the community. What makes an atheist anyway? An atheist is usually someone who has been very hurt by another human being, so finds it difficult to believe in a loving God. A similar question is, "Why do people believe in Hell?" People need the concept of Hell as a place to put someone who has hurt them terribly. They themselves can hope for heaven, but they cannot be happy in heaven with their torturer there, so they must locate the torturer in some other place. In a well-run earth which accepted the message of God's love, there would be little need to believe in Hell or to refuse to believe in the goodness of God.

If all persons were given the formal opportunity to covenant with God, or express before another person the good that they wished to do or become, the earth would be a more peaceful place. As an example of a small controlled experiment today, of expressing a covenant, we could take the prison situation. Unfortunately, many individuals participate in societal wrong doing. Some go undetected, but those that are apprehended should be interrogated at a detention center. Problems in their past could be discovered, and positive possibilities for their future could be discussed. The person could have an opportunity to look at himself and his relationship with God and others. He could make a contract for his future, admitting to himself what realistic hopes he has, and how he plans to achieve them. A person can make such a covenant in his heart, but it is good to discuss it with a wise counselor who has the time to listen and to advise. It is even better to affirm this belief in one's self before a supporting community. If the man is to be incarcerated for a period of time, his plan should include those prison programs that he will use in order to rehabilitate himself. If he is to serve his sentence in society, he will need members of the outside community who will remind him of his value commitments. Different prison and rehabilitation programs using these approaches, find that their application reduces recidivism.

For teen agers coming of age, we have the positive examples of confirmation and bar mitzvah. Unfortunately, many teens are not exposed to the ideas of commitment expressed in such ceremonies. Often such a *religious* commitment is seen by the average teenager as a promise to support the ministerial group and to pay for the church heating and repairs. He may feel it has nothing to do with the oppressed in other countries and finds it irrelevant to our secular way of life. Frequently teen agers will stop going to church because symbols, for them, have lost their relevancy, and they have been given no solid thoughts of God to fill the void. Just when a covenantal relationship with God becomes very important, the average American young person experiences the Santa Claus syndrome of feeling that he has been duped. If at this point the person made a covenant and was accepted into the consentaneous government of the community, he would be able to feel his partership with God, and his responsibility for the care of God's creation.

Our democratic form of government doesn't have to be changed very much in order to become consentaneous and covenantal. We must have town meetings where everyone's voice is heard, and not merely bow to the whim of the majority. Television is an excellent device for airing many points of view, but there must be feed back from everyone concerned. All those who represent us at any level, must make known their covenantal commitment to the true justice of consideration for and understanding of others. It is questionable as to whether we need one supreme leader who supposedly speaks with authority for all. As soon as you delegate authority, you are giving up freedom. What a consentaneous government needs to carry out its business, is a clerk or a series of clerks, to analyze just what the will of the people is, and to discover ways to implement that will.

The communist form of government does not need much change either. It needs more freedom in selecting representatives from its local groups to attend larger area *quality circles*. If the citizens of Chernobyl had been consulted, and given proper information, they would never have chosen to have an atomic power plant in their midst. Likewise, our communities seem to have little choice of whether or not we will host such energy plants, even though those in authority are well aware of their potential for disaster, especially in time of earthquake disturbance.

It seems a little thing to ask our governments to change their ways, and listen to God's wisdom speaking through the people. How could our leaders refuse, when the prize is so great,- a livable world! On the other hand, the alternative is that we will be unworthy of the land.

God gets involved in government when people do those just acts that please God. Isaiah 58:6-12 describes certain aspects of the holy society; we are the ones who have to make sure that God's justice is activated in our communities.

Is not this the sort of fast that pleases me
- it is the Lord Yahweh who speaks -
to break unjust fetters
and undo the thongs of the yoke,
to let the oppressed go free,
and break every yoke,
to share your bread with the hungry,
and shelter the homeless poor,

to clothe the man you see to be naked
and not turn from your own kin?

Then will your light shine like the dawn
and your wound be quickly healed over.

Your integrity will go before you
and the glory of Yahweh behind you.
Cry, and Yahweh will answer;
call, and he will say, "I am here."

If you do away with the yoke,
the clenched fist, the wicked word,
if you give your bread to the hungry,
and relief to the oppressed,

your light will rise in the darkness,
and your shadows become like noon.
Yahweh will always guide you,
giving you relief in desert places.

He will give strength to your bones
and you shall be like a watered garden,
like a spring of water
whose waters never run dry.

You will rebuild the ancient ruins,
build up on the old foundations.
You will be called "Breach-mender,"
"Restorer of ruined houses."

Isaiah describes the covenanted individual or group, and we must interpret for our particular day and age, how these directives are to be implemented. We must work out wise ways to relate to others in governing common territory. We will have to be innovative when building on the old societal structures (the ancient ruins), yet we will have a source of energy (an everlasting spring of water) that will never fail. The scripture passage does not seem to advocate depending on militarism or political machinations.

Seeing the old structures are tilting in the wrong directions, we must re-examine their foundations. If the supports are solid, then what is required of us is to reconstruct and mold the surface areas, so that the building is usable for us today. Where governmental structures are concerned, we should encourage politicians to listen to the integrated consensus of their constituents, and to heed the anguished cries of their minorities. Where religion is the issue, we must insure that God's love pours in free flowing channels, unconstricted by elitist liturgies or divisive symbols.

When the environment is mistreated, we must be foresighted enough to change our priorities. An example of wasted resources is our military build-up and use of land areas in states such as Nevada, for weapon proving grounds. We can relate this waste to a second waste, the sedentary manpower and womanpower in prisons. Putting these two wasted resources together, we could come up with a plus. Instead of polluting vast areas of desert with weaponry, have those citizens who have been legally sentenced to a process of wasting time in prisons yet who are still mentally and physically capable, go to these desert areas and transform them into cities and lush gardens. Let us be creative and constructive rather than fearful and destructive.

God can be brought into these political and environmental situations. If the earth is to survive, God must be brought into these dilemnas. As people, we are God's hands. We must be the ones who bring God's love and wisdom in the turmoil.

Times have changed. The world turns and turns. The rice harvest is still important, but today the flow of human life depends more on the human ability to be loving and considerate of one another, than it does on food supply. As we have seen in the countries in Africa, tons of foodstuffs can be shipped to a people, only to be diverted by graft, government, soldiers, and weapons.

If we are to believe that God made the world, then we must accept that God also made what some would call the devil. God gave us the freedom to choose the manner in which we think and act. If we make proper choices, we help in God's process of building the earth. If we fearfully underestimate our self worth, and act so as to destroy the other, we will annihilate both ourselves and that other. Devil worship is inherently self-centered and directed towards the exclusion or extermination of the imagined oppresser. Like weapon worship it does nothing to promote the flow of life and love. It grows out of our fears, and doesn't allow our positive expansion or fulfillment. Yet we are each given the freedom to choose our course of action. The security of our physical, social, and political environment, the continuance of our earth, is up to each one of us.

The thesis of this book is that the world is designed to run on creativity and consideration, and that God is a loving process in which we can all participate. If we admit these opinions, it seems that something is required of us. We must *cooperate* with this process God. We must *commit* ourselves to what we see as God's future. *Commit* and *cooperate* are actions words. They speak of a covenant in the heart. We dedicate ourselves to care for God's earth, and to encourage society to move in positive directions.

We are both the *CHOSEN* and the *CHOOSER*. The Jew, as *CHOSEN* specifically for this caring task as described in his Holy Scriptures, should *CHOOSE* to gift the world with understanding and acceptance of human diversity. The Christian, as believing himself the Spiritual seed of Abraham, should also take steps to inspirit and enoble the world. The Muslim, whose whole way of life is dedicated to Allah, has certainly pledged himself to be part of God's loving process.

None of us are born with this commitment. We *CHOSEN ONES* are born with freedom to *CHOOSE* the direction in which we will go. We are also born into a cultural milieu that pressures us into certain rejections and acceptances. Our culture encourages us to love our country, right or wrong. It builds up prejudices against those outside our group. As normal human beings we have fears for our safety, and are influenced into still other actions that may temper our commitments.

A good way to strengthen personal commitments, and to make wise decisions in regard to what is good for the well being of self, family, nation, and world, is to gather in discussion groups at the base community level. Nations, instead of being run from the top, on hierarchical or dictatorial models, should accept directions from the collective wisdom of the people.

As an experiment in shifting priorities in slightly more positive directions, the Jews could reorganize their state with circular advisory consensus communities, so that the Spirit of God would be given room to operate. God's wisdom resting in the people could lead their total community to endorse just actions towards both the stranger in the land, and to all peoples on earth. Soldiers, instead of being given authority from the top, to molest and subdue, would be given the job of *servant to the citizen* and their duty would be to expedite peaceful solutions to problems. In a dispute between citizens, soldiers could be used to assist in a mediation process, so as to bring about possible *both-gain* situations.

The Catholics in their code of canon law possess the directives which could reorganize their church in a covenantal and consentaneous manner. They have the regulations, and they should have the commitment, to let the wind of the Spirit blow freely in order to show forth what is truly important in a God serving community. Priests and others who desired to serve the Catholic community, could be trained in social services and mediation techniques. Every member of the Catholic Church could be a covenanted servant willing to serve God, his or her fellow human, and the environmental needs of planet earth.

In mentioning these specific examples of the Jewish people, and the Catholic church, I do not want to exclude the many other positive religious groups who already serve God through some measure of covenant and consensus. Specific examples are being given here as illustrating possibilities of what might be. The state of Israel-Palestine and the Catholic Church are well known, and thus more observable. Both the Catholic Church and the nation of Israel have responsibility to move in the direction of being open and caring communities, organizations truly guided by God's spirit, rather than by conventional politics, traditional reasoning, and fear. Who will be able to encourage the development of both the Israeli state and the Catholic Church into true *holy* communities? Only when communities act in the Spirit of the Messiah will messianic events happen.

Governments of today, because of seemingly insurmountable fears of others, seem to feel the need for weapons and armies. Such display of power was formerly thought to be unseemly by religious institutions who advised participants in their communities to put their trust in God. As weapons become more sophisticated, humankind has become less trusting with God's ability to preserve. Catholicism has grown from excluding members of the Roman army as participants in their communities, to maintaining its own honorary Swiss guard, and accepting police protection from various governments.

The Israeli state has sought after every new and horrendous weapon that has been invented. The government of Israel has no need for such a variety of weapons. Weapons are useful if you plan (either consciously or sub-consciously) to make war on your neighbors, or to subdue minorities (or majorities) in your domain of influence. The political group (or the individual) that procures weapons no longer has the need to think clearly in order to maintain peace. It automatically trusts to its weapons to keep order. Surely, there must have been discovered a less demonic way than raw power, to govern a nation, in the last two thousand years.

Israel should be encouraged to develop a caring community that does not employ weapons to threaten or subdue. Elders of villages in Israel-Palestine do not need young nervous soldiers with weapons stationed in their areas. Each village should be self govern-ing and should have a representative who meets consentaneously with representatives from other villages in the region to discuss larger area problems. It seems that in the land of Israel, today, and also in Ireland, South Africa, and Central America, no one is listening to the problems of the other, but frantically grabbing whatever privileges and property are available, for himself.

To fight for possession of dead relics or material objects, while ruining living people who are the true bearers of holy impulses and abilities, is to be deluded. The future of any God-inspired belief in the land of Israel-Palestine depends on the qualities of mercy and love in the local people, not on the holy stones.[2] It is important to recognize that people are the building blocks of loving community, and that the coveted sacred places are merely structures set in place by human ancestors, inspired by love for their community. Think for a moment on these ancestors. They certainly would be pained to know that their building project was causing dissension and being fought over. Which alternative is the greater objective set down in Holy Scriptures:- the Jews' religious claim to the stones of Israel-Palestine; or the Jews' God given responsibility to establish loving community in that country? Is not the greater commitment to be chosen by God to show the rest of the world how to dwell in harmony on the earth that God has given to all of us? Surely, the ancestors were hoping for harmony rather than discord.

There is no need to rebuild the physical temple in Jerusalem, or to construct any symbolic building to remind us of God our Creator. The temple humankind is to fashion is made from living stones. It is the *holy community* made of covenanted individuals working together in consensus. The stones of the physical temple are always subject to being utterly thrown assunder, but seeming calamities of this sort, are what inspire the people to band together in order to best love and serve one another. This presence of love in the community is the Spirit of God acting within the creation, encouraging that creation to be holy.

12.6 HOW TO TRANSFORM A WORLD

If we become a community which feels that God has a certain purpose for the world, we, as that community, will try to put this purpose into place and to act from principles of guiding love. Today we are threatened by nuclear holocaust which is more devastating than the recent holocaust of the Jewish people in Nazi Germany. Man's inhumanity to man often seems to sneak insidiously upon us under the noble guise of what is good for a particular individual or for a particular community or country. We hear world leaders explaining righteously that we must have peace, and therefore it is necessary to make tremendous weapons to protect ourselves and to destroy the other. They shout loudly, "This is good for us! This is good for our nation and for our allies." But is this threat to others, this horrendous un-love, really good for the whole world? In building armaments, we deprive our poor. We store away potential disasters as in Chernobyl. Surely, all our hate for the other will return to fall on our own heads in a possible calamity such as nuclear winter.

How can the community of love such as we have been describing come to pass on this earth with our wars and rumours of wars, and our ability to self-destruct? Zbigniew Brzezinski states that individuals and nations cannot forget the knowledge of nuclear weaponry, and thus we must live in a world where arms control is a reality. He quotes John Paul II as saying that "Christians know that in this world a totally and permanently peaceful human society is unfortunately a Utopia and that ideologies which hold up that prospect as easily obtainable are based on hopes that cannot be realized ..." Dr. Brzezinski suggests using limited strategic defense and first strike capabilities which is a step in the positive direction, as this suggestion considers what is a slightly improved situation for the civilian populations of the world.[3] He does not seem to feel that the Spirit of God can help to make friends and fellow creators out of our former enemies.

Does our human susceptibility to and knowledge of modern weaponry, mean that we should give up on our Christian beliefs in the Millenium? Shall we admit failure in our task of having a loving community in control of the earth? The search for a universal messianic spirit will only be rewarded in a world where justice and peace dwell. At first glance it doesn't seem like first strike capabilities have much to do with the person resting on his land in security under his fig tree, but on closer scrutiny, we might see in Dr. Brzezinski's thought, a tilting towards our messianic destiny. In this precise instance there is the opportunity to mold the city of Babylon towards the form of the New Jerusalem. In joining to limit our weapons, we take a first step towards trust in one another, and thus to trust in the Spirit of God working in each other.

The fact that we have so recently had the Nazi disruption of society shows that religious people have failed to bring the message of God's love and acceptance for all people to the mass of humankind. With present day knowledge and understanding of human psychology and the rising levels of communication, it should not be difficult to take actions that would make this long desired messianic community a reality in our world. God seems to expect that we have the capability to transform the world. God sends God's Spirit or *message*, and God's Messenger or *Messiah*, in order that we will be able to transform the poor situations in which we find ourselves. The messianic community is commissioned to transform our environment (with which God has blessed us and which humankind in its freedom has warped and deformed) into a world where love reigns, where God reigns.

In order to transform a world, first it is necessary to transform ourselves and our attitudes. This is an on-going process and takes a continual striving on our parts. The next step is to survey the scene around us to see where some improvement can be made. Observing the messianic dictums of Saint Francis, we should strive to illumine the situation when there is darkness and uncertainty. When there is injury, we should attempt to heal. When there is despair, we must give cheer. This, too, is a process. We do not heal for all time, because in a world full of interacting people, there are always new hurts to comfort.

If all of us follow the above proceedures, the messianic

community should gradually fall into place. This may have been the idea that was in the mind of the person, Jesus, about two thousand years ago, when he stated that the Kingdom of God was within people. However, this kingdom/queendom, or this messianic community does not have a definite time or location. It is comparable to a state of mind. It requires a willingness on the part of humanity to work with fluctuations and to steer uncertainties into positive directions.

As we are all created in God's image, all of us have this ability to transform, built in. The God whom we image, transformed the void into a pulsing universe teeming with life. We also are to transform voids into fulfillments. When we were too young a creation to understand fully, God sent messenger prophets to guide us towards the messianic community where all would live in justice and peace. Today humanity can see hope for that community on the horizon in spite of individual imperfections. We must remember that God trusts and hopes for the fulfillment of each and every one of us. If we decide to accept the invitation and make our personal covenant, God has fashioned each one of us for partnership in messianic love. This love can be best grasped through the encouragement of a loving community.

This world, a specific material place, seems to be in reasonably good shape in spite of human misunderstandings and a dearth of those willing to be carriers of God's spirit. There are hummingbirds. There are whales. There are people who do marvelous deeds for one another. There are those who make music and those who think great thoughts. There are little children to keep us honest. What needs to be transformed? Perhaps it is our attitudes that need to be transformed, for instance, our attitude towards the individual terrorist. If we could have an embodied representation of God's message, such as Jesus Christ, who saw injustice and used the example of himself to enlighten us on how to deal with injustice, cannot we show a terrorist who sees injustice, the messianic ideal? Hopefully, our messiahs, either individual or communal, need no longer be warlike in their leadership. They are those who have the goodness of the whole earth at heart. The messianic community which we are in the process of forming, should understand the root problem behind the terrorist's action, and in exercising justice, convert the terrorist to active membership in the peaceful community. If the messianic ideal is to encourage all peoples to work for the good of all peoples, there would be no need for terrorism in this process.

Perhaps it is in the most drastic threats to our well being that our most creative responses are drawn forth. Possibly the threat of nuclear annihilation is what is necessary to draw the populations of the world together in an active search for peace. The plague of AIDS may drive us into empathy with those facing death. The horror and waste of addiction to drugs and alcohol may lead us to new commitments of service to others. Perhaps a certain amount of darkness is necessary to encourage us to walk towards the light.

The messianic community must be continually striving to resolve situations through love. We cannot expect a perfect, static existence. To make a weapon free world, we must go through a loving, cleansing process. If we do achieve a world free from terror, there will still be individual differences to soothe and explain. If we keep the Spirit of the Messiah in our hearts, God will continue to help us to be able to deal with all situations.

Jews and Christians look forward to a time when God's message of justice and love for all peoples will permeate the world. If this is to be the earth's mode of action, all those who believe in this dream must have respect for themselves and others, and continually seek to maximize the good in every situation. Peacemakers must be constantly healing the rifts that develop in every normal community. They must be understanding of both sides of every question. "The way to peace is to do justice in the work at hand."[4] Hearts covenanted to the ideals embodied in God's word to the human, will be able to form a community that can be described as governed by God. Then God's Spirit can be said to rule in Israel and in all the earth!

FOOTNOTES

Chapter 1
1. *Order and History, Volume II: The World of The Polis*, Eric Voegelin, Baton Rouge: Louisiana State University, 1962, pp. 144-149.
2. *ibid.*, p.150.
3. *Sollicitude Rei Socialis* as given in the *National Catholic Reporter*, May 27, 1988.
4. Raimundo Panikkar, "The Invisible Harmony" in *Towards A Universal Theology of Religion*, Leonard Swidler, ed. (Maryknoll: Orbis, 1987), p. 147.

Chapter 2
1. W. Henry Kenney, *A Path Through Teilhard's Phenomenon*, (Dayton, Ohio: Pflaum Press, 1970), p. 266.
2. James M. Robinson, Ed., *The Nag Hammadi Library*, (San Francisco: Harpur and Row, 1977), p. 124. Gospel of Thomas: They saw a Samaritan carrying a lamb on his way to Judea. Jesus said to his disciples, "Why does that man carry the lamb around?" They said to him, "So that he may kill it and eat it."
3. Julian of Norwich, *Enfolded in Love*, (New York: Seabury Press, 1981), p. 37.
4. Disobedience to authority is often mentioned as the sin, but as this is a myth with a figurative tree, it is debatable whether there was a disobedience or if the purpose of the myth was to describe an evolutionary threshhold being crossed. Those interested in maintaining authority, might desire to interpret this *sin* as a lack of respect for an invisible *authority*.

Chapter 4
1. This process that went against nature had been put in the same class as homosexuality, and thus in the Bible we have the possibility of pre-captivity celibate priests being spoken of as sodomites, and being driven from the temple (II Kings 23:7).
2. Teilhard, *Christianity and Evolution*, translated by Rene Hague, (New York: Harcourt, Brace, Jovanovich, 1971), p. 170.
3. Over 900 followers of the Reverend Jim Jones committed mass suicide in British Guiana, November 1978, by drinking poisoned Kool-Aid.
4. Kathleen Nash, "Obadiah: Past Promises, Future Hope," in September, 1987, *The Bible Today, Vol 25#5*.

Chapter 5
1. George W. Forell, *Christian Social Teachings*, (Minneapolis MN: Augsburg Publishing House, 1971), p. 73.

Chapter 6
1. Stone, Andy, "Our Man in Managua" in *Sunday Camera Magazine*, May 29, 1988.
2. St. Thomas Aquinas, *Summa Theologica*, First Part of The Second Part, Question XVIII, Article 4, Objection 3.
3. Gutierrez, Gustavo, *A Theology of Liberation* (Maryknoll: Orbis, 1973).

4. *Sollicitudo Rei Socialis: Encyclical on Social Concern*, sections 39, 40, & 45.
5. *New York Times*, August 26, 1988, p. A9.
6. *Sollicitudo Rei Socialis: Encyclical on Social Concern*, section 42.

Chapter 7
1. Eugene Kennedy, *The Now and Future Church*, (Garden City, NY: Image Books, 1985), p. 145.
2. Robert McAfee Brown in "Theological Reflection on Accompaniment" quoted by Richard A. Howard in "Accompaniment: An Invitation," *America*, December 12, 1987, p. 456.
3. Alasdair Clayre, *The Heart of the Dragon*, (London: Harvill Press & William Collins Sons, 1984) p. 36.
4. Bukkyo Dendo Kyokai, *The Teaching of Buddha*, (Tokyo, Japan: Kosaido Printing Company, 1985), p. 273.
5. Lee Kwang Soo in article by Youn Yong Hae, "Following Buddha," *Maryknoll*, January, 1988, p. 62.
6. A. L. Basham, *The Wonder That Was India*, (New York: Taplinger Publishing Co., 1966), p. 309.

Chapter 8
1. Monika Hellwig, *Christian Women In A Troubled World*, (New York: Paulist Press, 1985), p. 53.
2. Canon Law Society of Great Britain and Ireland, *The Code of Canon Law*, (Grand Rapids, Michigan: William B. Eerdmans Publishing Co., 1983).
3. James Provost "Revising Canon Law: Where Do We Stand?" *America*, Nov. 7, 1981, p. 275.
4. Ladislas Orsay, "The New Canon Law: A Practical Proposal," *America*, Sept. 1981, p. 155.
5. *ibid.*, p. 156.
6. *loc.cit.*
7. John Alesandro, "The Revision of Canon Law: Conflict and Reconciliation," *The Jurist*, 1980, p. 9.
8. *ibid.*, p. 10.
9. Thomas Stahel, "More Action Than They Called For: The Detroit Meeting: A Call To Action," *America*, Nov. 1976, p. 296.
10. Ronald Modras, "Roman Law In A Universal Church," *America*, Dec. 17, 1983, p. 390.
11. Richard Rohr, *Salvation and Community*, a video production.
12. Acts 5:29.
13. Patrick Granfield, "Consilium and Consensus: Decision Making in Cyprian," *The Jurist*, 1975, p. 402.
14. *loc.cit.*
15. John Alesandro, *op.cit.*, p. 2.
16. South African Catholic Bishops Conference, *Official Catholic Teachings: Update 1977*, (Wilmington, NC: A Consortium Book, McGrath Publishing Company, 1980), p. 66.

17. Patrick Granfield, "Changes In Religious Life: Freedom, Responsibility, Community," *America*, Sept. 15, 1984, pp. 120-123.
18. Gloria Faizi, *Introduction to Baha'i Faith* (Wilmette, Ill., 1972), pp. 94-97.
19. *loc.cit.*
20. *loc.cit.*
21. Patrick Granfield, *loc.cit.*, p. 122.

Chapter 9
1. William LaDue, "A Written Constitution for The Church," *The Jurist*, 1972, p.1.
2. Willis Barnstone, Ed., *The Other Bible*, (San Francisco, 1983), p. 15.
3. Robert Howes, "Parish Councils: Do We Care?" *America*, Nov. 1976, p. 371.
4. Anne Buckley, "A Voice In The Plans," *Catholic New York*, November 1, 1984, p. 18.
5. Richard McBrien, *Catholicism*, (Minneapolis: Winston, 1980), p. 621.
6. *ibid.*, p. 791.
7. *ibid.*, p. 1082.
8. Code numbers mentioned in this chapter are from *The Code of Canon Law*, (Grand Rapids, MI: William B. Eerdmans, 1983).

Chapter 11
1. Mandell Creighton, *Theosaurus of Quotations*, ed. Edmund Fuller (New York: Crown Publishers, 1941), p. 727.
2. David Philipson, *The Reform Movement in Judaism*, (New York: Macmillan, 1907), pp. 496-7.
3. John K. Cooley, *The War Over Water*, ABC News correspondent, p. 5.
4. En-Gedi (Spring of The Kid) is a warm water spring 330 feet above the western slope of the Dead Sea, or Sea of Arabah. The Dead Sea contains no fish, at present, due to its heavy mineral content.
5. The valley of the acacias or shittah trees is probably the lower part of the valley of Kidron, the watercourse from Gihon Spring originating under the temple mount. This is comparable to the waters of Shiloah of Isaiah 8:6 and Psalm 46:4.
6. *Arena Newsletter*, #88, Winter 1990.
7. Daniel Deudney, *Worldwatch Paper #44, Rivers of Energy*, p. 24.

Chapter 12
1. Genesis 24:3, See *Interpreter's Dictionary of The Bible, Volume R-Z*, Article "Sex," (New York: Abingdon Press, 1962), p. 298.
2. Article on Elias Chacour in *Catholic Near East*, Winter 1987, "Today's Prophetic Voices in The Holy Land" by Michael Healy, p. 5.
3. Zbigniew Brzezinski, *America*, May 31, 1986.
4. Elias Chacour, *loc. cit.*, p. 6.